Anglais pour psychologues

PSYCHO SUP

Anglais pour psychologues

Sous la direction de
Laurence Masse
Wendy Pullin
Edward Hughes
Rebecca Shankland

DUNOD

ISBN 978-2-10-055143-9

LISTE DES AUTEURS

Ouvrage réalisé sous la direction de :

Laurence MASSE	Maître de conférences à l'Université Paris 8-Vincennes-Saint-Denis
Wendy PULLIN	Professeur à l'Université Concordia College d'Alberta (Canada)
Edward HUGHES	Chargé de cours à l'Université Paris 8-Vincennes-Saint-Denis et traducteur
Rebecca SHANKLAND	Maître de conférences à l'Université Pierre-Mendès-France (Grenoble)

Avec la collaboration de :

Colette AGUERRE	Maître de conférences à l'Université François Rabelais (Tours)
Philippe Arvers	Docteur en médecine et chercheur à l'Institut de Recherche Biomédicale des Armées (La Tronche)
Ingrid BANOVIC	Maître de conférences à l'Université Paris Ouest-Nanterre-La Défense
Virginie BEAUCOUSIN	Maître de conférences à l'Université Paris 8-Vincennes-Saint-Denis
Laurent BÈGUE	Professeur à l'Université Pierre-Mendès-France (Grenoble)
Marine BLONDEL	Université de Reims Champagne-Ardennes, psychologue
Céline BONNAIRE	Maître de conférences à l'Université Paris-Descartes
Sandra BRUNO	Maître de conférences à l'IUFM de Versailles
Catherine BUNGENER	Professeur à l'Université Paris-Descartes
Arnaud CARRÉ	Université de Reims Champagne-Ardennes, psychologue
Denis CORROYER	Maître de conférences à l'Université Paris Descartes
Fanny D'AMBROSIO	Université de Reims Champagne-Ardennes, psychologue
Aurélie DOCTEUR	Université Paris 8-Vincennes-Saint-Denis, psychologue
Romain DUGRAVIER	Pédopsychiatre, CHU Bichat, AP-HP (Paris)
Benjamin GALLAIS	Docteur en psychologie à l'Université Paris 8-Vincennes-Saint-Denis
Daniel GILIBERT	Maître de conférences HDR à l'Université de Bourgogne (Dijon)
Fabien GIRANDOLA	Professeur à l'Université de Bourgogne (Dijon)
Sabine GUÉRAUD	Maître de conférences à l'Université Paris 8-Vincennes-Saint-Denis
Mikkel HANSEN	Maître de conférences à l'Université Paris 8-Vincennes-Saint-Denis

Sonia HARRATI	Maître de conférences à l'Université Toulouse 2-Le Mirail
Robert-Vincent JOULE	Professeur à l'Université de Provence (Aix-Marseille 1)
Lubomir LAMY	Maître de conférences à l'Université Paris 11
Muriel LEZAK	Professeur à l'Université de Portland (Oregon, USA)
Céline MANETTA	Docteur en psychologie, Université Paris 8-Vincennes-Saint-Denis
Pascal MARCHAND	Professeur à l'IUT de Toulouse
Raphaëlle MILJKOVITCH	Professeur à l'Université Paris 8-Vincennes-Saint-Denis
Sébastien MONTEL	Maître de conférences à l'Université Paul Verlaine (Metz)
Michèle MONTREUIL	Professeur à l'Université Paris 8-Vincennes-Saint-Denis
Gabriel MOSER	Professeur à l'Université Paris-Descartes
Etienne MULLET	Professeur à l'École Pratique des Hautes Études (Paris)
María Teresa MUÑOZ SASTRE	Professeur à l'Université Toulouse 2-Le Mirail
Félix NETO	Professeur à l'Université de Porto (Portugal)
Ahogni NGBALA	Maître de conférences à l'Université Paris Ouest-Nanterre-La Défense
Jean-Louis PÉDINIELLI	Professeur à l'Université de Provence (Aix-Marseille 1)
Sophie RICHARDOT	Maître de conférences à l'Université Picardie Jules-Verne (Amiens)
Edith SALÈS-WUILLEMIN	Professeur à l'Université Paris 8-Vincennes-Saint-Denis
Silke SCHAUDER	Maître de conférences HDR à l'Université Paris 8 -Vincennes-Saint-Denis
Baptiste SUBRA	Maître de conférences à l'Université Paris-Descartes
Anne TCHERKASSOF	Maître de conférences à l'Université Pierre-Mendès-France (Grenoble)
Makeda THOMAS	Université Paris 8-Vincennes-Saint-Denis, psychologue
Claire TOURMEN	Maître de conférences à AgroSup (Dijon)
Didier TRUCHOT	Professeur à l'Université de Franche-Comté (Besançon)
Isabel URDAPILLETA	Professeur à l'Université Paris 8-Vincennes-Saint-Denis
David UZZELL	Professeur à l'Université de Surrey (Grande-Bretagne)
Isabelle VARESCON	Professeur à l'Université Paris-Descartes
David VAVASSORI	Maître de conférences à l'Université Toulouse 2-Le Mirail
Jean-François VERLHIAC	Maître de conférences HDR à l'Université Paris Ouest-Nanterre-La Défense
Jacqueline WENDLAND	Maître de conférences à l'Université Paris-Descartes

TABLE DES MATIÈRES n°1 / TABLE OF CONTENTS Nr 1[1]

Textes et films

1. Les textes et films sont classés par domaine de recherche (texts and films are classified by research area).

TABLE DES MATIÈRES N°2 – DVD/TABLE OF CONTENTS Nr 2 – DVD

Films, textes electroniques et textes audio/films/texts in electronic format, and texts in audio format

Les films classés par niveau de difficulté

Les textes électroniques et audio

Audio 8 : Video game addiction : a real addiction ? (*cf.* texte 20 du livre)
Audio 9 : Psychopathology of drug addiction : substance abuse and dependence (*cf.* texte 24 du livre)
Audio 10 : Theory of mind (*cf.* texte 28 du livre)
Audio 11 : Obesity and body image (*cf.* texte électronique 11 du DVD)
Audio 12 : A psychiatric and psychopathological approach to delirium and hallucinations (*cf.* texte électronique 12 du DVD)
Audio 13 : Rewarding and praising children (*cf.* texte 31 du livre et tout le texte en version électronique 13 du DVD)
Audio 14 : The impact of early mother-infant interaction on the development of infant attachment (*cf.* texte 32 du livre)
Audio 15 : Introduction to attachment theory (*cf.* texte électronique 15 du DVD)
Audio 16 : Health psychology (*cf.* texte 38 du livre)
Audio 17 : The locus of control : contributions and limits (*cf.* texte électronique 17 du DVD)
Audio 18 : Learning to work : an introduction to professional didactics (*cf.* texte électronique 18 du DVD)
Audio 19 : The neuropsychological examination (*cf.* texte électronique 19 du DVD)
Audio 20 : Coping and quality of life in relation to depression and anxiety in Parkinson's disease (*cf.* texte électronique 20 du DVD)
Audio 21 : The relation between cognition and brain functioning : an introduction to neuroscience (*cf.* texte 50 du livre)

PRÉFACE

Ce manuel est destiné **aux étudiants de psychologie et à leurs enseignants d'anglais**, ainsi qu'**aux professionnels de la psychologie**, chercheurs et praticiens qui souhaitent apprendre et se perfectionner en **anglais pour psychologues**.

De plus en plus, l'exercice actuel du « métier » d'étudiant et par la suite, de celui de psychologue, nécessite fréquemment la lecture d'ouvrages et d'articles en anglais. Or ces écrits sont rarement traduits dans notre langue. De plus, les communications des chercheurs lors de colloques internationaux se font très souvent en anglais, nécessitant une bonne maîtrise de cette langue.

Par ailleurs, l'ouverture des frontières européennes et les nombreux accords passés entre nos universités françaises et des universités anglophones rendent possible la préparation de diplômes à l'étranger. Pour ce faire, il est parfois demandé aux étudiants français de justifier de leur niveau de langue par des tests comme le TOEIC, le TOEFL, le IELTS, le FCE, pour citer les plus connus. La maîtrise de l'anglais s'avère donc un atout incontestable tant au niveau des études qu'au niveau professionnel.

L'objectif de cet ouvrage est de vous fournir un outil de travail à la fois écrit et oral vous permettant d'aborder les théories et concepts en anglais présents dans les différents champs de la psychologie.

Pour ce faire, cet ouvrage est composé d'un **recueil de textes** accompagné d'un **DVD**. Ce dernier comprend :

– **des vidéos de cours filmés et des expériences de psychologie à voir et à reproduire chez soi ; elles sont indiquées par le sigle** ;
– **les versions audio de certains textes du livre, indiquées par le sigle ;**
– **des textes électroniques indiqués par le sigle et leur version audio.**

PRÉSENTATION DES TEXTES ÉCRITS ET DES TEXTES AUDIO

Les auteur(e)s des textes

Nous avons sollicité un ensemble de spécialistes des différents champs de la psychologie appartenant à de nombreuses universités françaises ou étrangères. Ils se sont exprimés dans de courts textes de 3 à 4 pages sur leurs thèmes de prédilection, qu'ils soient classiques ou contemporains. Les textes que vous lirez sont écrits, tantôt en anglais britannique, tantôt en anglais américain, reflétant ainsi la diversité des appartenances géographiques des auteurs.

Les textes et leur version audio

Vous disposerez des textes du livre et des textes électroniques du DVD pour pouvoir suivre les **textes audio**.

Avertissement au lecteur : afin de faciliter la lecture des textes présents sur le DVD, nous les avons parfois légèrement remaniés. La version « audio » de ces textes peut donc s'écarter parfois sensiblement de la version écrite présente dans le livre ou sur le DVD.

Les textes sont accompagnés d'exercices de compréhension

Les réponses aux exercices sont données dans la partie « Réponses » (« Answers ») en fin d'ouvrage.

Les textes sont accompagnés d'un lexique de vocabulaire

Les **termes de spécialité** seront traduits **de l'anglais vers le français et du français vers l'anglais** dans la partie lexique (« Lexicon ») en fin d'ouvrage. Vous trouverez également des **définitions** relatives à certaines théories ou concepts.

PRÉSENTATION DES FILMS

Des cours et des expériences de psychologie

Certains textes ont donné lieu à des cours ou à des expériences de psychologie filmés. Pour la plupart, ces cours ou expériences sont illustrés par des

« diaporamas » projetés pendant le film, vous permettant de suivre l'exposé oral du professeur. De plus, certains de ces films vous permettront de réaliser ces expériences chez vous.

Ces films seront indiqués par le sigle 

La réalisation et les intervenants des films

Les expériences sont animées par **Wendy Pullin**, Professeure de Psychologie à l'université Concordia Collège d'Alberta au Canada et par deux chargés de cours d'anglais pour psychologues à l'Université Paris 8 : **Christina Cosmos et Edward Hughes**.

Les cours sont donnés par Wendy Pullin.

Réalisation des films : Laurence Masse.

Montage : Stéphane Ténier.

Prise de vues : Jean-Louis Ténier.

Les films sont classés par niveaux de difficulté

Niveau 1 : « débutant » indiqué par le sigle *

Niveau 2 : « intermédiaire » indiqué par le sigle **

Niveau 3 : « confirmé » indiqué par le sigle ***

Logiciel de lecture de fichiers multimédias

Pour être en mesure de lire les fichiers audio et vidéo contenus sur le DVD-Rom, vous pouvez télécharger le logiciel VLC Media Player.

Ce logiciel gratuit et libre est disponible à l'adresse suivante :

www.videolan.org

Vous pouvez également lire ces fichiers multimédias sur une platine DVD de salon acceptant les fichiers aux formats MP3 pour les fichiers audio et MPEG4 (H.264) pour les fichiers vidéo.

REMERCIEMENTS

Je remercie Stéphane Ténier pour son professionnalisme : sans son travail acharné, sa grande disponibilité et sa patience, rien du contenu de ce DVD n'aurait pu voir le jour.

Je remercie Christina Cosmos, Agathe Brochard, Sabine Guéraud, Marine Gardeur et Florentin Lesellier pour leur participation active et enthousiaste à ce projet.

Mes remerciements vont également à Corinna Kohler, Carole Josodola et Wendy Pullin pour leur aide soutenue et leur amitié indéfectible tout au long de ce projet.

Enfin, je remercie Jean-Louis Ténier pour sa généreuse mise à disposition des moyens audio-visuels et Maryl Azzoug pour son accueil chaleureux au sein de la SCUIO.

Je remercie pour finir les collègues BIATOSS ainsi que les étudiants pour leur aimable participation : Nicolas Abejean, Anne Barrachin, Sancia Bikindou, Céline Bilhaud, Mélissa Bouzidi, Cindy Camart, Morgane Chauvin-Pagesy, Sébastien Danve, Laura-Marianne Decreuse, Mailin Dittman, Anne Duhin, Maud Feret, Manon Gautran, Rémi Gils, Pierre Gris, Bomi Kim, Camille Kis, Fanny Laclef, Christelle Lavialle, Thomas Lukowski, Sarah Maes, Myriam Messika, Camille Monteltagot, Imen Ouasti, Jean-Sébastien Petrucci, Céline Pinto, Catherine Rumebe, Ibrar Sarwar, Jamila Soulaymani, Clio Stavropoulos, Pauline Thomas, Alexandria Vide, Laurence Wozniak, Chahrazade Zekri.

En résumé :

Table des matières n° 1 : textes et exercices classés par domaine de recherche.

Table des matières n° 2 : films, textes électroniques et versions audio du DVD classés par domaine de recherche.

: voir le film sur le DVD

Pour les films :

*   Niveau 1 : « Débutant »

**   Niveau 2 : « Intermédiaire »

*** Niveau 3 : « Confirmé »

: voir le texte électronique sur le DVD

: écouter la version audio sur le DVD

Mots ou expressions de spécialité : reportez-vous aux deux LEXIQUES de vocabulaire anglais/français et français/anglais en fin d'ouvrage.

Solutions aux exercices de compréhension : reportez-vous à la partie « Réponses » en fin d'ouvrage.

We hope that you enjoy reading this book and find it useful for your acquisition of psychological concepts and English terminology.

Laurence Masse

Chapitre 1

PSYCHOLOGIE SOCIALE/ SOCIAL PSYCHOLOGY

Social psychologists cover a wide range of topics in their research. The topics are all connected by the desire of researchers to understand and explain how individuals are influenced by the actual, imagined, or implied presence of other individuals or groups. In other words, social psychologists are interested in the impact that both the social environment, and social interaction with other people, have on someone's attitudes and behaviours. In the wide field covered by social psychologists, some of the major topics include : social cognition, attitudes and how they change, aggression/violence and its counterpart-prosocial behaviour, prejudice and discrimination, social identity, group behaviour, persuasion techniques, and social influence. Research based on both traditional and more recent topics will be covered in this section.

1 THE REASONS FOR LOVE AND FRIENDSHIP : CONSCIOUS OR UNCONSCIOUS ? ♫ (AUDIO 1)

Love, friendship, and interpersonal attraction have been the focus of social psychology research for over 50 years. They offer a sharp contrast between scientists', experts' explanations and taxonomies, "and" spontaneous, often implicit theories or relational schemas related to feelings of attraction.

Theories of love and friendship

Love entails a variety of concepts (Lamy, 2007), sometimes very broad and unspecified (*e.g.*, "It is an emotion"), sometimes more specific and possibly contradictory. Love is supposed to bring intense joy, but also suffering.

It unites and destroys. It can be viewed as intrusive and obsessive thinking about the beloved one, or intense longing for his/her presence. Conversely, in later stages of the relationship or in other persons, it is conceptualized as a kind of serene friendship or secure attachment. Love can be selfish or altruistic. Lovers tend to idealize their partner – wear *"rose-colored glasses"* – but they also develop greater empathy towards them than towards strangers.

The representation of friendship includes three components (Maisonneuve, 2004) : friends are those with whom we can truly communicate, and who understand us ; they are faithful ; they help each other – *"true friends are those who remain when things go wrong"*.

Differences are visible, similarities go unnoticed

Most people believe both that "birds of a feather flock together", and that "opposites attract". Previous research, however, has shown that only the first adage is true. Friends or lovers are more alike than random strangers measured demographically on age, sex (for friendship), education, religion, social status. They share similar values and attitudes. They tend to resemble each other in personality, and in their cognitive and emotional style. Moreover, people tend to believe that similar others will like them and that dissimilar others will dislike them, which, in turn, leads to an overestimation of similarity among close partners.

Similarity can be interpreted as a reward or belief validation : the agreement between the partners appears to testify for both of them that they are right to think or behave the way they do. But similarity is also an underlying factor, because we are constantly surrounded by people who resemble us : same residential location, same job, same educational level, same age, same leisure activities, etc. Therefore, the field of eligible individuals from which we choose our mate or friends is mainly composed of similar others. However, it remains unnoticed that, even if we have the right to love or like any human being, we don't have the opportunity to meet any (or every) human being. Moreover, these choices among physically close or similar others appear to be "natural" because we tend to feel more attracted to familiar – as opposed to unfamiliar – others (*mere exposure effect*).

Physical attractiveness is more visible than the reasons why we long for it

Male and female attractive targets are presumed to have more desirable traits than physically unattractive targets, to be more socially skilled, to represent exciting dates, to be involved in happier marriages. Despite the fact that ratings of attractiveness are often considered personal and largely non-consensual among adults, people tend mostly to agree about who is attractive and who is not. However, they are unaware that criteria of physical beauty fit the main assumptions of evolutionary psychology (Buss, 1999). Men prefer women with a WHR (waist-to-hip ratio) of 0.7, and women whose WHR nears 0.7 are those who get pregnant more easily and have the highest likelihood of being in good health. Further, men and women are attracted to people whose faces and bodies are most symmetrical, which signals good genes and good health. Women prefer men who display cues of high status, good earning, and high commitment to the relationship, because it ensures that their offspring will be protected and will survive.

Friends and lovers are matched with individuals of similar levels of physical attractiveness, but – with the exception of men recording interest in female partners – persuade themselves that their choices are only based on the inner qualities and skills of those they like or love.

Relationship experts *versus* withdrawers

Regarding love and friendship, women have been described as being more aware of relationships compared to men. They display more emotion and value closeness and intimacy. They have an interdependent self-construal, *i.e.*, relationships are part of their identity. In contrast, men have an independent self-construal, *i.e.*, their self-definition is based on their own unique attributes and on a sense of autonomy from others (Markus & Kittayama, 1994). Men have more difficulty explaining personal relationships. Married men tend to talk about their relationships in order to fix a conflict, whereas wives consider relationship talk as an end in itself. Women also spend more time thinking about relationships and describe them in a more sophisticated fashion. They have a better memory for relationship events, *e.g.*, a first date. Women are more pragmatic and more cautious during relationship initiation, while men endorse romantic beliefs more frequently, such as *"love at first sight"* or *"predestination of soul-mates"*. Thus it can be asserted that women have a better consciousness of the reasons why people get involved in – or put an end to – personal relationships.

When empathic accuracy comes to be an enemy

Both men and women may exhibit reduced empathic accuracy when it allows them to maintain positive – though unrealistic – beliefs about their partners or about their current relationships. Realistic views may have a destructive impact on intimate relationships, thus inducing partners to prefer inaccurate mind-reading. For example, dating partners tend to avoid awareness of their mate's possible interest in an attractive alternative partner. Men and women also tend to overestimate how similar their partner's opinions, feelings, and personality traits are to their own. When attracted to someone, they try to guess the probability of being liked or loved in return, but the probability of a realistic evaluation decreases when the need for love increases.

Idealization in couples is connected to satisfaction regarding the relationship : those who perceive their partners more positively than the partners view themselves receive more emotional benefit from their relationships. Therefore, such *positive illusions* (Murray, Holmes, & Griffin, 1999) are a means by which people can maintain long-term relationships.

CAUSES OF ATTRACTION MAY BE WORTH THINKING ABOUT, CONSEQUENCES GO UNNOTICED

Previous research, just as natural thinking, has focused almost exclusively on the antecedents of attraction : why do we like or love ? Which people are likely to be attracted to each other ? However, an epistemological shift is needed, in order to clarify the possible consequences of love and friendship. Now, it is well-documented that social ties may be linked to mental and physical health (mortality and morbidity). However, such epidemiological studies are based on marital status or social networks, and thus loosely connected to the cognition of love. Consequences of feelings on memory or judgment are well documented too, but research is mostly restricted to positive versus negative moods, and to other feelings than love (*e.g.*, fear, disgust, or anger).

Recent research (*e.g.*, Lamy, Fischer-Lokou, & Guéguen, 2008) has found that the mere suggestion of the idea of love may trigger increased helpfulness. Therefore, further research will need to test for cognitive, emotional, and behavioral effects that may occur when the idea of love is made salient.

Selective references for further reading

Buss, D. M. (1999). *Evolutionary psychology : the new science of the mind*. Boston : Allyn & Bacon.

Lamy, L. (2007). *L'amour ne doit rien au hasard*. Paris : Eyrolles.

Lamy, L., Fischer-Lokou, J., & Guéguen, N. (2008). Semantically induced memories of love and helping behavior. *Psychological Reports*, *102*, 418-424.

Maisonneuve, J. (2004). *Psychologie de l'amitié*. Paris : PUF.

Markus, H. R., & Kitayama, S. (1994). A collective fear of the collective : Implications for selves and theories of selves. *Personality and Social Psychology Bulletin*, *20*, 568-579.

Murray, S. L., Holmes, J. G., & Griffin, D. W. (1996). The benefits of positive illusions : Idealization and the construction of satisfaction in close relationships. *Journal of Personality and Social Psychology*, *70*, 79-98.

Exercise 1

Fill in the blanks in the sentences below with the most appropriate term from the following list.

List of terms

(a) positive illusions ; (b) "rose-coloured glasses" ; (c) "true friends are those who remain when things go wrong" ; (d) "birds of a feather flock together", (e) "opposites attract" ; (f) mere exposure effect ; (g) intrusive and obsessive thoughts.

Sentences with blanks

In terms of the two familiar myths, research demonstrates that (1) __________________ but not that (2) __________________. When people idealize their lovers, we say they are wearing (3) ______________ ______________. When people fall in love they often experience (4) ____ ____________________________ about the person they love. One of the most important findings about friendship is that (5) ________________ ________________. We tend to feel more attracted to familiar – as opposed to unfamiliar – others. This could be a (6) ______________________. (7) ______________________ consist of viewing our partners more positively than they view themselves.

2 PROSOCIAL BEHAVIOR

The starting point of modern research on prosocial behavior is known as the *"Kitty Genovese incident"*. On March 13, 1964, when returning to her home in Queens (New York), a 29-year old woman was attacked and stabbed over a 45-minute period while witnesses were listening or watching from their apartments without intervening. Diffusion of responsibility is one of the key concepts that were proposed in order to explain this *"bystander apathy"*: people feel less personally accountable for helping when they believe other persons are present and might intervene.

HELPING AND ALTRUISM

Prosocial behavior refers to helping and altruism. Helping is an action that provides a benefit or improves the well-being of another person (Dovidio *et al.*, 2006). Casual, substantial, emotional, or emergency helping can occur. It can be planned or spontaneous. Altruism is a motivational state (Batson,

1991) ; its goal is to increase another's welfare, with no (apparent) benefit to oneself. Altruism is triggered particularly when one feels empathy or sympathy for the person in need of help. When one has a sense of "oneness" with the person in need, *i.e.*, experiences with shared or interconnected identities, being altruistic toward the other is being altruistic towards oneself.

Evidence supports the view that true altruism exists, as well as self-benefiting helping behavior which is, for example, motivated by concerns to stop witnessing someone suffering, to improve one's own mood, to promote self-esteem by being helpful, and to expect social benefits such as fame or gratitude. It must also be emphasized that there are costs for not helping as well as for helping. When choosing not to help, one can feel guilty, selfish, or having contravened a social norm (*e.g.*, a man is expected to help a woman in distress in a public setting).

MEN AS HELPERS, WOMEN AS DESERVING HELP ?

Despite contradictory findings, research on sex differences and helping behavior has reached the conclusion (Eagly & Crowley, 1986) that men are more helpful than women, and that women receive more help than men. Also, men help women more than men and women seek help more than men do.

These differences have been interpreted in light of the social role theory of helping that states men and women behave according to their gender roles. The masculine gender role promotes helping that is heroic and chivalrous, whereas the feminine gender role promotes helping that is nurturant and caring. In line with these expectancies it has been found, for example, that men were more helpful than women to a man who fell in the subway, or to a person whose car had broken down. Women were more helpful than men if they were asked to help a friend or lover, or a person confronted with personal or emotional problems.

The salience of a helping norm also contributes to greater helping. According to the fact that most studies of helping behavior have been conducted in public, as compared to private settings, gender differences in helping behavior may be accounted for by social pressure that reminds potential helpers of the way they should behave. For example, in a city street, men should be brave and protect helpless persons. Men should be strong and independent, and therefore, avoid asking for help. Women should be cautious in public settings, and emotionally expressive in private, personal settings.

CHIVALROUS, OR PATERNALISTIC HELPING ?

Chivalrous helping has been defined as the protection granted to individuals who are *less able and powerful*. It can be considered a survival of medieval knights' code of honor, which was prescribed to protect "the widow and the orphan" and, more generally, the weak and defenseless – among whom, notably, are women. *"Archaic, symbolic, or anachronistic forms of chivalry"* (Lamy, Fischer-Lokou, & Guéguen, 2010) may have survived, in which the male is perceived as strong and a protector, while the female is perceived as weak, passive, and in need of protection.

Social norms and standards prescribe that men should be daring and courageous, especially when a woman is in need of help. In addition, in dangerous and emergency situations, another motive for intervening is one's physical strength. Previous research has found that male "heroes" who had prevented dangerous crimes were taller, heavier, and more experienced, compared to a group of men who didn't intervene to save or rescue someone.

Because women, as a group, are shorter, lighter, and less muscular than men, it can be asserted that women engage in heroic helping less frequently than men because they presume their intervention might be unsuccessful, and they risk being harmed. Conversely, men are stronger than women and socialized to be self-confident and powerful. Obviously, these gender roles and the reminiscence of an ideology of chivalry encompass paternalism and *benevolent sexism* (Viki, Abrams, & Hutchison, 2003), *i.e.*, a representation of women treated courteously in so far as they endorse women's subordinate role. And it remains unsure if these representations and behaviors can dissolve when men's fear of subordination to women, and women's desire to be courteously treated, remain unchanged.

Love and helpfulness

Helpfulness can be considered as a particular type of love, among many others. The concept of love is divided into subcategories such as romantic love, maternal love, affection, and so on. Therefore, activating the concept of love may result in the activation of its subcategories, thus reinforcing the awareness of helpfulness in a relevant situation.

In a line of research aimed at testing a possible increase of helpfulness among participants primed with the idea of love, Lamy (*e.g.*, Lamy, Fischer-Lokou, & Guéguen, 2009) found that participants induced to retrieve the memory of a love episode were more helpful than those induced to retrieve the memory of a piece of music. They more frequently helped a requester asking for money to take the bus, or a person who had inadvertently lost a stack of CDs, or a lost person who needed directions. Moreover, increases in helpfulness were obtained only when the requester was female and the helper was male, *i.e.*, in the case where chivalrous helping was needed. In another study (Lamy, Fischer-Lokou, & Guéguen, 2010), male participants who were asked for the direction of Valentine Street, as compared to Martin Street, were more helpful to a female confederate whose cell phone had been taken by a group of four disreputable-looking male confederates who refused to return it.

It was hypothesized that the activation of the concept of love may enhance the awareness of gender roles which, in turn, would enhance men's chivalrous helping. Also, when reminded of "Valentine", spreading of activation to related concepts would reinforce the awareness of love and gender-congruent roles.

Along with the social role theory of helping and socio-cognitive explanations, we suggested that mood-maintenance effects could explain the above-mentioned findings. Participants prompted to remind themselves of love or "Valentine", feel good, and thus might be actively helpful in order to maintain their good mood. An alternative explanation is that positive moods are related to faster, less analytic information-processing, which leads participants to decide more quickly, and with less awareness of possible consequences, to give their help. These findings, however, show that the mere activation of "love", or "Valentine", in the absence of any romantic context, is sufficient to trigger enhanced helpfulness.

Selective references for further reading

Batson, C. D. (1991). *The altruism question : toward a social-psychological Answer*. Hillsdale, NJ : Lawrence Erlbaum Associates.

Dovidio, J. F., Piliavin, J. A., Schroeder, D. A., & Penner, L. A. (2006). *The social psychology of prosocial behavior*. Mahwah, NJ : Lawrence Erlbaum Associates.

Lamy, L., Fischer-Lokou, J., & Guéguen, N. (2009). Induced reminiscence of love and chivalrous helping. *Current Psychology*, *28*, 202-209.

Lamy, L., Fischer-Lokou, J., & Guéguen, N. (2010). Valentine street promotes chivalrous helping. *Swiss Journal of Psychology*, *69*, 167-170.

Viki, G. T., Abrams, D., & Hutchison, P. (2003). The "true" romantic : Benevolent sexism and paternalistic chivalry. *Sex Roles*, *49*, 533-537.

Pour en savoir plus sur le comportement d'aide, reportez-vous au DVD contenant le film intitulé :

Film 1 : When do people help ? Diffusion of responsibility

3 THE POWER OF CONFORMITY

How do others' opinions affect us ? How likely are people to conform in social groups ? When in a group, we often "go with the flow" while at the same time having some private reservations about what we are doing. Asch (1951, 1952, 1956) conducted a series of experiments to investigate how, and to what extent, social forces constrain people's opinions and attitudes. He felt that conformity can "pollute" the social process and that it is important for society to foster values of independence in its citizens. He wanted to find out just how powerful the need to conform is in influencing our behaviour.

ASCH'S EXPERIMENT ON GROUP PRESSURE UPON DISTORTION OF JUDGEMENTS

Method

Participants in groups of 7 to 9 young men, all college students, were assembled in a classroom for a "psychological experiment" in visual judgement. They were given the following instructions : *You see two large white cards in front of you. On the left is a single line (standard line) ; on the right are three lines of various lengths (comparison lines). They are numbered 1, 2, 3 in order. You have to choose the one that is of the same length as the standard line on the other card (see Figure 1).*

The task was a simple one. The subjects announce their answers one at a time, in the order in which they are seated. However, only the last individual in the sequence is a real subject ; the others are in league with the experimenter (confederates) and respond according to a prearranged plan. For the first pairs of cards, everyone gives the correct answer. For the second set of cards, the group is again unanimous. But on the third trial, the other "subjects" choose the wrong line. And they *all* choose the *same* wrong line. Each study had 18 trials, for 12 of which the confederates gave unanimous incorrect answers. They gave correct answers occasionally so that the participant did not suspect collusion. In this situation, "*two alternatives were open to the subject : he could act independently, repudiating the majority, or he could go along with the majority, repudiating the evidence of his senses*" (Asch, 1955, p. 33).

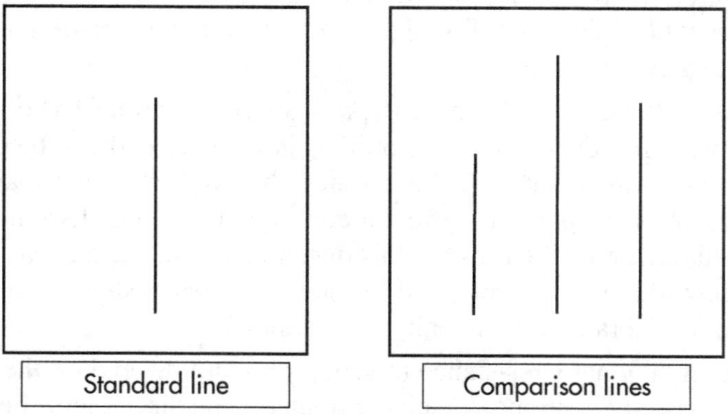

Figure 1

Results

Under ordinary circumstances (control group), when all the participants were naïve subjects, individuals made mistakes less than 1 % of the time, but under group pressure the participants accepted the wrong judgements in 36.8 % of the cases. Only 29 % of participants remained completely independent. Whether the participants yielded or remained independent, for the most part, they were deeply disturbed by this discrepancy between what they saw and what they believed others saw.

Of course, individuals differed markedly in their responses : some subjects were completely independent, and never agreed with the erroneous judgements of the majority, whereas other subjects conformed almost all the time. Each participant was interviewed at the end of the experiment. Explanations given for participants' nonconformity included : confidence in one's own judgment or the obligation to stick to their answers. Conformists gave explanations such as : *"I am wrong, they are right"*, *"not to spoil your results"*, or the idea that something was wrong with them for seeing the answer differently, so they wished to hide it.

Factors affecting the degree of conformity

After completing the initial study, Asch conducted additional research to see which aspect of group influence was most important - the size of the majority or its unanimity.

In one series, the size of the opposition was varied from one to 15 persons. When a participant was confronted with only a single individual who gave a wrong answer, s/he answered independently in almost all of the trials. However, when the subject faced two people giving wrong answers, s/he answered incorrectly 13.6 % of the time. With three confederates answering incorrectly, participants gave erroneous answers 31.8 % of the time. However, further increases in the size of the majority did not result in a substantial increase in conformity. Asch found that the size of the opposition only had an effect up to a certain point.

To explore the effect of unanimity, a supporting partner (who gave right answers) was introduced in the group. This decreased the subject's incorrect answers to one quarter of the number observed when the majority was unanimous. Was the partner's effect a consequence of his dissent, or was it related to his accuracy ? To answer this question, a confederate was instructed to disagree with both the group and the subject. Results showed that, even in this situation, the rate of conformity was reduced.

Does an individual's resistance to group pressure depend on the degree to which the majority is wrong ? Asch manipulated the discrepancy between the standard line and comparison lines. He tried to reach a point where the error was so blatantly obvious that the subject would be sure to choose the correct answer, despite the majority. But he observed that even when the difference between the lines was as much as seven inches, there were still some participants who went with the majority.

Cultural differences and conformity

Has the level of conformity changed over time since the 1950s ? An analysis of American studies found that levels of conformity in general had steadily declined since Asch's studies (Bond & Smith, 1996).

Does the level of conformity vary from one culture to another ? Using a modified form of the Asch-type group pressure technique, Stanley Milgram (1961) compared the conformity rates of Norwegian and French participants. He noted that Norwegians have a strong feeling of group identity and social responsibility and he hypothesized that social cohesiveness of this sort could go hand in hand with a high degree of conformity. In contrast, he noticed that French society has a tradition of dissent and a greater diversity of opinions, which could help participants resist group pressure. In line with these predictions, Milgram observed conformity in 62 % of Norwegian subjects and 50 % of French subjects.

More generally, literature shows that individuals from collectivist cultures, rather than individualist cultures, are more likely to yield to the majority, given the higher value placed on harmony in person-to-group relations.

Selective references for further reading

Asch, S. E. (1955). Opinions and social pressure. *Scientific American, 193*, 31-35.

Bond, R., & Smith, P. B. (1996). Culture and conformity : a meta-analysis of studies using Asch's (1952, 1956) line judgment task. *Psychological Bulletin, 119*, 111-137.

Milgram, S. (1961). Nationality and conformity. *Scientific American, 205*, 45-52.

Pour en savoir plus sur la conformité et l'expérience de Asch, reportez-vous au DVD contenant les films intitulés :

Film 2 : Power of conformity. Asch's experiment : effects of group pressure on distortion of judgements

Film 3 : Conformity

4 DESTRUCTIVE OBEDIENCE TO AUTHORITY

As car drivers, we obey the signals of traffic police, school pupils respond to the instructions given to them by their teachers and soldiers obey the orders of their commanding officers. Some system of authority is a requirement of all communal living and the very life of society is predicated on its existence. Obedience may be ennobling and educative, as well as destructive.

Stanley Milgram's experimental studies on *destructive obedience to authority* (1974) are among the most famous in all of psychology's history. Milgram's idea for this research grew out of his desire to investigate scientifically how people could be capable of carrying out great harm to others simply because they were ordered to do so. He was referring specifically to the atrocities committed under orders during World War II. In the limited form possible in laboratory research, the question becomes : if an experimenter tells a subject to hurt another person, under what conditions will he refuse to obey ? The idea was thus to study the reactions of the individual placed in the centre of a conflict between his conscience and authority. The study produced some shocking and disturbing findings.

MILGRAM'S BASELINE EXPERIMENT

The experiment took place at Yale University in the 1960s. The subjects were males between twenty and fifty years of age and covered a wide range in educational background and occupational status. They were recruited through newspaper advertisements seeking subjects to be paid participants ($ 4.50) in a scientific study about learning and memory.

Each subject and another person (introduced as a second subject, but in reality a confederate of the experimenter) were asked to draw slips of paper to determine each person's role in the experiment : either "learner" or "teacher". In fact, the draw was rigged so that the subject was always the teacher and the confederate the learner.

The experimental procedure is as follows : the learner is strapped into a chair and electrodes attached to his wrists. Electrode paste to avoid burns is applied by the experimenter.

The experimenter then takes the teacher into another room and seats him in front of a shock generator equipped with 30 switches graded from 15 to 450 volts. Clearly indicated below the switches are the words *"slight shock"*, *"moderate shock"*, *"strong shock"*, *"very strong shock"*, *"intense shock"*, *"extreme intensity shock"*, *"danger : severe shock"* and finally *"XXX"*. The teacher has in front of him a list of thirty adjective-noun word pairs. His task is first to read the thirty word pairs (*e.g.*, blue/sky) to the learner and then present one of the words to the learner who has to reply with the pair-word (*e.g.*, blue… sky). The experimental situation permits communication from one room to another.

The experimenter explains to the teacher that each time the learner makes a mistake, he must give him an electric shock (the learner gives a predetermined set of responses to the word pair test, based on a schedule of approximately three wrong answers to one correct answer). He specifies that the level of the shock must increase in intensity with the number of mistakes. The experiment is planned so that the teacher receives feedback from the learner each time he administers an electric shock and according to its intensity : at 75 volts the learner begins to grunt and moan ; at 150 volts he demands to be let out of the experiment ; at 180 volts he cries out that he can no longer stand the pain ; at 300 volts he refuses to provide any more answers. In response to this last tactic, the experimenter instructs the naïve subject to treat the absence of an answer as equivalent to a wrong answer, and to follow the usual shock procedure. Each time the teacher hesitates, the experimenter urges him to continue and if, after the fourth encouragement, the subject refuses to obey, the experiment is stopped.

The learner, in fact, was not connected to the generator and received no shocks at all. His reactions – which sounded very convincing and whose authenticity was not questioned by the naïve participants – were pre-recorded so that each learner was exposed to a standardized set of protests from the victim. Each naïve subject was given a sample shock (45 volts) prior to beginning his run as the teacher. This further convinced the subject of the authenticity of the generator.

After the subjects finished the experiment, they received a full explanation (called a debriefing) of the true purpose of the study. In addition, they were interviewed as to their feelings and thoughts during the experiment and the confederate "learner" was brought in for a friendly reconciliation.

Results

A measure of obedience was obtained simply by recording the level of shock at which each subject refused to continue. Results showed that 62.5 % of the subjects placed in this situation continued administering shocks until 450 volts. This is not to say that the subjects were enthusiastic about what they were doing. Many exhibited signs of extreme stress and concern for the man receiving the shocks, and even became angry with the experimenter. Yet they obeyed.

These were average, normal people, not sadistic, cruel individuals in any way. So why did they behave like this ? For Milgram it is not the person but rather the "power of the situation" that is the major lesson of the experiment.

The power of the situation

The power of the situation was demonstrated in an extensive research program consisting of 17 situational variations on the basic paradigm. These variations helped Milgram identify some of the conditions that strengthen or weaken the obstacles to challenging authority – the binding and opposing forces that push the level of obedience up or down.

Obedience decreased :

(1) as the physical distance between the teacher and learner decreased (if the learner was in the same room rather than another one) ;

(2) as the physical distance between the participant and experimenter increased (if the experimenter was not physically present in the room but issued orders over a phone link) ;

(3) if other "teachers" (confederates) were introduced and seen to disobey the experimenter (the first one withdrew at 150 volts and the second at 210 volts) ;

(4) if subjects faced a divided authority (two experimenters of apparently equal status ran the experiment jointly and, at the point at which the learner began to protest vehemently, experimenter 1 called for a halt and experimenter 2 instructed the teacher to continue) ;

(5) if the experiment was re-located from Yale University to a less prestigious office.

Obedience increased if the teacher's role was divided among two people (the shocks were administered by a man playing the role of another participant while the naïve subject performed subsidiary tasks which contributed to the experimental proceedings but did not require him to press the lever of the shock generator). Milgram repeated the procedure with women subjects and he found similar results.

Some explanations of obedience

According to Milgram, the *socialization* of obedience is of enormous significance. From early childhood throughout our lives, we are taught to obey authority and are rewarded for doing so. We learn to *value* obedience. Obedience becomes an unquestioned operative norm in countless institutions and settings (military, medicine, education, and corporation). In addition, he considered that we have two states of consciousness : the *agentic state* and the *autonomous state*. In the latter state, individuals are aware of the consequences of their actions and therefore voluntarily engage in, or disengage from, behaviour. In the agentic state, they see themselves as subordinates in an otherwise hierarchical system and, as a result, they don't feel responsible for what they are doing.

Selective references for further reading

Blass, T. (2002). *The man who shocked the world*. New York : Basic Books.

Milgram, S. (1974). *Obedience to authority*. New York : Harper & Row.

Pour en savoir plus sur la soumission à l'autorité, reportez-vous au DVD contenant le film intitulé :

Film 4 : Destructive obedience to authority

5 ATTITUDES, ATTITUDE CHANGE AND PERSUASION

ATTITUDES

The study of attitudes has been central to the field of social psychology for a long time (Allport, 1935), and the concept has been viewed in diverse ways over the decades. Most often, researchers adopt this definition of attitude : *"Attitude is a psychological tendency that is expressed by evaluating a particular entity with some degree of favor or disfavor"* (Eagly & Chaiken, 1993). Psychological tendency refers to a state that is internal to the person. It predisposes the person toward evaluative responses that are positive or negative. Attitudes toward an object can be based on different classes of information : affective (the emotions it evokes), cognitive (reasoned analysis of the consequences that accrue from selecting an option among those available) and behavioral information (experiences and observation of our own relevant behavior).

Research concerning attitudes has been able to progress as a result of advances made in the measurement of attitudes. A Likert scale consists of a series of declarative statements about some attitude object, followed by a continuum of choices ranging from *"strongly agree"* to *"strongly disagree"*. A respondent's attitude is represented by the average of his or her responses to all the declarative statements in the scale. The *semantic differential scale* or SDS (Osgood, Suci and Tannenbaum, 1957) asks respondents to evaluate an attitude object along a series of bipolar adjective scales (good-bad, favorable-unfavorable, pleasant-unpleasant, etc). Respondents are asked to check the scale point that best represents their evaluation of the attitude object. The sum of averages across the items serves as the respondent's attitude score.

At present, there is an interest in implicit attitudes due to the development of implicit measures. Implicit measures seek to obtain an estimate of an individual's attitude without directly asking him/her to consider it. Implicit measures involve responses or processes that are automatic or difficult to control. Greenwald *et al.'s* (1998) *Implicit Association Test* (IAT) has led the way and is driving theorizing about the nature of the attitude construct.

ATTITUDE CHANGE AND PERSUASION

Persuasion and, therefore, attitude change, constitutes one of the most fundamental processes of social communication. By changing people's attitudes we can change how they think about other people, groups, objects, or issues. Persuasive communication often involves a number of elements, such as the communicator (*e.g.*, source credibility), the receiver (audience), the medium (*e.g.*, writing, video), the type of message (*e.g.*, long or short) and the context (*e.g.*, distraction).

Early research concerned the *"Yale Model"* (Hovland, Janis & Kelley, 1953). Communication is analyzed in terms of *"who says what, via what medium, to whom, and directed at what kind of behaviour"* (Lasswell, 1948). Any one variable (*e.g.*, an expert source) is expected to have just one effect on persuasion, either enhancing or reducing it. Are expert people more persuasive than non-expert people ? Researchers have demonstrated that any one variable (*e.g.*, an expert source) was shown to be good for persuasion in some studies but detrimental in others.

Later, the *cognitive response model* (Greenwald, 1968) emphasized the mediating role of the thoughts (cognitive responses) that people generate as they receive and reflect upon persuasive communications. Thoughts mediate the effect of persuasive messages on attitude change : favourable recipient-generated thoughts should be persuasive, unfavourable thoughts should be unpersuasive. Variables could increase or decrease persuasion by influencing the likelihood that people would elaborate or think about the arguments presented. For example, variables like source credibility might enhance persuasion by leading people to be more favourable in their thoughts to the message than if the source was not mentioned or was low on credibility.

The *Elaboration Likelihood Model* or ELM (Petty & Cacioppo, 1986) and the *Heuristic-Systematic Model* or HSM (Chaiken, 1987) postulated that persons subjected to persuasive messages process information, and thus change attitudes, via one of two routes. According to ELM, when people are motivated and able to think about an issue, they are likely to take the central route to persuasion – focusing on the arguments. Yet, sometimes people are not motivated enough or able to think carefully. Rather than noticing whether the arguments are compelling, people might follow the peripheral route to persuasion – focusing on cues that trigger acceptance without much thinking (*e.g.*, expertise of the source, "experts can be trusted"). For example, when motivation and ability to think were low, positively valenced variables such as source expertise would be used as simple cues (peripheral route) leading to more persuasion regardless of the quality of argument in the message.

A NEW WAY TO AFFECT ATTITUDE CHANGE : SELF-VALIDATION

According to ELM, the way in which a person processes information may be more important in determining persuasion than the content of the information itself. We know from Greenwald (see above) that people generate negative or positive thoughts (first-level thoughts) as they receive persuasive communications. However, following a thought, people can also generate other thoughts that occur at a second level (metacognition), involving reflections on the first-level thoughts. Two people might have the same first-level thought in response to a persuasive message ; but one person might have greater confidence in that thought than the other person. This is the self-validation hypothesis : generating first-level thoughts is not sufficient for them to have an impact.

Confidence in a thought (second-level thought, or metacognition) is important because the greater the confidence, the greater its impact on attitude.

For example, Petty and Briñol (2008) proposed that source credibility can influence persuasion by affecting the confidence people have in the thoughts they generated in response to a message. When one has already thought about information in a message, and then discovers that it came from a high- or low-credibility source, one's thoughts are also validated or invalidated by the source information. Tormala *et al.* (2006) presented people with either a strong or a weak quality message promoting a new pain relief product, and then revealed information about the source (low vs. high in credibility). When the message was strong, people generated positive thoughts. High source credibility led to more favorable attitudes than low source credibility because of greater confidence in the positive thoughts generated. However, when the message was weak, the credibility effect was reversed. When the message was weak, people generated negative thoughts. High source credibility led to less favorable attitudes than low source credibility because of greater confidence in the negative thoughts generated.

All of these models assume that information does exert an important impact on attitudes. Moreover, these models have a relation with the content of attitudes (they may express different beliefs and emotions), their structure and strength (attitudes reflect the intensity of feelings and beliefs to a greater or lesser extent), and their function (attitudes may serve different psychological motivations, such as the need to be correct or the need to be liked by others).

Selective references for further reading

Bohner, G., & Wänke, M. (2002). *Attitudes and attitude change*. Psychology Press.

Girandola, F. (2003). *Psychologie de l'engagement et de la persuasion*. PUFC.

Maio, G. R., & Haddock, G. (2009). *The psychology of attitudes and attitude change*. London : Sage.

Petty, R. E., & Briñol, P. (2008). Psychological processes underlying persuasion : A social psychological approach. *Diogenes*, *217*, 52-67. [Lien en anglais : www.psy.ohio-state.edu/petty/documents/2007DiogenesEnglishPettyBrinol.pdf] [Lien en français: www.psy.ohio-state.edu/petty/documents/2007Diogenes.pdf]

Exercise 2

Questions

1. List two types of attitude measurement.
2. If someone is persuaded by an attractive speaker with a poor argument, which "route to persuasion" did s/he take ?

3. Which term in the text could be defined as "thoughts about thoughts" ?
4. Which three types of information can serve as the basis for attitudes ?
5. What term refers to attitudes of which a person is unaware ?

6 PREJUDICES, STEREOTYPES AND DISCRIMINATION

Discrimination means treating a target[1] individual favourably or unfavourably because s/he is a member of the source's[2] own group (the *ingroup*) or a different one (the *outgroup*), for example in terms of his/her ethnic origins, skin colour, age, religion, language, sexual orientation, weight, etc. Discrimination takes various specific forms, each of them related to a different prejudice (*e.g.*, racism, ageism, sexism, homophobia or weightism). Discrimination is always related to two other phenomena, prejudice and stereotypes.

A group's stereotypes can relate to the ingroup *(endostereotypes)* or an outgroup *(exostereotypes)*. Prejudice is a negative or positive attitude towards a target, expressed in the form of unreasoned rejection or approval, for instance *"I don't like trade unionists"* or *"I love Italian girls"*. Prejudices are linked to stereotypes, such as *"gay men are effeminate"*, *"black people are good athletes"*, *"women are intuitive"* which indicate the *direction* (positive or negative) of the prejudice. Studies such as the one conducted by Mackie & Smith (1998) show that a prejudice is different from a stereotype because it calls on the *affective* dimension of an attitude, whereas a stereotype is linked to knowledge and beliefs – the *cognitive* dimension. Discrimination is the result of prejudice and stereotypes, and concerns people's actions (the *behavioural* dimension).

Discrimination can be positive or negative, direct or indirect. Direct positive discrimination could involve giving a particular group special favours, or crediting it with responsibility for positive situations ; indirect positive discrimination would mean defending a group by trying to protect it from ending up in negative situations, or denying its responsibility for them.

Studies show (*e.g.*, Yzerbyt & Schadron, 1996 ; Bourhis & Leyens, 2001 ; Salès-Wuillemin, 2006) that positive forms of discrimination generally take place in favour of members of the ingroup, and negative forms towards members of outgroups ; although in certain cases the reverse phenomenon, favouritism towards the outgroup, appears when a target group is treated better than the source group (Clark & Clark, 1947). This can happen when

1. Someone towards whom discrimination is practised.
2. Someone who practises discrimination.

a minority group demonstrates particularly strong enculturation (Wright & Taylor, 1995), internalising and reproducing dominant social norms – which might help its members to limit conflict and maintain social equilibrium (Jost & Banaji, 1994).

Discrimination is present in many forms in businesses. Sometimes a particular task is associated with a specific ethnic group (usually less qualified and lower in social status, leading to the group being restricted to that task). The *"glass ceiling"* effect can make it impossible for members of certain groups to rise to the top jobs in a business.

A *"glass partition"* effect can also be observed in relation to key positions which lead *to* those top jobs. Then there is the *"swing door"* effect, which involves piling up problems for a colleague, so that in the end the target gives up trying to succeed, and thus confirms the negative stereotype.

Two social processes feed all these phenomena, *social reproduction* and *cooptation*. Social reproduction means that when a manager wants to recruit or promote someone, s/he gives preferential treatment to individuals with a similar educational, social or cultural background to him/herself. It gives the manager the false impression that s/he can *predict* how the other person will behave. Cooptation is similar, and involves preferentially recruiting or promoting people who are part of the "network" and thus "vouched for" by other close colleagues. It gives the manager the false impression that s/he will be able to control how the other person behaves.

There is a difference between explicit and implicit attitudes. For more than thirty years now, polls and studies have shown that prejudice and stereotypes are on the decline. Everything seems to show that the fight against racism is being won – which would be good news, were it not that the reality is quite different.

Studies in social psychology show that there is a latent phenomenon hidden behind the figures. It has been shown that reduced discrimination is mainly limited to studies which use *explicit* measures – for instance, people are asked to *say* whether they discriminate, or whether they think certain positive or negative traits are characteristic of a particular group. Participants can control their answers, because they can see what the study is all about, and so they conform to the anti-discrimination norm. But when they are unable to control their responses, or if the measurement is based on unexpected indicators, discrimination reappears. This shows that there are two types of attitudes : *explicit* attitudes which are accessible and measurable using traditional scales, and *implicit* attitudes which are less accessible and require more specific types of measurement. Among the most interesting of such measures are subliminal priming, measuring reaction times, and some kinds of language analysis (Devine, 1989 ; Maass, Castelli, & Arcuri, 2000 ; Dovidio, Kawakami, & Beach 2001 ; Gaertner & Dovidio 2005 ; Masse, Salès-Wuillemin, Bromberg & Frigout, 2008).

Various psychosocial theories have been advanced to explain the processes at work. One group of theories focuses on individuals and how they analyse information, while another is more based on relationships between groups.

At the individual level, there are three factors underlying prejudice, stereotypes and discrimination :

(1) Stereotypes enable people to reduce the amount of information they have to process, which limits the *"cognitive load"*, facilitates understanding (see Hoffman & Hurst's, 1990, *"naive scientist"* model, or Fiske & Taylor's 'cognitive miser', 1984), and decides what information coming from the environment is the most relevant (Fiske & Taylor's *"motivated tactician"* model, 1987).

(2) Because they are social, and, thus, the sign of a certain consensus, they allow people to make judgements which have more chance of being socially accepted (Schadron & Yzerbyt's *"social judgeability"* model, 1991).

(3) They are part of each individual's culture and are triggered automatically – although people who have been brought up to question stereotypes and prejudice may have some ability to control this process, if they have enough cognitive resources available to them (*"automatic activation"*, see Devine, 1989 and Dovidio, Kawakami & Beach, 2001).

At the collective level, two main factors come into play. Relationships between groups can become conflictual : (a) when resources are limited and groups have to compete for them, or (b) when, even if resources are not limited, groups are in a situation of comparative evaluation. In both cases, people have survival mechanisms which lead them to privilege members of their own group to the detriment of other individuals (*"real conflict"*, Sherif, 1966 ; *"social comparison"*, Festinger, 1954). These inter-group relations affect individual functioning for two reasons :

- First, when individuals suffer discrimination and they see the situation as unjust (Stouffer *et al.*, 1949) they tend to seek a better place in society. That can lead them to aim for individual or collective social mobility, and to take action aimed at improving their group's position in society, such as strikes and demonstrations.
- Second, individual members of dominant groups have their self-esteem enhanced by belonging to that group, if they are strongly attached to it. If they think this is legitimate, they will replicate the system, helping to maintain their group's privileges. On the other hand, if they find the situation unjust, they may try to change the system through individual or collective action (Social Identity Theory, Tajfel & Turner 1986).

Is it possible to fight prejudice, stereotypes and discrimination ? Any attempt to do so has to take into account the attitude concerned (*i.e.*, is it explicit or implicit ?) and the level at which action is to be carried out (individual or collective).

First, let's examine the fight against explicit discrimination. At the individual level, explicit attitudes can be modified by giving clear information about different forms of discrimination – these messages can be relayed by the media, or for younger targets via educational programmes in school (Dovidio & Gaertner, 1999). There are also more subtle techniques based on creating cognitive conflict, for example, by presenting people with information that contradicts a stereotype. However, such information is more effective if it relates to a large number of members of the stereotyped group ; if it only applies to one, targets are likely to see the case as an exception – which allows them to accept the information without changing their stereotype. At the collective level, bringing groups into contact might help. This will be more effective if the groups are put in a position of interdependence rather than competition, with a common goal – for example, getting members of various communities to work together on a common project. If the objective is also compatible with (or even indispensable for) people's individual goals (if they can put it on their CVs, for instance) the effect of contact will be maximised.

As for the fight against hidden forms of prejudice, less direct techniques are required, based on asking individuals to carry out an analysis or cognitive treatment of the situation. This should lead them to reconfigure their mental universe and see things differently, from a different point of view. This, too, can be done by using cognitive conflict with individuals and inter-group contact at the collective level (Dovidio & Gaertner, 1999).

For individuals, cognitive conflict arises from exposing the inconsistency between certain actions or emotions and their prejudices. This can be done using roleplay, where someone is confronted with a member of the group s/he is prejudiced against. The role play can be filmed, and analysing the film afterwards can reveal a gap between people's intentions and their actions. Resulting guilt feelings can motivate people to become more attentive, and subsequently control their prejudiced reactions (Devine & Monteith, 1993).

At the collective level, the process has to involve the group. Groups can be brought together and participants invited to conceive of themselves as individuals (*decategorization*) then, at a second time, to reorganise their social perception of constitutive groups and relations *(recategorization).*

Decategorization means reducing the feeling that there are fundamental differences between the groups, and this can be done by *differentiation* (showing the wide variation between members of the same group) and *personalisation* (showing that members of the group are individuals, not interchangeable units). Decategorization can be accomplished by getting people from the two groups to work on achieving a goal in pairs or small groups with different people.

Recategorization involves showing that each person can be seen as a member of one category according to one criterion (*e.g.*, a community), in addition to other categories according to other criteria (age, sex, etc.), and that ultimately everyone belongs to a single category, that of human beings. The main thing is to keep moving between these different levels of belonging, analysing each change of level to show the perceptual consequences of assigning someone to this or that group.

Fighting racism is not just a matter of laws. It involves taking into account the psychological and social processes at work, so as to understand them better and find appropriate measures to tackle them. Unless we do that, we will always be confronted with superficial conformism, since in the end *"the water is always the same shape as the vase"* (Japanese proverb).

Selective references for further reading

Bourhis, R.-Y., Leyens, J.-P. (éd.) (1999, 2e éd. 2001). *Stéréotypes, discrimination et relations intergroupes*. Liège : Mardaga.

Salès-Wuillemin, E. (2006). *La Catégorisation et les stéréotypes en psychologie sociale*. Paris : Dunod.

Scharnitzky, P. (2006). *Les pièges de la discrimination*. Paris : L'Archipel.

Exercise 3

Match the terms with the appropriate statement.

List of terms

(a) *"glass partition"* ; (b) prejudice ; (c) social reproduction ; (d) stereotypes ; (e) direct positive discrimination ; (f) affective ; (g) discrimination ; (h) behavioural ; (i) direct negative discrimination ; (j) cooptation ; (k) favouritism towards the outgroup ; (l) cognitive ; (m) *"glass ceiling"* ; (n) *"swing door"* effect.

Statements

1. Treating an individual favourably or unfavourably because s/he is a member of a specified group.
2. A negative *or* positive attitude towards a target, expressed in the form of unreasoned rejection or approval, for instance *"I hate children"* or *"I love black women"*.
3. Statements such as *"gay men are effeminate"*, *"black people are good athletes"*, *"women are intuitive"* indicating the *direction* (positive or negative) of the prejudice.

4. This dimension of an attitude is expressed by prejudice.
5. This dimension of an attitude is expressed by stereotypes.
6. This dimension is an action demonstrating prejudice.
7. Giving a particular group special favours, or crediting it with responsibility for positive situations.
8. Generally takes place towards members of outgroups.
9. Appears when an outgroup is treated better than an ingroup.
10. An effect that can make it impossible for members of certain groups to rise to the top jobs in a business.
11. An effect that can be observed in relation to blocking key positions which lead *to* those top jobs.
12. Piling up problems for a colleague, so that in the end the colleague gives up trying to succeed, and thus confirms the negative stereotype.
13. Means that when a manager wants to recruit or promote someone, s/he gives preferential treatment to individuals with a similar educational, social or cultural background to him/herself. It gives the manager the false impression that s/he can *predict* how the other person will behave.
14. Involves preferentially recruiting or promoting people who are part of the "network" and thus "vouched for" by other close colleagues. It gives the manager the false impression that s/he will be able to *control* how the other person behaves.

Pour en savoir plus sur la catégorisation sociale, reportez-vous au DVD contenant le film intitulé :

Film 5 : The effects of social categorization

7 CIVILITY IN URBAN ENVIRONMENTS : IS POLITENESS OUTDATED ?[1]

At the very beginning of the last century, Simmel was already writing that life in the city is characterized by egotistical behavior, detachment, and disinterest towards others. The *"Genovese case"* (Latané and Darley, 1970) and the conclusions of numerous research projects undertaken since then (Korte, 1980 ; Korte & Kerr, 1975 ; Krupat, 1985 ; Merrens, 1973 ; Moser, 1988) consistently demonstrate that the conditions of urban life reduce the attention given to others and diminish our behavioral availability to help others.

1. Moser, G. & Corroyer, D. (2001). Politeness in an urban environment: Is city life still synonymous with civility? *Environment & Behavior, 33(5)*, 2001, 611-625.

While in our society helping behavior reflects the rule of morality (it is "good" to help others), civil behaviors are an expression of codified and formal relations, and they involve more automated reactions than helping behaviors, which involve deliberate interaction with a particular, identifiable individual. Civil behaviors refer to tacit rules governing the regulation of social interaction, shared conventions concerning what it is appropriate to do in everyday life (Goffman, 1974). Civility finds its expression in politeness. Bernard (1995) emphasizes the disinterested nature of acts of civility. In fact, politeness concerns relations with people unknown to the actor, without the actor expecting any benefit in return for the behavior. It is a behavior which is largely automatic or even reflexive, not requiring the individual to make a deliberate decision.

Is politeness only an expression of a specifically urban way of life, and therefore independent of the target person and environmental and situational conditions ?

METHODOLOGY

Politeness was operationalized by holding open the door of a large department store for the person who entered after the research participant we were observing. It was studied in two different urban contexts, a large city and a small city. Research participants were observed at the entrances of large popular department stores. The entrances contained swing doors which opened both outwards and inwards. The central location of the shops allowed us to assume a strong heterogeneity of the population, this type of shop being frequented by all segments of the population.

Participants were observed as they entered the department store. They had to be alone, in an estimated age-range of 20 to 60, and have both hands free (so if someone was carrying a handbag it had to have a shoulder strap). They had to be followed by another person at a distance of four to six steps (measured by the experimenter and marked on the ground) – the other person also had to be alone with both hands free. The observation matrix included the following components :

- individual variables – (sex of the participant and the person following the participant) ;
- situational variables – the conditions in which the participant encountered the door of the store ;
- open – (held open by the preceding person entering the store) or closed (not held open or simply closed) ;
- the participant's behaviour – holding open, or not holding open, the door for a subsequent person entering the store.

RESULTS

A total of 880 observations were made, 480 in Paris and 400 in the provincial city of Nantes. On average, and over all conditions, participants held the door open for the next person in a little more than half the cases (54 % ; 476/880).

Analysis of the results concerned, first, the sex of the participant and of the target-person ; next, environmental and situational effects ; and then interaction effects.

Finally, for each of these questions, we are not only concerned with whether each has an effect, but also with its relative size (Corroyer & Rouanet, 1994). Our adopted criterion is that a difference of five percentage points or less is weak - or negligible – whereas a difference of more than five points is significant. In order to make such a statement on the importance of an effect, we include the traditional chi-square test of observed frequencies (which only indicates a real effect or an overall effect), as well as the Bayesian probabilities associated with this effect (Bernard, 1986 ; 1999). We used the program IBF2XK. The probabilities – or Bayesian inferences – are indicated by a "*g*", in order to distinguish them from probabilities based on frequencies shown by the letter "*p*". Our reference criterion of minimum Bayesian inference was $g = .95$ (95%).

(1) **Individual variables** : Forty-two percent of participants observed were men (366/880) and fifty-eight percent women (514/880). In general, men hold the door open more often for the next person entering the store than women do (61 % / 49 %; Pearson chi square = 10.875, $p = .001$). The real difference is greater than five percentage points ($g = .97$). But we did not find more civil behavior towards women than towards men, rather the opposite (53 % for women compared to 56 % for men). Overall, civil behaviour did not vary according to the sex of the participant and the target person.

(2) **Environmental conditions (the effects of urban size)** : Polite behavior occurs more frequently in the provincial city than in Paris. In Nantes, 60 % (238/400) show civil behavior while in Paris only half do so (50 % ; 238/480). This difference is significant (60 % / 50%; Pearson chi square = 8.64, $p = .0033$), and also greater than five points ($g = .93$).

(3) **Situational conditions (the effects of door held open for the participant or door closed)** : The situational conditions encountered by the participants have an effect on their respective behaviors. Participants encountered a closed door in a little less than two-thirds of cases (64 % ; 556/880 observations). In this case, they engaged in a civil behavior on about half of the occasions (188/314 : 51 %). For the 36 % of participants who found the door held open by a person preceding them, there was a tendency to replicate the behavior (60 % / 51%; Pearson chi square = 6.572, $p = .0104$). This phenomenon only seemed to hold true for Paris.

(4) Interaction effects of environmental and situational conditions : In Paris, participants' behavior varied depending on whether they found the door open or closed. When the door was closed, 45 % (153/338) held it open for the next person, while, when they found it open, 60 % (85/142) in turn held it open for the next person (45 % / 60 %; Pearson chi square = 10.59, p = .0002). One can conclude by inference that there is a difference greater than 5 points (g = .97).

In the provincial city, the behavior of participants did not vary depending on whether they encountered an open or closed door. In both cases, about 60 % held the door open for the next person (open-door condition : 103/172, 60 % ; closed-door condition : 135/228, 59 %).

The extent of these differences does not allow us to conclude with sufficient certainty that there is even a negligible difference between the two frequencies (g = .68). When the door was open, there was therefore no difference between Paris and Nantes : in both cities slightly less than two-thirds of participants held the door open for the next person (85/142, 60 % ; 103/172, 59 %). On the other hand, there was a difference between Paris and the provincial city when the door was closed. In this case, civil behavior was clearly less marked in Paris (153/338, 45 %) than in the provincial setting (135/228, 59 %). This difference is superior to 5 points (g = .98).

In other words, in Paris, the fact of finding the door closed reduced considerably the frequency of politeness behavior, compared to all other experimental conditions.

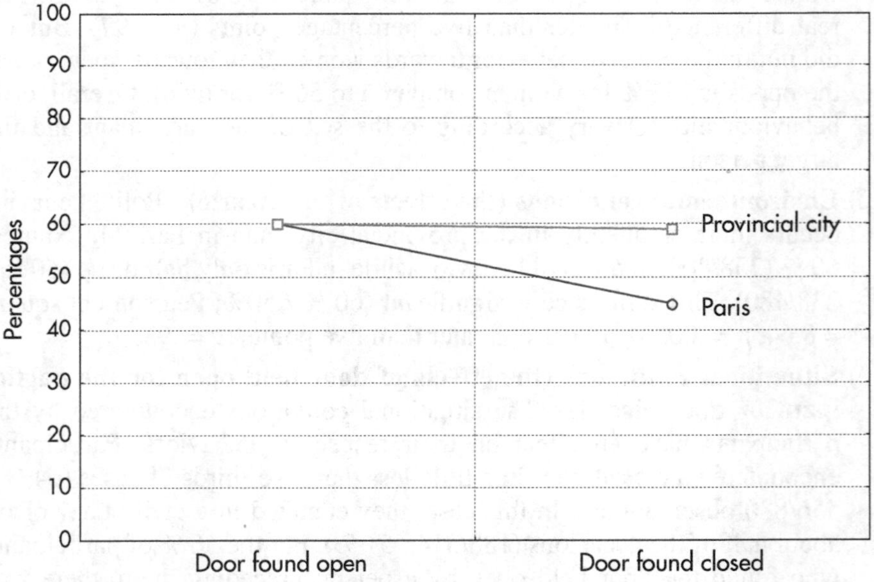

Figure 2

Interaction effects of environmental and situational conditions.

Discussion

Slightly more than half of our participants exhibited behaviors of politeness and held the door open to the person following them at the entry of a large department store. While men held the door open for the next person more often than women, politeness was equivalent whether the person following was a man or a woman. Contrary to helping behaviors, which have been found to vary according to the characteristics of the person to be helped (Moser, 2009), politeness is not dependent on the target person. These results demonstrate clearly that holding a door open to another person cannot be assimilated to a helping behaviour. Nevertheless, civility is affected both by general environmental conditions – it occurs less often in Paris than in an average provincial city – and is sensitive to situational conditions.

Politeness is more evident in the provinces than in Paris. While in the mid-sized provincial city nearly two-thirds of people hold the door open for another person, in Paris it is only one-half who do so. There is obviously a difference in spontaneous politeness between Paris and the provincial city, Parisians engaging significantly less often in civil behaviors. In Paris, the fact of finding the door open by the preceeding person strongly increases the behavior of politeness, regardless of the immediate population density (60 %/40%) while, in the provincial city, the behavior of participants is not influenced by this variable. So Parisians, but not the provincial sample, are influenced by the door being held open. This can be explained by behavioral contagion (Freedmann, 1975), itself attributable to the observation of the performance of a model (Bandura, 1973). Furthermore, participants become more likely to replicate this behavior due to its social desirability. Such effects have been frequently found in helping behaviors (Bryan & Test, 1967). In other words, the direct confrontation with a polite model appears to reactivate the norm of politeness in big city dwellers. To the extent that civil behavior in the provincial town does not depend upon observing a model, one can assert that the behavior conforms to an implicit social norm.

In conclusion, the large city is no longer synonymous with civility, and behaviors of respect towards others are not part of the daily repertoire any more. Yet, for the inhabitants of the large city, the fact of being confronted with a polite model reactivates their civility and their behaviors in this situation are similar to those living in small provincial cities.

Selective references for further reading

Bernard, Y. (1995). Les représentations sociales de la civilité dans le contexte urbain d'aujourd'hui. In M. Segaud (Ed.). *Espaces de vie, espaces d'architecture*. Paris : Éditions du Plan Construction, n° 64.

Corroyer, D., & Rouanet, H. (1994). Sur l'importance des effets et ses indicateurs dans l'analyse statistique des données. *L'Année Psychologique*, *94*, 607-624.

Goffman, E. (1973). *La Mise en scène de la vie quotidienne* : (vol. 1 : *La Présentation de soi* ; vol. 2 : *Les Relations en public*). Paris : Éditions de Minuit.

Milgram, S. (1970). The experience of living in cities : A psychological analysis. In F.F. Korten, S.W. Cook & J.I. Lacey (Eds.) *Psychology and the Problems of Society*. Washington DC : American Psychological Association.

Moser, G. (1992). *Les Stress urbains*. Paris : Armand Colin.

Exercise 4

Select the appropriate ending for each sentence.

Sentences

1. Politeness is an expression…
2. Approximately half of the individuals you meet in…
3. An expression of codified and formal relations…
4. Civil behaviours are social conventions that…
5. In our society, helping behavior…
6. Approximately two-thirds of the individuals you meet in…

Endings

a. reflects the idea that it is a moral act to help others.
b. of one of the tacit rules of civility.
c. are created by groups to regulate social interaction via tacit rules.
d. provincial cities in France are likely to hold the door of a big department store open for you.
e. Paris are likely to hold the door of a big department store open for you.
f. that involve deliberate interaction and automated reactions are called civil behaviors.

8 PSYCHOLOGY OF WOMEN : FROM THE MARGINS TO THE MAINSTREAM

NAMING THE BODY OF KNOWLEDGE

The terms *"psychology of women"*, *"feminist psychology"*, or the *"psychology of women and gender"* have all been used to refer to the body of knowledge about women and gender produced since the late 1960s (Marecek, 2001).

Individuals who have contributed to this field do not share a single ideological perspective ; not all are women ; and not all would label themselves *"feminists"*.

Woman as "Other" : critique of sex differences

In the 1960s, it was difficult for women to get accepted into graduate programs in psychology (Pullin & Stark, 1996). Consequently, feminist scholars provided research that challenged the claims that women were deficient in cognitive abilities and other qualities associated with success in work and public life (Matlin, 2007). Women were expected to become homemakers and support the careers of their husbands. Eventually, women overcame these ideological and structural barriers, supported by the feminist movement and resultant changes in societal attitudes. As the percentage of women in academic psychology increased, research articles and books that demonstrated that women and men are capable of the same work/social roles increased (Pullin & Stark, 1996).

In 1979, Unger (1979) noted that researchers studying perceptions, behavior, and personality characteristics were using the term *"sex differences"*, a term that implies relatively permanent biological differences. She noted that the term *"gender differences"* would be a more appropriate label for characteristics that are socially constructed.

Social construction refers to the fact that we are all shaped, or socially conditioned, to behave in ways that are appropriate for our sex (gender), in a given culture and context, at a particular point in history (and this is in continual evolution).

Another critique of sex/gender research is that the whole approach is paradoxical (Tavris, 1991). Researchers continue to refer to male attributes as the "norm". This highlights the unconsciously adopted cultural assumption of male/masculine characteristics as normal, and female/feminine characteristics as different. Paradoxically, the whole focus on gender differences falsely reinforces caricatures of both male and female characteristics.

Woman as caregiver : critique of the essentialist position

In the 1980s, many feminist authors focused on the concept that women possess a distinctive ethic of care, with a greater capacity for nurturing through empathic relationships. This ideology resonated with the political climate of the 1980s. American and European culture supported a psychology of feminine morality ; with women as virtuous mothers – good, caring, and essentially feminine.

In fact, neither the approach of exaggerating sex differences using male characteristics as the norm, nor the approach of defining women as essentially good caregivers served society well. In more recent work of feminist scholars, the whole process of searching for differences has been questioned because of the artificial opposition of the two genders and the reinforcement of sexist cultural bias.

An example of the potential difficulty associated with this *"Woman as Other/Woman as Problem"* was identified by Tavris (1991). She noted that many modern authors refer to the *"feminization of poverty"* (implying the problem of poverty is attached to being a woman) whereas very few authors refer to *"the masculinization of wealth"* (failing to imply there is a problem of wealth attached to being a man). That is not to say that either is true. However, the *"poor female as problem"* theme is visible and widely voiced ; *"the rich male as problem"* is not. The issue remains that whichever side is considered the norm, the other side will be perceived as deviating from it, and deviation is quickly enshrined as *"opposition"* (Tavris, 1991).

The post-modern woman : a social construction

In recent feminist literature, a post-modern perspective has been evident. In this perspective, socially constructed gender identities are continuously changing in a constantly-evolving culture. In addition, gender-related qualities and behaviors are continuously re-interpreted in the mind's eye of the observer, as the observer adapts and changes perspective. Innovative methodologies like pluralistic qualitative research (*i.e.*, using multiple qualitative approaches simultaneously) are used to promote the simultaneous consideration of multiple characteristics within a situational and cultural context. This prevents researchers from emphasizing artificial caricatures of gender characteristics divorced from their context.

Voicing critical ideas : breaking through mainstream barriers

In the 1970's, many gatekeepers of academic psychology were not open to women who questioned or criticized sex bias in the discipline. In 1970, a number of academics (who all happened to be women) discovered that their conference submissions to the national conference of the Canadian Psychological Association (CPA) had been rejected (Pyke, 2001). The reason for the rejection was cited as : *"the submissions did not fit into the established framework for the convention"*. In response, the scholars created a joint symposium of their papers, titled *"On Women, by Women"*. When this submission was, in turn, rejected by the gatekeepers, they booked a meeting room in the convention hotel to present their work at the same time as the conference. Their booking was cancelled due to pressure from the conference organizers. Refusing to be silenced, the scholars moved their meeting to an adjacent hotel. Convention delegates came in large numbers to hear their presentations on : sex stereotypes in children's literature ; fear of success ; and sex bias in social psychology journals. Today, it is hard to believe that scholars would be silenced from voicing their ideas on these topics. These topics have moved from the margins (an alternative symposium) to inclusion in the mainstream (traditional conferences, textbooks, and journals).

The whole history of the psychology of women and gender is one that has involved research and writing *« in the margins »* (Austin, Rutherford, & Pyke, 2006). Feminist scholars dared to challenge the existing sexist assumptions of mainstream psychology. Feminist journals welcomed alternative theories while encouraging the adoption of critical standpoints and alternative methods such as qualitative or narrative approaches. Despite feminist scholars' best efforts, however, the psychology of women and gender is still relatively invisible in many mainstream journals and course textbooks. Fortunately, for the motivated reader, a treasure trove of challenging reading and reflective critical thinking awaits you, if you actively search for interesting feminist literature in psychology (cf. Matlin, 2007 ; Lorber, 2009).

Selective references for further reading

Lorber, J. (2009). *Gender Inequality : Feminist Theories* (4th edition). Oxford University Press.

Matlin, M. (2007). *La Psychologie des femmes*. Bruxelles : DeBoeck. (Translation and cultural adaptation by W. Pullin & C. Blatier).

Pyke, S. (2001). Feminist psychology in Canada : Early days. *Canadian Psychology/Psychologie canadienne*, (Special issue : *Looking forward, looking back : Women in psychology*), *42* (4), 268-275.

Pour en savoir plus sur des expériences mettant en évidence le rôle du langage dans la perception des différences hommes-femmes, reportez-vous au DVD contenant le film intitulé :

Film 6 : Sexist language and cognition

Pour le texte de Wendy Pullin, voir le cours filmé intitulé :

Film 7 : Psychology of women : From the margins to the mainstream

9 ALCOHOL AND AGGRESSION : THREE MAIN PERSPECTIVES

The association between drinking and aggression has been recognized for centuries (Hanson, 1995). Today, alcohol is known as the psychotropic substance most frequently related to aggressive and violent behavior (Boles &

Miotto). For example, in a study aggregating more than 9 300 criminal cases from 11 countries, Murdoch, Pihl, and Ross (1990) showed that 62 percent of violent offenders were drinking at the time they committed the crime, or shortly before. In a nationwide American survey, Coleman and Strauss (1983) showed that rates of marital violence were 15 times greater for husbands who were often drunk, compared to those who had never been drunk during the past year. Among female victims of violence, alcohol consumption represents an important risk factor (Bègue *et al.*, 2010). In the past 25 years, more systematic and extended research has been undertaken to understand the correlation and the causal processes linking alcohol consumption and aggressive behavior. In this chapter, we will focus on three current social cognitive explanations of the effect of acute alcohol consumption on aggression.

The cognitive disruption model

The cognitive disruption model posits that alcohol intoxication affects controlled, effortful processing by impairing executive cognitive functions. Whereas a sober individual can consider a range of more or less salient information before responding to a social situation, an intoxicated individual will be less concerned with considerations that are distant in time and place, because s/he will be caught in an impoverished version of reality – the breadth, depth, and time line of his/her understanding will be affected.

Various studies show that intoxicated people no longer have the requisite processing skills to attend to all the multiple cues involved in social behavior (Streufert, Pogash, & Gingrich, 1993). As attentional impairment is generally more pronounced in people who are not used to drinking alcohol (Carpenter, 1962), they are accordingly more aggressive following a high dose of alcohol intake than moderate or heavy drinkers (Laplace, Chermack, & Taylor, 1994). Herzog (1999) showed that when asked to focus on the dispositions of others, intoxicated participants tended to exaggerate the extent to which these dispositions were influencing their behavior.

Another study showed that intoxicated individuals interpreted more acts as intentional than sober people did (Bègue *et al.*, 2010). Their study tested the hypothesis that alcohol magnified the intentionality bias by disrupting effortful cognitive abilities. Using a 2 x 2 balanced placebo design in a natural field experiment disguised as a food-tasting session, participants received either a high dose of alcohol (target BAC =.10%) or no alcohol, with half of each group believing they had, or had not, consumed alcohol. Participants then read a series of sentences describing simple actions (*e.g., She cut him off in traffic*), and indicated whether the actions were done intentionally or accidentally. As expected, intoxicated people interpreted more acts as intentional than sober people did. Such an inclination potentially contributes to a hostile information-processing pattern induced by alcohol (Ogle & Miller, 2004), which is proximal to aggressive behavior (Zelli, Dodge, & Lochman, 1999).

An intoxicated person may therefore not correctly perceive the reasons for other people's behavior, making the actions of others appear more provocative than they would to a sober perceiver. Another inhibiting cue that is also blurred by alcohol consumption is the perceived future consequences of one's action (Sayette, 1993).

The attributional model

According to the attributional model, drinkers are using alcohol to mitigate perceived personal responsibility by attributional processes. Drinking can thus have consequences that are mediated not by alcohol effects, but by the self-fulfillment of expectations about alcohol's effects or by the use of drinking to excuse reprehensible behavior (Critchlow, 1986). MacAndrew and Edgerton (1969) especially argued against the notion of alcohol as a pharmacological disinhibitor by showing that there were societies whose members' drunken behavior failed to exhibit the unrestrained behavior supposed to follow alcohol consumption. They also highlighted that the behavioral consequences of alcohol had undergone marked transformations over time and were radically different from one site of socially ordered situations or circumstances to another. The excuse value of alcohol was also underscored. A premise of the attributional perspective is that a layperson expects alcohol to have specific consequences on him/herself and others.

The automaticity model

Finally, the model of automaticity implies that alcohol representations stored in long term memory potentially automatically trigger aggressive thoughts and behavior without the individual being aware of it. Automaticity refers to a process that is unintentional (the individual does not start the process by an act of will), uncontrollable (the process cannot be stopped), efficient (consumes minimal attentional resources), and occurs outside awareness (Bargh, 1994). For instance, social knowledge is automatically (implicitly) activated in memory during the natural course of perception without people's awareness or intention. Knowledge activation, in turn, shapes and guides people's impressions, judgments, feelings, and intentions without people being aware that such influence is occurring (Ferguson & Bargh, 2004). Applied to the alcohol-aggression link, the automaticity perspective implies that alcohol cues could implicitly activate alcohol expectancies, which will affect social judgment and behavior in line with these expectancies.

Two experiments tested whether alcohol-related cues automatically activated aggressive thoughts and increased aggressive behaviors (Subra *et al.*, 2010). In a first study, participants made faster lexical decisions concerning aggression related words following alcohol-related primes or weapon-related primes, compared with neutral primes.

In another study, participants exposed either to alcohol or aggressive subliminal primes were more aggressive toward the experimenter than participants exposed to neutral subliminal primes, and the effect even lasted a few days in participants exposed to alcohol subliminal primes. Therefore, just seeing bottles of alcohol increased aggressive thoughts and actions. Such a result is consistent with a study of the physiological and expectancy effects of alcohol consumption on the aggressive behavior of 116 general-population individuals (Bègue *et al.*, 2009). In this study, males aged 18-45 years were analyzed separately in a naturalistic field experiment using a 3x3 Balanced Placebo Design (BPD). Participants were given a non-alcoholic drink, a drink targeting a Blood Alcohol Concentration (BAC) of .05 %, or a drink targeting a BAC of .1 %. Within these three groups, three expectancy levels were induced regarding the quantity of alcohol ingested. Aggressive behavior was measured through retaliation against an aggressive confederate, in the form of amounts of hot sauce and salt administered in a taste test. The results showed that what participants were told about the amount of alcohol they received had a greater effect on their aggression than what they actually received. Thus, one reason why alcohol contributes to aggression is that people assume it will do so, regardless of the true alcohol content of what they drink.

Selective references for further reading

Bègue, L., Subra, B., Arvers, P., Muller, D., Bricout, V., & Zorman, M. (2009). The message, not the bottle : extrapharmacological effects of alcohol on aggression. *Journal of Experimental and Social Psychology*, *45*, 137-142.

Bègue, L., Perez-Diaz, C., Subra, B., Ceaux, E., Arvers, P., Bricout, V., Roché, S., & Swendsen, J. (2010). The role of alcohol in female victimization : findings from a French representative sample. *Substance Use and Misuse*, in press.

Subra, B., Muller, D., Bègue, L., Bushman, B.J., & Delmas, F. (2010). Automatic effects of alcohol and aggressive cues on aggressive thoughts and behaviors. *Personality and Social Psychology Bulletin*, *36*, 1052-1057.

Bègue, L., Bushman, B., Giancola, P., Subra, B., Rosset, E. (2010). There is no such thing as an accident', especially when people are drunk. *Personality and Social Psychology Bulletin*, *36*, 1301-1304.

Videos

http://telegrenoble.kewego.fr/video/iLyROoafJhUu.html

http://www.lexpress.fr/actualite/sciences/alcool-et-violence-un-lien-jusqu-ou_570650.html

Websites

www.sante-sports.gouv.fr/IMG/pdf/etude_evaluative.pdf

http://www.lexpress.fr/actualite/sciences/alcool-et-violence-un-lien-jusqu-ou_570650.html

Exercise 5

Questions

1. Which model suggests that people become aggressive when drunk because their information-processing capacity is reduced ?
2. Who showed that aggression after drinking is relative to one's society ?
3. According to Begue and colleagues'research (2009), what has a greater effect on aggression, the amount of alcohol consumed or the amount *thought* to have been consumed ?
4. What term describes a process that uses relatively little of a person's attentional resources ?
5. Does alcohol consumption tend to increase or decrease situational attributions ?

10 REGRET : ITS ROLE IN OUR LIVES (AUDIO 2)

Conceptual aspects

Imagine this happening to you : during the sales, you visit a store and buy a nice suit that is selling for 40 % less than the original price. At home, a friend of yours sees the suit and tells you he likes it ; he wants to buy the same one, so you take him to the store the following day. There you find out that the suit is now being sold for 60 % less. What would your reaction be ?

Now imagine the following situation : after a party where you have a few drinks, you decide to drive home. On the way, you fail to stop at a stop sign. You do not see that another car is coming across the intersection at right angles to you. The other driver makes a sudden move to avoid crashing with you, but cannot avoid crashing into an electricity pole. He is in shock, and has to be taken to an emergency room where he is kept under observation for 24 hours. You later learn that the other driver is not seriously hurt, but he did miss a job interview appointment that was scheduled for the day he was at the hospital. What would your reaction be ?

Definition

According to theorists, you will more than likely feel regret in both cases. There are as many definitions of regret as disciplines treating it (Gilovitch & Medvec, 1995 ; Zeelenberg & Pieters, 2007). We will content ourselves with Landman's (1993) definition, which seems broad enough to cover most of the aspects of this phenomenon : *"Regret is a more or less painful cognitive and emotional state of feeling sorry for misfortunes, limitations, losses, transgressions, shortcomings, or mistakes. It is an experience of felt-reason or reasoned-emotion. The regretted matters may be sins of commission as well as sins of omission ; they may range from the voluntary to the uncontrollable and accidental ; they may be deeds actually executed, or entirely mental ones, committed by oneself or by another person or group ; they may be moral or legal transgressions or morally and legally neutral."* (p. 36)

This definition emphasizes four dimensions of regret. One, it is a painful emotional experience, which renders regret an aversive emotion. Two, it has a cognitive aspect, in the sense that we need to think practically and in-depth about the context of the decision we regret. Three, we are likely to feel regret when we believe that we made the wrong decision, when we feel responsible for causing harm to ourselves or others, and blame ourselves for it, and when we feel like undoing or correcting what happened. Four, regret may be intrapersonal, focusing on the harm we cause to ourselves, or interpersonal, based on the harm our behavior causes others. The fictitious situations described above illustrate both types of regret respectively.

Regret shares some similarities with several other aversive emotions, and is sometimes confused with them. They include guilt, shame, disappointment, remorse, embarrassment, and so on. However, the emotions that have most commonly been investigated in parallel with regret are guilt and disappointment. Below, we describe the relation between regret and these emotions.

Differences between regret and related emotions

Regret and guilt

Guilt is defined as "an unpleasant emotional state that involves a feeling of self-reproach, repentance, and remorse resulting from realizing that one has caused harm, loss, or distress to another, or violated some moral standards" (Leith & Baumeister, 1998). Guilt and regret seem to be interchangeable emotions because they both originate from the same factors ; both are painful emotions that motivate avoidance behaviors. Indeed, people experiencing guilt or regret are likely to apologize, try to compensate the victim, and make a promise of good conduct in the future (Baumeister *et al.*, 1994 ; Manstead, 1991). However, while guilt and regret are indiscriminately reported in situations of interpersonal harm, only features specific to regret are reported in intrapersonal harm situations (Zeelenberg & Breugelmans, 2008). In other words, regret is a broader emotion than guilt. Moreover, while regret more likely results from a non-normative act being carried out, guilt can also arise from non-normative intentions (*e.g.*, the desire to sleep with one's brother's girlfriend).

Regret and disappointment

Like regret, *disappointment* is also associated with decision-related loss, but they are different emotions. Specifically, *"disappointment is caused by comparing an outcome with prior expectation"* (Bell, 1985, p. 2), especially when the outcome hoped for seemed highly likely. It is displeasure about the non-occurrence of a desired outcome (van Dijk, Zeelenberg, & van Der Pligt, 1999). Disappointment is relatively free of self-blame because the outcome of the situation is appraised as beyond one's control ; and the individual feels powerless to face its outcome. More importantly, while the initial cause of regret or disappointment may be the individual's behavior, it is not necessarily so. For example, if your parents give you a pair of Keni tennis shoes for your birthday, while you expected a pair of the Nikes which most young people like, you'll be disappointed.

Pour la suite de cet article concernant les théories actuelles sur le regret, reportez-vous au DVD contenant le **texte** et la **version audio 2** intitulés :

Regret : Its role in our lives

Conclusion

People are likely to experience regret when they realize or imagine that their current situations would have been better if they had made a different decision, when they cause harm to themselves or others. Because regret is a negative emotion, people seek to avoid it through various means. As a result, they may make decisions that seem irrational with regard to available information, or make more prudent decisions, or refrain from acting. Moreover, individuals feeling regret for their wrongdoing may amend their actions, and act more normatively. Considering the effects of regret on our decisions, a question that may be asked is : how negative is regret ?

Selective references for further reading

Gilovitch, T. & Medvec, V. H. (1995). The experiences of regret : what, when and why. *Psychological Review*, *102*, 379-395.

Landman, J. (1993). *Regret : The Persistence of the Possible*. Oxford University Press.

Zeelenberg, M. & Pieters, R. (2007). A theory of regret regulation 1.0. *Journal of Consumer Psychology, 17*, 3-18.

Pour des exemples mettant en jeu des situations de regret anticipé ou réel, reportez-vous au DVD contenant le film intitulé :

Film 8 : Examples of decisions influenced by regret, whether experienced or anticipated

11 FREE WILL COMPLIANCE AND BINDING COMMUNICATION

Is it possible to influence someone to the point of making him/her freely modify his/her ideas and behaviors ? The answer is *"yes"*.

FREE WILL COMPLIANCE AND FOOT-IN-THE-DOOR EFFECT

From a practical point of view, the paradigm of free will compliance (Joule & Beauvois, 1998) can be defined as the study of the techniques likely to lead an individual to freely modify his behaviors.

The effectiveness of several techniques is now well established (Joule & Beauvois, 2002), particularly that of the foot-in-the-door (FITD). The principle of the FITD technique is based on asking for a little (preliminary act) before asking for a great deal (expected behavior). In one of their experiments, Freedman and Fraser (1966), using the pretext of a telephone survey, first asked young women to answer some innocuous questions about their consumer habits (preliminary act). Three days later, the same young women were again solicited by phone. This time they were asked to receive a team of several pollsters at home for about two hours for a survey on household consumption (expected behavior). The probability that this particularly costly request would be accepted was significantly higher with this technique (53 %) than in the control condition in which the young women had not been solicited beforehand to participate in the telephone survey (22 %). In another experiment, the expected behavior was for participants to display a large sign in their gardens encouraging people to *"Drive Carefully"*. The highest rate of compliance came from participants who had been asked two weeks earlier to display a small sign encouraging driver safety (preliminary act), compared to participants who were directly requested to display the large sign (76 % and 17 % respectively). Compliance with the expected behavior dropped off when the initial request was either to engage in a different behavior (sign a petition) or support a different cause *("Keeping California beautiful")*.

Studies carried out on the FITD technique show the interest of gaining compliance to preliminary acts ; carrying out such acts increases the probability that the persons who did them will accept other requests of a similar nature, even if these requests are more costly and therefore more difficult to satisfy.

COMMITMENT THEORY

Based on the theory of commitment (Kiesler, 1971), the effects of the preliminary acts will be modulated by the context in which they are performed. This context can involve more or less commitment, or even no commitment at all. For instance, Tybout (1978) asked participants to simply sign a petition or, at a deeper level of commitment, they signed the petition and were asked to explain their personal reasons for signing to the experimenter. Compliance with the expected behavior was higher when the preliminary act was at a high level of commitment. According to Kiesler (1971), *"commitment is the pledging or binding of an individual to behavioural acts"*. According to Joule and Beauvois (1998), the objective characteristics of a situation may or may not commit an individual in his/her acts, and hence help establish a relationship between an individual and his/her acts. Joule and Beauvois offer a definition that takes account of the effect of a situation on commitment : *"commitment corresponds, in a given situation, to the conditions in which the completion of an act can only be charged to the individual who completed the act"*. The commitment variable can be handled using factors in two categories :

(1) Act visibility and importance : this category includes five factors :

a- public nature of the act : an act carried out in public commits more than an anonymous act ;

b- act irrevocability : an irrevocable act that cannot be canceled commits more than a revocable act ;

c- act repetition : a repeated act commits more than an act carried out once. Act repetition is a commitment factor likely to increase resistance. According to Kiesler, the commitment adds up with the acts ;

d- act consequences : the more serious the consequences, the higher the commitment ;

e- act cost : an act commits what it costs. Lending a car costs more than lending a pen.

(2) Reasons for the act and freedom context

The reasons behind what one does or is about to do can be external (for example : circumstances or the situation) or internal (an individual's personal will). External reasons decrease commitment, they loosen the relationship between an individual and his/her acts. For instance, the stronger the reward and the punishment, the more behavior is justified. Internal reasons tighten the relationship between an individual and his acts. Finally, the context in which the individual lives should give him or her a "free" subject status. Commitment theoreticians regard freedom of choice as the main commitment factor.

For example, Joule and Beauvois (1998) tested the commitment efficiency by asking job-seekers to attend training sessions and encouraging them to look for a job. In one control group, the trainers acted as usual : they informed the participants of the mandatory character of the sessions, indicating that any unjustified absence would result in salary deductions. In the experimental group, the rules were different : the trainers emphasized that the participants were free to attend the training sessions or not. The results of this simple commitment manipulation show first that the absenteeism rate is no higher in the experimental group than in the control group (15 %). Secondly, the experimental group has more positive views on the training. Finally, the placement rate is significantly higher in the experimental group (56 % participants found jobs) than in the control group (25 %). In the long run, three month later, the placement rate was 69 % in the experimental group and 35 % in the control group.

BINDING COMMUNICATION

Preliminary acts could have another interest : making the individuals who performed them more or less susceptible to information they may receive later. Binding communication (Joule, Girandola and Bernard, 2007) confronts someone with a persuasive message in order to measure the effects, but this confrontation is made after the individual has complied with the request and carried out a preliminary act going in the same direction as the information contained in the message, such as signing a petition to outlaw smoking in public areas before reading a message about passive smoking. There are still questions to be dealt with in the paradigm of binding communication, as there are in the framework of persuasive communication : *"What is the best information to convey to the target ?"*, *"Which arguments will the target-individual be sensitive to ?"*, *"What are the most appropriate channels, tools, media etc ?"*, and another essential one can be added : *"What are the preliminary acts to be obtained beforehand ?"*. The binding communication approach is distinguished from that of persuasive communication because it takes into account this last question, thus, giving the target the status of an actor rather than a mere receiver.

Deschamps, Joule and Gumy (2005), for example, used binding communication to get Swiss citizens to vote in elections. They were divided into three groups. All three groups were exposed to a speech condemning electoral abstention. In addition to this, participants in two of the three groups were asked to carry out a preliminary act : filling in a questionnaire on their opinions and voting practices, or drawing up an argument against abstention. A significantly higher number of students in the two groups that carried out preliminary activities actually participated in the vote (questionnaire : 77 % ; argument : 79 %) compared with the group that had simply been subjected to the anti-abstention speech (50 %). Binding communication attempts to show that by resorting to a preliminary act before diffusing a persuasive message, it is possible to obtain behavioral changes that would not be obtained without resorting to such acts. It is not just about presenting targets with information and arguments. Efforts are put into encouraging targets to carry out preliminary actions and to make specific commitments.

Binding communication supports the development of studies seeking to integrate both research on the role of commitment and free will compliance, and research dealing with communication in general and with a focus on persuasive communication in particular.

Selective references for further reading

Deschamps, J. C., Joule, R. V., & Gumy, C. (2005). La communication engageante au service de la réduction de l'abstentionnisme électoral : une application au milieu universitaire. *Revue Européenne de Psychologie Appliquée*, *55*, 21-27.

Girandola, F. (2003). *Psychologie de la persuasion et de l'engament*. PUFC.

Joule, R.-V., Girandola, F. & Bernard, F. (2007). How can people be induced to willingly change their behavior ? The path from persuasive communication to binding communication. *Social and Personality Psychology Compass*, *1*, 493-505.

Joule, R.-V., & Beauvois, J.-L. (1998). *La soumission librement consentie*. Paris : PUF.

Joule, R.-V., & Beauvois, J.-L. (2002). *Petit traité de manipulation à l'usage des honnêtes gens*. Grenoble : PUG.

Pour en savoir plus sur la technique d'engagement du pied-dans-la-porte, reportez-vous au DVD contenant le film intitulé :

Film 9 : Free will compliance and foot-in-the-door effect

12 "TALKING ABOUT SOMETHING" OR "TALKING TO SOMEONE" ?

Saussure's General Linguistics (1916) identified two types of relations, both *"indispensable to the life of language"*, and which defined the verbal items :

- Words are associated in the memory by relations of different types. To take up Saussure's own example, the word *enseignement* "teaching" relates to the words *enseignant* "teacher", *enseigner* "teach", *instruction* "teaching", *éducation* "education"..., which stem from the same paradigm. This will be referred to as the *paradigmatic* relation.
- Language rules out the possibility of pronouncing two words simultaneously, and consequently imposes/requires a linear sequence of the elements into syntagms, according to the language rules. This will be referred to as the *syntagmatic* relation.

According to Jakobson and Halle (1956), "the locutor selects words and combines them into sentences according to the syntactical system of the language he is using" (pp. 45-46). The operations of selection (the paradigmatic relation in which words are replaceable with others) and the process of combination (the syntagmatic relation in which words are arranged in sequences on the chain of speaking) seem to function independently and to be specifically centred on one relation or the other. They appear to be independent to such an extent that they enable a distinction of two language pathologies (Jakobson, 1955) : disorders of word-selection (or similarity : Wernicke's aphasia) and disorders of word-combination (or contiguity : Broca's aphasia).

In the field of language learning, earlier studies by Miller (1951) based on free association tests showed that a child's intellectual development, and especially his or her categorical capacities, led him or her to move gradually from syntagmatic associations to paradigmatic associations that are more characteristic of adults. However, the results obtained by Pichevin and Noizet (1968) and Beauvois and Ghiglione (1972) showed that paradigmatic associations increased steadily up to 9-11 years old, and that beyond this age, a sudden shift from syntagmatic to paradigmatic associations occurred. It did not result from a process of maturation but rather from the investment in language as an object triggered in response to educational demands. Primary school teaching, in giving priority to lexical skills (and language decoding tasks), led implicitly to answers that were more paradigmatic, whereas in upper grades, where the focus was on communication skills (and on the pupil as interlocutor), the syntagmatic register reappeared : "language was considered as a tool for decoding the world before being fully used as a tool for communication".

The study of language acquisition takes the same direction, notably with works by Nelson (1981), who identified a fundamental distinction between *referential* strategies (analytical and nominal strategies, centred on content, words and particularly substantives) and *expressive* strategies (holistic strategies, which favour language form and function, particularly pronouns and social phrases). The implementation of one strategy or the other depends on the type of interaction style between the child and his or her surroundings : referential strategies correspond to a didactic interaction style (centred on knowledge of the world), whereas expressive strategies result from a socio-affective style (focusing on relationships between individuals).

The child's age must be taken into account, but a difference in interaction styles is likely to emerge between firstborn and later children in the same family. Nelson observed that late-born children tend to use more socio-regulative language than firstborn children do : *"their mothers used less metalingual speech than did mothers of firstborns"*.

Beauvois and Ghiglione (1981, 1983) put forward the hypothesis that there are two registers of attitudes towards language : a paradigmatic (P_A) and a syntagmatic (S_A) attitude. *"In P_A attitude, language is concerned as a self-regulated and self-referring code ; in S_A attitude language is concerned as a communication tool" (Ghiglione & Beauvois, 1983, p. 97). More specifically, "paradigmatic attitude (P_A) corresponds to an attitude that gives priority to language used as a tool for systemic decoding of the world ; syntagmatic attitude (S_A) corresponds to an attitude giving priority to language used as intermediary between speakers"* (p. 98).

Like every object of attitude, each individual is liable to be characterised (through a word association test) either as mostly *paradigmatic* or mostly *syntagmatic*. When subjects who had previously been identified as *paradigmatic* or *syntagmatic* were asked to do free association or writing activities, Ghiglione & Beauvois observed that : *"Whereas the P_A Ss created sentences whose reference was located at the level of lexical code (metalinguistic sentence), the S_A Ss produced sentences whose reference was located at the level of potential communication (communicative sentence)"*.

In a different activity involving text improvement, results showed that the subjects who manifested a P_A attitude behaved toward the text by accentuating the metalinguistic character or by reducing the interlocutory character of a given text to a greater extent than subjects manifesting a S_A attitude. Furthermore, regardless of their P_A or S_A inclination, subjects can be presented with a text, which is, itself, either P_A or S_A orientated. When asked to make a report on the recorded P_A and S_A text, the subjects recalled more literal units whose discursive texture was consistent with their language attitude. The reception of a persuasive message is seen to be affected by congruence between speech attitude and the discursive texture of the message.

In a persuasive communication situation, they noted that a P_A text created a persuasive effect only on P_A subjects and a S_A text only on S_A subjects. The effectiveness of a persuasive message depends upon the interaction of its discursive texture with the language attitude of the receiver. P_A subjects proved to be more receptive to a message in which metalinguistic potentialities predominated ; S_A subjects were more receptive to a message in which interlocutory potentialities predominated. A similar effect was also observed concerning the text source image : P_A evaluators found texts by P_A writers more convincing, and likewise, S_A evaluators found texts by S_A writers more convincing.

Finally, we must keep in mind that the expression of a particular attitude may also constitute an answer to the requirement of the situation (*e.g.*, formal or communicative). When encountering unexpected difficulty during discussions, some female students were inclined to withdraw from the problematic situation and tended to invest in the paradigmatic register. This result allowed the authors to give another interpretation of the well-known *"Conference situations"* carried out by Moscovici and Plon (1966 ; see Beauvois and Ghiglione, 1981, p. 180).

In our own studies in the political field, we used the principles as defined by Beauvois and Ghiglione, to see how they may be applied to more recent lexicometric and morphosyntactic methods of analysis. By analyzing the speeches of candidates for the French Presidential elections, we have shown that the two attitudes towards language predict different behaviour in performing a similar discursive task (signing the "ecological pact" and explaining motivations for doing so – Marchand, *in press*). We also showed that French Prime Ministers revealed a paradigmatic attitude when they were in a high popularity context and a syntagmatic attitude when they were in a low popularity context (Marchand, 2007).

It confirms the psychosocial dimension of the model : the attitude towards language is determined by the *"subject * situation"* interaction and implies both normative expectations and contextual marking.

Selective references for further reading

Ghiglione, R. & Beauvois, J.-L. (1981). Speech-markers and attitude toward language as an object. *International Journal of Psycholinguistics*, *8-1*, 51-73.

Ghiglione, R. & Beauvois, J.-L. (1983). Language attitudes and social influence. *The Journal of Social Psychology*, *121*, 97-109.

Jakobson, R. & Halle, M. (1956). Fundamentals of language. La Haye : Mouton (trad. fr. Éditions de Minuit, 1963).

Marchand, P. (in press). Attitudes towards language : new perspectives. *International Review of Social Psychology*.

Miller, G. A. (1951). *Language and communication*. New York : McGraw Hill (trad. fr. Paris : CEPL, 1973).

Nelson, K. (1981). Individual differences in language development : Implications for development and language. *Developmental Psychology*, *17*, 170-187.

Exercise 6

Questions

1. Which proposed attitude to language sees it as a self-regulating code ?
2. Around what age do children generally shift towards a more syntagmatic approach to language ?
3. What kind of aphasia is associated with difficulties with syntax ?
4. "Politicians tend to emphasise language as a communication tool when surrounded by their supporters." True or false ?
5. Are people with a syntagmatic attitude to language more susceptible to its metalinguistic or its interlocutory aspects ?

13 ENVIRONMENTAL PSYCHOLOGY : SCOPE AND UTILITY OF A CONTEXTUALISED PSYCHOLOGY[1]

One of the shortcomings of much psychological research is that it treats the environment simply as a value-free backdrop to human activity and a stage upon which we act out our lives. It is seen as expedient in psychological investigations and experiments to remove as much extraneous noise as possible, in case it affects the "purity" of our results. This is understandable and desirable in many situations ; but when it comes to understanding human perceptions, attitudes and behaviours in real-world settings, the environment is a critical factor that needs to be taken into account. As Wilpert (2006, p. 71) states, *"Psychological phenomena cannot be thought of but as being contextualised, i.e., being embedded in different environments"*.

The environmental setting is not a neutral and value-free space ; it is culture-bound. It is constantly conveying meanings and messages, and is an essential part of human functioning and action. The environment embodies the social and cultural values of those who inhabit it (Getzels, 1975), it provides us with opportunities and constraints which we can choose to draw upon (Gibson, 1979). Of course, not everybody will perceive the same affordances in a single environment, and neither will similar environments generate the same perceptions and evaluations in a single person (Wohlwill & Heft, 1987).

1. Extended abstract from : Moser, G. and Uzzell, D. (2007). "Environmental Psychology", in R. Baumeister and K. D. Vohs (eds.), *Encyclopedia of Social Psychology*, San Francisco : Sage.

The environmental context – in which perceptions occur, attitudes are formed and behaviour takes place – also has a temporal dimension. We cannot understand space and place without taking time into account. We experience places not only in the present, but as having a past which impinges upon, and colours, our interpretation of the present.

The nature and scope of environmental psychology

Individuals and groups in their physical and social context, are studied by environmental psychologists. They focus on the effects of environmental conditions on behaviour, as well as how individuals perceive and act on the environment. Physical and social factors are inextricably linked in their effects on individuals' perceptions and behaviour (Altman & Rogoff, 1987). In order to achieve this effectively, environmental psychology research aims to identify processes in real-world situations which regulate and mediate the individual's relationship to the environment. Theories are generated from what can be observed, and from data unearthed by research in the real world.

The conceptual model by which our perceptions, representations and behaviour are interdependent with the physical and social environment has frequently been mentioned in psychology. Brunswick (1959) and Gibson (1950), in their work on perception, referred to the role of the environment ; Tolman (1948) used the concept of the *"mental map"* to describe the cognitive mechanisms which accompany maze-learning ; and Lewin (1951) elaborated the theory of the environmental field, conceived as a series of forces which operate on the individual. The first milestones of environmental psychology date from the late 1960s (Barker, 1968 ; Lee, 1968 ; Proshansky, Ittelson & Rivlin, 1970 ; Craik, 1970). The human-environment relationship is dependent on the evolution of both the individual and the socio-cultural context, and the way the individual perceives them. In conclusion, environmental psychology can be considered as the study of the interrelation of the individual with the physical and social aspects of the environment, taking into account the cultural and temporal dimensions.

Domains of environmental psychology

Environmental psychology, because of its very focus, has been, and remains above all, the relation to space. The discipline operates, then, at several levels of spatial reference enabling the investigation of people-environment interactions (at the individual, group or societal level) at each echelon (*cf.* table 1).

Obviously the terms of analysis, and the problems encountered, are of a different nature according to each level. The respective relations can best be understood through perception, needs, opportunities, and means of control.

Table 1

Type of spaces, physical and social aspects

	Physical environment	Social environment
(1) Micro-environment	private space habitat private working place	individual and family level
(2) Proximal environment	semi-public spaces neighbourhood space open to the public	interindividual level communities users, clients
(3) Macro-environment	public spaces cities, villages, etc. countryside, landscape	inhabitants aggregates of individuals
(4) Global environment	nation, planet natural resources	society, population

The people-environment relationship at different levels

Private spaces

Personal space and **privacy** are important for individual and community well-being and quality of life. Altman (1975) defines privacy as the *"selective control of access to the self or one's group"*. Thus, privacy implies control over the immediate environment. Steadily, or transitionally, occupied places produce place attachment and are often accompanied with ties to personal objects like furniture, pictures and souvenirs which mark the appropriation (Korosec-Serfaty, 1976).

Territoriality is visibly delimited by boundaries and tends to be home- or workplace-centred. It is a demarcated and defended space and, invariably, an expression of identity and attachment to a place (Sommer, 1969). Territories have an essential function in providing and promoting security, predictability, order, and stability in one's life.

Semi-public/semi-private environments

Rows of houses or apartment blocks, the immediate neighbourhood, the work-place, and leisure areas in the immediate surroundings of the home are referred to as semi-public spaces, which means that control over them is shared within a community. The degree of satisfaction felt with neighbourhood attributes like green spaces, the aesthetics of the built framework and degree of noise, has an effect on the affectivity developed towards it, as well as feelings of well-being. The feeling of being at home in one's neighbourhood is linked to the frequency of encounters, the extent of the sphere of close relations, the nature of local relationships, and satisfaction with them.

Besides the home and neighbourhood environments, other domains involve a problematic congruence between people and their environment, for example, work, classroom, and institutional environments (hospitals, prisons, homes for children or the elderly). Increasing attention is being paid to the design of the workplace so that it matches more effectively the organisation's goals and cultural aspirations, as well as employee needs, job demands, and performance.

Public environments

Cities concentrate novelty, intensity and choice - more so than smaller towns and villages. They provide a variety of cultural, recreational, and educational facilities. Equally, it is argued, cities have become more dangerous, since they concentrate all sorts of crime and delinquency, and are noisy, overcrowded and polluted. Living in metropolitan areas is considered as stressful. The analysis of behaviour in cities has concentrated on noise, density, living conditions (difficulty of access to services), high crime and delinquency rates. A series of conceptual considerations (environmental overload, environmental stress and behavioural constraint) has been proposed to understand the consequences of these stressors for typical urban behaviour like paying less attention to others, and being less affiliative and less helpful.

Urban residents often seek nature, and research consistently points to its positive psychological function (Staats *et al.*, 1997 ; Staats *et al.*, 2000). Green spaces and the natural environment can provide not only an aesthetically pleasing setting, but also restorative experiences (Kaplan, 1995) including a positive effect on health (Ulrich, 1984 ; Moore, 1982).

THE GLOBAL ENVIRONMENT

Local agendas are increasingly informed by global perspectives and processes (Lechner & Boli, 1999). The most significant topic analysed at the level of global environment is without doubt individuals' attitudes towards, and support of, sustainable development. A major challenge for environmental psychology is to enable the understanding and development of strategies to encourage environmentally friendly behaviour. There is consistent field research in environmental psychology about ways to encourage environmentally responsible behaviour concerning resource conservation (*e.g.*, energy and water), littering and recycling. The effect of environmental education, commitment, modelling, feedback, rewards and disincentives, are on the whole effective only if such behaviour is reinforced and opportunities are provided which encourage environmentally friendly behaviour.

Growing ecological concern in our societies is attributed to a series of beliefs and attitudes favourable to the environment. Yet, it is clear from research that pro-environmental attitudes do not necessarily lead to pro-environmental behaviours. Environmental problems can often be conceptualised as *"commons dilemma"* problems (Vlek, *et al.*, 1993 ; Van Lange, *et al.*, 1998). Social dilemmas are typically collective problems. People, therefore, neither feel personally responsible for the problems, nor do they feel in control of the solutions.

PERSPECTIVES

The issues at the forefront with reference to sustainability – well-being and preoccupation with preserving the environment – need to be addressed in a more integrated way.

Environmental anchoring and appropriation leading to identity, are progressive processes and are essential for individual behaviour in favour of sustainable development. The appropriation of the urban space helps to favour environment-friendly behaviours (Moser *et al.*, 2002 ; Uzzell *et al.*, 2002). According to the *"City Identification Sustainability Model"* (Pol, 2002), people identifying themselves as urbanites are more likely to engage in pro-environmental behaviour. Achieving sustainable cities requires putting citizenship at the centre of public life. The implementation of sustainable development in the context of "agenda 21" implies that city-dwellers feel they belong to an urban entity. In a context of increasing cultural heterogeneity, it is essential to go beyond the appropriation of home and neighbourhood, and to assess how individuals identify with the urban community in its totality and diversity. Environmental psychology has to consider the individual's relation to the environment as a whole, from habitat, through the city to the global environment.

Selective references for further reading

Moser, G. (2009). *Psychologie Environnementale*. Bruxelles : De Boeck.

Moser, G., & Weiss, K. (2003). *Espaces de vie : Aspects de la relation homme-environnement*. Paris : Armand Colin.

Moser, G. (2004). La psychologie environnementale : de l'analyse à l'intervention. *In* : C. Louche & P. Pansu : *La psychologie appliquée à l'analyse des problèmes sociaux*, Paris : PUF, p. 231-254.

Moser, G. (2006). Psychologie environnementale et territoires urbains. *In* : K. Weiss & D. Marchand (Eds.). *Psychologie sociale de l'environnement*. Rennes : Presses Universitaires de Rennes, p. 19-22.

Exercise 7

Questions

1. What could be described as a person's "defined space" ?
2. What is the definition of a "semi-public space" ?
3. Why does the text suggest that a more positive attitude towards the environment does not always lead to more environmentally-friendly behaviour ?
4. To what does the term "micro-environment" refer in its social aspect ?
5. What reasons does the text give for city-dwellers seeking green spaces ?

D'autres thèmes de la psychologie sociale à découvrir sur le DVD :

Pour en savoir plus sur le domaine des émotions, reportez-vous au DVD contenant le **texte** et la **version audio 3** intitulés :

📖 ♫ **emotion**

Pour en savoir plus « le pardon » dans le contexte des relations intergroupes, reportez-vous au DVD contenant le **texte** et la **version audio 4** intitulés :

📖 ♫ **Seeking forgiveness in an intergroup context**

Chapitre 2

PSYCHOLOGIE COGNITIVE/ COGNITIVE PSYCHOLOGY

Cognitive psychologists study internal mental processes, including : memory, perception, language processes, thought processes, and problem-solving. A major goal of this area of psychology is to better understand and explain how people acquire information and process it, in order to store it in memory and recall it when needed. Some applied areas of cognitive psychology include : improving educational programs to enhance learning ; developing better models for problem-solving ; developing better techniques to store and retrieve information in memory ; and designing virtual realities and video simulations that mimic human thought processes. This area of psychology has close ties to neuropsychology, psycholinguistics, computer processing, and human factors engineering. A number of interesting topics in cognitive psychology will be covered in this section.

16 RETRIEVING INFORMATION FROM MEMORY

Memory is probably one of the broadest areas of cognitive psychology research. Researchers interested in memory try to develop a better understanding of how we acquire new knowledge. For example, they describe : (a) cognitive processes involved in storing new information in memory ; (b) how memory is structured or knowledge is organized ; (c) factors that contribute to a better storage of information in memory ; and (d) how we retrieve information from memory. A complete review of research and theories related to memory would require more than a few pages. Thus, the present paper will focus on a single aspect of memory – the retrieval process.

Retrieving information from memory

Retrieval is the process that allows an individual to gain access to information that is stored in memory. Indeed, once information has been encoded and stored in memory, later use of this information requires bringing it back into our conscious awareness. In the terminology of cognitive psychologists, when a piece of information is stored in memory, it is said to be inactive. In order to use it, this inactive information has to become activated. The retrieval process is the process responsible for this change of state of information. It allows inactive information to become activated. Cognitive psychologists have developed interesting models to explain how the retrieval process works.

One of the major processes that is responsible for retrieving information from memory is called *"spreading of activation"* (Collins & Loftus, 1975). When information is inactive in memory, it can be seen as *"sleeping information"*. It will wake up, that is, it becomes activated if it receives a sufficient amount of activation. Once this information has been activated, the activation spreads to other information that is related (semantically, categorically, contextually…) to that former information, and this information becomes activated in return. The main property of the spreading activation mechanism is that it is automatic. It is fast and does not emerge in conscious awareness and, once triggered, it cannot be stopped.

The principal experimental evidence in favor of the spreading activation process is what are called priming effects. These effects can be studied through a well-known paradigm in cognitive psychology – the priming paradigm. It consists of presenting two pieces of information one after another, then examining to what extent the processing of the first piece of information facilitates (speeds up), disturbs (slows down), or has no influence on the processing of the second piece of information that follows. The first piece of information is called *"the prime"* and the second piece of information is called *"the target"*. The factor that is manipulated is the prime – target relation.

Facilitation priming effect refers to a situation in which the prime facilitates the processing of the target ; or the reverse, inhibitory priming effect refers to a situation in which the prime disturbs processing of the target.

You might wonder how this relates to the spreading activation mechanism. Because it is assumed that activation spreads further to semantically or contextually related information, when the prime is semantically or contextually related to the target, processing of the target is facilitated (speeds up) compared to a situation in which the prime has no direct link with the target. For example, we automatically gain access to the word CAT when it is preceded by the word MOUSE but not when it is preceded by the word NURSE. Because priming effects are very strong effects that have been broadly studied, priming may be considered to be one of the most fundamental processes by which information is retrieved from memory. Nevertheless, everybody has experienced situations in which they were unable to retrieve information from memory. We will now turn to these situations of memory retrieval "failures" and specifically briefly discuss a well-known one : the tip-of-the tongue phenomenon.

The tip of the tongue phenomenon (TOT)

The TOT phenomenon refers to a situation in which we are unable temporarily to retrieve a word or a name from memory, while (a) we are certain that we possess this knowledge, and (b) the word or name seems to be close to emerging in our conscious awareness. Thus, it feels as if the word or name is on the tip of our tongue. Although it is difficult to evaluate precisely how often TOT experiences occur, it is clear that everyone experiences TOT regularly. Diary studies[1] of TOT occurrences estimate the TOT rate as about a once-a-week occurrence in everyday life for young individuals. The rate increases as people get older.

Typically in a TOT situation, we gain access to some properties of the word or name searched such as the first letter, the number of syllables, and sounds ; or to others words similar in sound or meaning. Thus, it appears that when experiencing TOT, fragmentary information of the word becomes activated but the word is not directly accessible to consciousness.

There are currently two main competing hypotheses to explain TOT experiences – the incomplete activation hypothesis and the blocking hypothesis.

Incomplete activation hypothesis

Within the incomplete activation view, word retrieval from memory results from a simultaneous accumulation of information from several sources that provide a sufficient amount of activation for the word to become activated. A TOT experience occurs when the amount of activation is not sufficient to lead to the word activation. More specifically, it is assumed that the amount of activation received is sufficient to allow semantic information activation (*i.e.*, meaning of the word) but not to activate the phonological information necessary to pronounce the word. This explains why, when experiencing TOT, we gain access to some properties of the word only and to semantically related words.

Blocking hypothesis

Within the blocking hypothesis view, TOT experiences correspond to a situation in which the memory search process takes a wrong track and results in retrieving a word that is not the intended one. This incorrect retrieved

1. To see how the TOT phenomenon can be studied experimentally, go to the "Tip of the Tongue" video.

word competes with the intended one and prevents its retrieval. However, the memory search does not end up with the incorrect retrieved word accidentally ; most of the time, the incorrect word shares phonological or semantic properties with the searched one. Therefore, it seems as if the memory search took the right track at first but ends up retrieving a word that sounds like, or is semantically related to, but not, the intended one.

Although it could be irritating to experience TOT or other memory retrieval "failures" as slips of the tongue or slips of the pen, these phenomena do not constitute memory dysfunctions but are fundamental aspects of human memory.

Selective references for further reading

Brown, A. S. (1991). A review of the tip-of-the-tongue experience. *Psychological Bulletin, 109* (2), 204-223.

Collins, A. M. & Loftus, E. F. (1975). A spreading activation theory of semantic processing. *Psychological Review, 82*, 407-428.

Pour en savoir plus sur le phénomène du « mot sur le bout de la langue », reportez-vous au DVD contenant le film intitulé :

Film 10 : Tip of the tongue exercise

17 CAN OLFACTORY EXPERIENCES BE SHARED BY INDIVIDUALS ? VARIABILITY AND STABILITY OF OLFACTORY PERCEPTION ♫ (AUDIO 5)

Traditionally, in the field of perception, five senses are discussed (sight, hearing, touch, taste, and smell). Paradoxically, the sense of smell, the least studied of the senses, raises numerous questions about psychological models of perception. On the one hand, odors differ from other stimuli in terms of physiological characteristics. In comparison to the range of visual or auditory stimulation[1], the range of olfactory stimuli has not been established (it is usually considered that about 10,000 different odors exist in the world, but this number is constantly changing due to advances in chemistry). On the other hand, the main idea found in psychological literature is that the

1. The ranges of stimulation for sight and hearing are known: only wavelengths between 350 and 750 nanometers are visible to the human eye, and only frequencies between 20 and 20,000 hertz are audible to the human ear.

cognitive processes associated with the perception of odors (*e.g.*, discrimination, memory, and identification of odors) are highly variable and diverse among individuals. Given these characteristics, is it possible to share our olfactory experience ? We are especially interested in the way people describe their olfactory perception, since experience-sharing is generally done through language.

The perception of odors is variable and global

The sense of smell is chemical, based on contact between volatile molecules released from substances and receptors contained in the olfactory cell membrane. Unlike sight, however, for which there is only one type of receptor perceiving color, there is a wide diversity of olfactory receptors and individuals do not all have the same amount of receptors. Thus, some individuals can be sensitive, and others completely insensitive, to the same molecules. Odor detection also varies among individuals. Detection thresholds, *i.e.*, the thresholds at which an odor can be perceived, depend on endogenous factors such as gender, age, internal state (satiety, level of attention, etc.) and exogenous factors such as experience, familiarity, and culture. Odor perception appears to be global. Whereas visual stimuli are assessed through various dimensions, (height, color, orientation in space, etc.), this seems not to be the case for odors. Our ability to discriminate basic compounds of a mixture is limited to three or four compounds. Laing (1991) showed that even with training, participants cannot recognize olfactory compounds of a mixture in more than 3 % of trials, a very small proportion. So the perception of a mixture does not correspond to the sum of its basic compounds, it is more global (Holley, 1999).

These results are confirmed by experiments on olfactory memory. Memory for odors is global in the sense that olfactory memories include the encoding context, *i.e.*, some elements of the scene in which the odor was perceived. Further, odors are particularly powerful and evocative memory cues, as established by the *"Proust phenomenon"* (Chu & Downes, 2000), named after the oft-quoted anecdote in Proust's, *"A la recherche du temps perdu"*, in which the author describes how he was vividly reminded of childhood experiences by the smell of a little cake dunked in his tea. Odors can spontaneously trigger autobiographical memories and the sense of smell is commonly considered idiosyncratic, related to individual and personal perception. The sense of smell seems global, personal, and highly variable between individuals. In these circumstances, is it possible to experience the same olfactory perceptions and share them ?

The description of odors

It is currently well-accepted that the expression of olfactory experiences through identification or description of odors is difficult, compared to the same process in relation to the other senses. Although it is quite easy to describe a picture or a sound, the labels available to name odors are limited. It is difficult to identify an odor, and we can get stuck when we try. Lawless and Engen (1977) referred to this phenomenon as the tip-of-the-nose state (as opposed to the tip of the tongue) : when we smell an odor, we might know we have experienced it before, but find we cannot precisely reach its exact label.

Despite this major linguistic difficulty, some experimental results have shown the possibility of expressing an olfactory experience verbally. Urdapilleta, Giboreau, Manetta and Richard (2006) studied the characteristics of denominations used to describe odors by grouping them into semantic classes (*i.e.*, according to their meaning). They demonstrated that the vocabulary used to describe odors is based on a variety of classes referring to many dimensions, such as *source*, *intensity*, *temporality* (the way the odor changes in time), *use* (its assigned function) and also the *hedonistic value* (pleasantness/unpleasantness) or *emotion* (the effect produced by the odor on the subject). Thus, even if the labels used to describe odors vary from person to person, they refer to the same semantic dimensions and convey the same sort of meanings.

What about sharing olfactory experiences ? According to Chrea, Ferdenzi, Valentin and Abdi (2007), the variability of the description depends on the nature of the odor. The authors rely on the notion of *codability* to revisit the relation between odor perceptions and language. This notion refers to the ease and degree of agreement with which people can name a referent (*i.e.*, an odor in this case). In their experiment, the authors assessed the consensus between French, American and Vietnamese participants in a free identification task of 40 odors from daily life *(e.g., lavender, wintergreen, ginger, garlic, anise* and *soap)*. Participants were asked to identify odors using single words, and avoiding general terms whenever possible. The results show that some odors are more *codable* than others – they are more readily identified by specific names, and these names give rise to stronger agreement in each culture. For instance, *anise*, *garlic* and *lavender* were highly consensual for French participants, but not for American and Vietnamese subjects. The authors suggest that the *codability* of a fragrance is related to its familiarity in a culture : fragrances associated with an important label consensus are familiar in French culture but are less frequently encountered in the other two.

Thus, we can see that difficulties observed in describing odors are related to the sensory and cognitive characteristics of the sense of smell. Nevertheless, the results showing between-subjects' consensus suggest that these difficulties do not prevent individuals from agreeing about how to identify or describe at least a few odors. It may be possible to some extent, then, for people to share their olfactory experiences. However, since few experiments have examined olfactory processing or shared olfactory perceptions, the question remains open.

Selective references for further reading

Chrea, C., Ferdenzi, C., Valentin, D., & Abdi, H. (2007). Revisiting the relation between language and cognition : A cross-cultural study with odors. *Current Psychology Letters*, *22*, 1-14.

Chu, S., & Downes, J. J. (2000a). Long live Proust : The odour-cued autobiographical memory bump. *Cognition*, *75*, 41-50.

Holley, A. (1999). *Éloge de l'odorat*. Paris : Odile Jacob.

Urdapilleta, I., Giboreau, A., Manetta, C., Houix, O., & Richard, J. F. (2006). The mental context for the description of odors : A semantic space. *European Review of Applied Psychology*, *56*, 261-271.

Exercise 8

Match the following terms to the appropriate blank in the sentences below.

List of terms

(a) chemical ; (b) range ; (c) codability ; (d) insensitive ; (e) memory ; (f) color ; (g) sensitive ; (h) cognitive processes (i) dimensions ; (j) volatile ; (k) odors.

Sentences with blanks

(1) ________________ differ from other stimuli in terms of physiological characteristics.

The (2) ________________ of olfactory stimuli has not been established.

The (3) ______________ associated with the perception of odors (*e.g.*, discrimination, memory, and identification of odors) are highly variable and diverse among individuals.

The sense of smell is (4) ___________, based on contact between (5) __________ molecules released from substances and receptors contained in the olfactory cell membrane. Unlike sight, however, for which there is only one type of receptor perceiving (6) _____________, there is a wide diversity of olfactory receptors and individuals do not all have the same amount of receptors.

Thus, some individuals can be (7) ________________________, and others completely (8) _____________________, to the same molecules.

Whereas visual stimuli are assessed through various (9) _______________ (height, color, orientation in space, etc.), this seems not to be the case for odors.

(10) ________________ for odors is global in the sense that olfactory memories include the encoding context, *i.e.*, some elements of the scene in which the odor was perceived.

(11) ________________ of a fragrance is related to its familiarity in a culture. For instance, *anise*, *garlic* and *lavender* are more easily identified by French than American or Vietnamese coders.

Pour en savoir plus sur la catégorisation, reportez-vous au DVD contenant le **texte** et la version **audio 6** intitulés :

Categorisation : A fundamental process

Pour en savoir plus sur la catégorisation des odeurs, reportez-vous au DVD contenant le **texte** et la version **audio 7** intitulés :

Do categories for odors exist ? The contribution of categorisation to the study of odor perception

D'autres thèmes de la psychologie cognitive à découvrir sur le DVD :

Pour en savoir plus sur l'effet Stroop, reportez-vous au DVD contenant le film intitulé :

Film 11 : Stroop effect

Pour en savoir plus sur les lois de la perception, reportez-vous au DVD contenant le film intitulé :

Film 12 : Gestalt theory : Laws of perceptual organization

Pour vous entraîner au mécanisme de chunking, reportez-vous au DVD contenant le film intitulé :

Film 13 : Learn how « chunking » improves recall

Pour en savoir plus les différents niveaux d'encodage des informations, reportez-vous au DVD contenant le film intitulé :

Film 14 : Differences between structural, phonemic and semantic encoding : a depth processing effect

Chapitre 3

PSYCHOLOGIE CLINIQUE ET PSYCHO-PATHOLOGIQUE/ CLINICAL PSYCHOLOGY

Clinical psychologists work to understand, prevent, and treat psychological problems. When people are distressed, unable to cope with problems due to stress, or engage in behaviours that are maladaptive in their social context, clinical psychologists are available to assist them. They assess clients, form diagnoses, and provide appropriate treatments. The goals of diagnosis and treatment are to observe and understand the difficulties experienced by people of all ages and to assist them by promoting subjective well-being, adaptive behaviours, and/or ongoing personal development. Psychologists can work with clients who have been diagnosed with serious psychological disorders or clients who are average individuals who wish to improve some aspect of their personal development. In the series of texts presented in this section of the book, authors will discuss a range of issues covered by clinical psychologists, including diagnosis and classification of personality disorders, different types of psychopathology, and how to cope with some of these difficulties.

20 VIDEO GAME ADDICTION : A REAL ADDICTION ? ♫ (AUDIO 8)

Existing research on video gaming tends to focus on two main areas : the negative effects of playing video games, and whether video games can be used for pedagogical purposes. It is clear that video games have some positive effects : they can improve sensorimotor tasks, visual acuity, and attention, as well as aid in the recovery of motor skills after physical trauma. Thus video games should be considered as platforms for learning. They also contribute to children's development, and their maturation to adulthood. For example, teenagers can try out situations they have not yet had to deal with, but that could happen later in life. In doing so, they could learn how to deal with those situations. In another example, adolescents could learn how to deal with social interactions. Some video games require increasing cooperation, helping a young person work in a team – a skill which could be very useful in the professional world.

Video games also have a negative side, however. Over the last few years, there has been increasing interest in Massively Multiplayer Online Role-Playing Games (MMORPGs). They are the latest Internet-only computer gaming experience, consisting of a multi-player universe with a richly detailed visual and auditory world. Some researchers and clinicians suggest that playing MMORPG is an addictive behavior for some people, similar to substance dependence. Video games provide anonymity, and that anonymity gives those with low self-confidence the chance to create a virtual life for themselves on the Internet. Then playing MMORPG can become a substitute for real-life social interaction, giving the user an escape from reality. MMORPGs such as "Everquest" or "World of War Craft" have been categorized as "heroinware" by some of their users.

In Chappel *et al.*'s study (2006), most participants who played "Everquest" displayed core components of addiction, such as salience, mood modification, tolerance, withdrawal symptoms, craving and relapse. Nevertheless, no single account mentioned all the core components of addiction. The result of this research could be that the "addiction" narrative players use to describe their problematic behavior is an example of a functional attribution, whereby individuals pathologize their behaviour as a way of eliminating self-blame and "excusing" their behavior. In the same way, for some clinicians, it is difficult, or even dangerous, to use the word "addiction" for video gaming. Indeed, most individuals who have difficulties with video games are adolescents. Research on cerebral imaging has shown that impulse control is established at the end of adolescence – around age 25 – as a result of multiple factors, among which environment plays a central role. This is later than researchers first imagined and a lack of control in adolescence is quite normal ! So, together with the lack of evidence, it is probably better to talk about "excessive players" other than addicts.

There are features of video game playing that have the potential to absorb some players' attention to the extent that their perception of time is altered. Studies have found that regular video game players often report playing for longer periods than they intended. So it seems that a number of features of those video games could be seen as addictive characteristics :

- The notion of a persistent world : while traditional videogames end at some point or become repetitive and boring, MMORPGS are endless. By definition, a persistent world is a world that exists independent of the users. In an MMORPG, the world exists before the user logs on, and continues to exist when the user logs off. Thus users could be preoccupied by the game without connection to it because events and interactions occur in the world even when the user is not logged on to the persistent world.

- The avatar (the character representation of the player in the virtual word) receives narcissistic reinforcement in the form of recognition by other players (if the player is any good !) and a potential sense of prestige and power from having other players comply with the avatar's orders. The worldwide aspect of these video games signifies that the recognition received is planetary. Returning to the real world could be difficult.
- Social interaction in MMORPGs is highly essential. Most forms of advancement in MMORPG require increasing cooperation or dependence on other users. You must collaborate with other players in the game to succeed in more complex goals, otherwise you cannot go up a level. A player needs to join a "guild" or "clan" of other players to advance in the game.
- These video games demand a high level of time investment. If you want to belong to a guild, and, if possible, an elite guild, you must spend a lot of time playing almost every day.
- Excitement/arousal produced by the game is promoted by constant stimulation and unexpected situations. According to Jacob's *General Theory of Addiction* (1986), the relation between an individual and his/her addictive behavior is rooted in a need to increase or decrease arousal levels. In other words, an addicted person takes part in the chosen activity to escape from the reality of existence. Therefore any activity that has the capacity to be either arousing and/or relaxing, and that can allow a person to be distracted from his/her normal life, is likely to be engaged in excessively by some individuals. Some researchers have shown that some gamers engage in online gaming as a means of coping with problems in their everyday lives. These findings support Jacob's theory that suggests people who play excessively are either over- or under-aroused and use online gaming, or other reinforcing behaviors, as a means of escape and to relieve depressive states.
- Finally, the reward component of video games can be compared to a "virtual Skinner box". Rewards, as well as difficulties, increase progressively and this reinforces the commitment of the gamer. This reward cycle could generate dependence.

While certain video games have some positive effects, others could be dangerous for some individuals. While it is difficult and inappropriate to talk about pathological gamers (especially for adolescents), some features of MMORPG lead to negative effects on gamers. Further research that focuses on both positive and negative effects is necessary. This could help in developing prevention programs in order to avoid or reduce possible detrimental effects on the well-being of gamers. Research could also help clinicians obtain a better understanding of the difficulties encountered by adolescent gamers that would allow them to develop better treatments for these individuals.

Selective references for further reading

Hussain, Z., & Griffiths, M. D. (2009). Excessive use of Massively Multi-Player Online Role-Playing Games : A pilot study. *International Journal of Mental Health and Addiction, 7*, 563-571.

Stora, M. (2007). *Les écrans, ça rend accro...* Paris : Hachette Littératures.

Tisseron, S. (2008). *Qui a peur des jeux vidéo ?* Paris : Albin Michel.

Valleur, M. (2009). La cyberaddiction existe-t-elle ? *Psychotropes, 15*, 13-19.

Yee, N. (2006). The demographics, motivations, and derived experiences of users of Massively Multi-User Online Graphical Environments. *Presence, 15*, 309-329.

Exercise 9

Questions

1. What is a MMORPG ?
2. List three of the core components of addiction.
3. What is a "persistent world"?
4. Which writer has suggested that addiction represents an escape from too much or too little stimulation ?
5. What is an "avatar" ?

21 POSITIVE PSYCHOLOGY : AN INTRODUCTION

WHAT IS POSITIVE PSYCHOLOGY ?

Positive psychology is the scientific study of the strengths and virtues that enable individuals and communities to thrive (Gable & Haidt, 2005). Originally inspired by Humanistic Psychology (Carl Rogers), this more recent field was founded at the beginning of the 21st century on the belief that people want to lead meaningful and fulfilling lives and to cultivate what is best within themselves. When he was president of the *American Psychological Association* (APA), Seligman worked hard to promote this approach, as evidenced by the subsequent creation of several scientific associations (*International Positive Psychology Association, Association Française et Francophone de Psychologie Positive*, etc.) and exchange networks (*e.g., European Network of Positive Psychology* or ENPP). Contrary to most studies carried out in psychology, positive psychology is more focused on what works than on the problems observed. Hence, mental health is no longer seen as the absence of anxiety and depressive symptoms, but as a particular state of well-being (of complete physical, mental and social health) which enables individuals to overcome the inevitable current life tensions and to accomplish fruitful work and contribute to social life.

The goals of positive psychology

Positive psychology has three central concerns (Seligman, 2002) : positive emotions, positive individual traits, positive institutions and relationships. Understanding positive emotions entails the study of contentment with the past, happiness in the present, and hope for the future. Understanding positive individual traits consists of the study of strengths and virtues, such as the capacity for love, courage, compassion, resilience, creativity, curiosity, integrity and self-control. Understanding positive institutions entails the study of the strengths that foster better communities, such as justice, responsibility, civility, parenting, nurturing, work ethic, teamwork and tolerance. The main goal of positive psychology is to build a science of optimal human functioning that enables a better understanding of positive outcomes : for example, families and schools that allow children to flourish, workplaces that foster satisfaction and productivity, communities that encourage civic engagement and therapies which develop the patients' strengths.

Is positive psychology opposed to other fields of psychology ?

Since World War II, psychology has focused almost exclusively on psychological problems and how to remedy them. Great strides have thus been made in understanding and treating psychological disorders. However, one consequence of this focus on psychological disorders is that psychology has little to say about what makes life most worth living. Positive psychology proposes to correct this imbalance by focusing on strengths without ignoring weaknesses. It should not be considered as a replacement for traditional psychology, but merely as a supplement to the hard-won gains of traditional psychology. Psychology's concern with reducing problems should not be abandoned and this demands scientifically informed solutions. Suffering and well-being, however, are both part of the human condition, and psychologists should be concerned with both.

Basic themes, assumptions, and early missions of positive psychology

One of the major themes that define positive psychology is a focus on the factors and conditions that contribute most to a well-lived life and which encourage human flourishing – in other words, the characteristics and predictors of the "good life". This focus inevitably concerns human qualities that enrich our lives, make life worth living, foster strong character and promote psychological growth, but also nurture genius and talent. Today, psychologists identify 24 psychological strengths (Peterson). These are grouped into six areas : knowledge and wisdom, courage, humanity, justice, temperance and transcendence. According to Seligman (2002), these personal qualities are the guarantee of authentic happiness when they help us to accomplish our goals and when they are used to benefit others.

What is not related to happiness and well-being ?

Positive psychology is grounded in empirical and replicable scientific studies. Although some findings may come close to common sense, others can be counter-intuitive and quite surprising. For example, it is often believed that wealth makes people happy. However, data shows that whilst economic output in the UK has nearly doubled in the last 30 years, happiness levels have remained identical. Research studies highlight that wealth is only weakly related to happiness, both within and across nations, particularly when income is above the poverty level (Diener & Diener, 1996). Equally, being well-educated or being young is not necessarily a guarantee of happiness. In fact, contrary to popular belief, older people are more constantly satisfied with their lives than younger individuals. Furthermore, not surprisingly, married people are generally happier than singles, but perhaps because they were happier in the first place !

What kinds of life experiences contribute to well-being ?

Most pleasurable activities (such as shopping, watching TV, eating good food, or making money) can make people joyful, but do not lead to psychological growth or to the human flourishing in the long term, probably because they do not require any ability or provide little challenge. It is more interesting to experience situations that present challenges, more specifically, which help us to develop or improve skills (*e.g.*, becoming a better chess player), through the achievement of previously set goals (*e.g.*, reading a book, winning a game).

"Flow" is a state of well-being that can be experienced through dealing successfully with small daily challenges which are freely chosen (intrinsic motivation). This term, coined by Mihaly Csikszentmihalyi (2006), refers to a state of absorption in one's work that is characterized by intense concentration, loss of self-awareness, a feeling of control, and a sense that "time is flying". It is possible to induce this state by living optimal or *"peak experiences"*. This kind of activity generates positive emotions that we are able to build upon, and which have lasting benefits for the individual, helping him/her to cope better with adversity.. Other studies also suggest that traumatic experiences (*e.g.*, serious illness) can sometimes be instructive and may later provide a sort of psychological immunity against adaptative difficulties.

How can we become happier, build our resources and develop resiliency ?

There are numerous ways to develop happiness and well-being. Seligman recommends identifying individual strengths and virtues in order to find new ways to build upon them. Increasing self-awareness of personal qualities helps to decide the extent to which one wishes to change in order to achieve long-term well-being. Sonja Lyubomirsky (2008) proposes using strategies that foster positive emotions, such as practicing acts of altruism or kindness, engaging in forgiveness, and developing a grateful and mindful disposition. Another way to cultivate well-being is to build positive social relationships which can play a protective role.

The future of positive psychology

Seligman (2002) predicts that in this new century positive psychology will help us better understand the factors that allow individuals, communities, and society to flourish, and not only to endure stressful situations or to thrive after a trauma. In this perspective, further efforts should be made to identify human strengths and classify them in the same way as the *Diagnostic and Statistical Manual of Mental Disorders* (DSM-IV), which would become a universally adopted tool for practitioners.

It also becomes crucial to create reliable assessment tools to evaluate personal assets and to conduct appropriate longitudinal studies or experiments in order to understand why and how these individual strengths may increase through daily actions. Positive psychology can also use scientific methods to investigate the consequence of living a life based on the adoption of certain human values (*e.g.*, altruism, integrity, tolerance). Ultimately, it is essential to develop and to test clinical interventions and structured programs to build or enhance these psychological strengths and virtues.

Selective references for further reading

Lecomte, J. (dir., 2009). *Introduction à la psychologie positive*. Paris : Dunod.

Seligman, M. E. P. & Csikszentmihalyi, M. (2000). Positive psychology : An introduction. *American Psychologist*, *55*, 5-14.

Snyder, C. R., and Lopez, S. J. (2001). *Handbook of positive psychology*. Oxford University Press.

Exercise 10

Fill in the blanks. Choose the most appropriate term from the list below.

List of terms

(a) flow ; (b) meaningful work ; (c) positive institutions ; (d) absence of anxiety and depression symptoms ; (e) positive psychology ; (f) state of well-being ; (g) social life ; (h) positive emotions ; (i) qualities that enrich our lives ; (j) positive individual traits.

Sentences with blanks

(1) ______________ is the scientific study of the strengths and virtues that enable individuals and communities to thrive. Mental health is no longer seen as the (2) ______________, but as a particular (3) ____________ (of complete physical, mental and social health) which enables individuals to engage in (4) ________ and contribute to (5) __________. Understanding (6) _____________________ entails the study of contentment with the past, happiness in the present, and hope for the future. Understanding (7) _________________ consists of the study of strengths and virtues, such as the capacity for love, courage, compassion, resilience, creativity, curiosity, integrity and self-control. Understanding (8) _________________ entails the study of the strengths that foster better communities, such as justice, responsibility, civility, parenting, nurturing, work ethic, teamwork and tolerance. Human (9) _________________ can be grouped into six areas : knowledge and wisdom, courage, humanity, justice, temperance and transcendence. (10) _________________ refers to a state of absorption in one's work that is characterized by intense concentration, loss of self-awareness, a feeling of control, and a sense that "time is flying".

22 FACTORS IN JUVENILE DELINQUENCY

Juvenile delinquency is an important social concern and clinical psychologists have increasingly been called upon to address problems associated with juvenile delinquents/young offenders. Delinquency among young people, and particularly reoffending minors, has to be studied in connection with the period of adolescence. Delinquent acting-out is not the result of chance, but rather of a combination of different factors – individual, environmental and social – in the turbulent context of adolescence. One warning before we begin, however : even if processes which are in play during adolescence can be explanatory factors, not all adolescents are potential delinquents !

Adolescence is above all a period of change – physical and psychological – which makes it a period of risk taking (Jeammet, 2001). In a context which is inadequate to meet their needs, psychologically or environmentally, adolescents often express psychological conflict as violent or aggressive behaviour directed towards others (aggression and violence) or turned against the self (suicide attempts and self-mutilation). This pattern demonstrates it is easier for an adolescent to act out his/her suffering than to think about it.

During this fragile period, the biggest risk is repetition of deviant, aggressive, or violent behaviours. For an adolescent, repeating transgressive acts can become the only way available of escaping psychological suffering and preserving some degree of equilibrium. Reinforcing this psychological pattern of behaviour can lead a person towards what Selosse (1980) calls a *"negative identity"* which gives the young person a certain satisfaction : *"I'm the craziest ; I'm the one who's done the most crimes ; I'm the one who's taken the most substances"*. Multiple convictions and sanctions only confirm this position of gang-leader in the eyes of the peer group. The only way forward for such a young person is to become a reference ; sanctions then become a recognition by society of his/her capacity to be the "best" in the path s/he has "chosen". (This behaviour is frequently associated with an attitude of being all-powerful, and of feeling omnipotent, which expresses narcissistic fragility).

In terms of the young person's level of vulnerability, a delinquent's "career" can take on different forms and characteristics. Some authors (Blatier, 2002 ; Favard, 1985 ; Frechettes & Leblanc, 1987 ; Pinatel, 1987) have distinguished different types of delinquency characterised by repetition ; we shall consider two of them.

Transitory delinquency

Delinquency is considered transitory when the frequency and (usually) seriousness of offending is low, during a limited period in the person's life. There is, then, a transitory delinquency which is limited to adolescence and which remains connected to the process of challenging values and institutions which is common to all adolescents – their search for independence via challenging adult authority. It is mostly characterised by offences that involve stealing, during a period of three or four years. In this context, we can directly connect the act of transgressing with the adolescent's psychological tensions, for which repetitive aggressive acts are a less costly response than thinking or talking about psychological difficulties. Many adolescents leave this transitory delinquency behind them at about the age of eighteen, as they prepare for their professional future, or as they invest themselves in their affective or professional lives.

Persistent delinquency

Persistent delinquents present characteristics quite distinct from those who only show a short period of delinquency. Persistent delinquency starts early ; during adolescence it gives rise to ten or more offences per year (Elliott *et al.*,

1989) and the offences are of different natures (delinquent polymorphism) – at least one of them being offences against persons.

The seriousness of offences increases progressively (Frechette and Leblanc's *process of aggravation*, 1987), starting with simple theft, moving on to breaking and entering, then carjacking and violent offences against persons. The motivation of offences is both utilitarian and hedonist.

The dimension of persistence increases the probability of a wider variety of acts and more serious acts being committed. There are some adolescents who pursue their delinquency well into adulthood. Delinquency will last longer, with increasing commitment from the delinquent, and a higher likelihood to be accompanied by violence, the earlier it begins in childhood.

Characteristics of persistent delinquents

Examining the different factors which are involved in persistent delinquency takes us, for the most part, to three main areas : organisation of the personality, socio-cognitive processes, and social factors.

(1) Organisation of the personality

The more persistent delinquency is, the greater the role played by elements of personality. In addition to circumstances, the immediacy of situations are involved to a considerable extent in acts committed. Certain characteristics of persistent delinquent personalities are grouped around the following traits (Favard, 1991) :

- aggressiveness
- affective indifference
- lability (instability)
- egocentricity

Affective indifference and aggressiveness have been found to be the strongest predictors for delinquent acts and recidivism (Favard, 1991).

(2) Cognitive distortions

Another particularity of persistent delinquents points concerns a certain number of cognitive distortions, generally beliefs pre-existing their actions. They consider that the action was caused by the victim's attitude. They think they did the victim no harm – or even that they did him/her some good. This is the case, for example, for delinquents who :

- say they didn't steal because they weren't the end beneficiaries of what they stole,

- see a bank as not being a person, and therefore incapable of being personally attacked or robbed (Blatier, 2002).

Persistent delinquents feel little or no guilt because their psychological functioning (characterised, among other things, by a lack of internalised prohibitions) prevents them feeling such a sentiment (Blatier, 2004). They rarely consider themselves responsible, attributing responsibility to emotions, or to a personal state which justifies their action :

- a feeling of injustice
- having to defend a friend
- loyalty towards their family in front of an intruder, etc.

Committing an act sometimes has the objective of dealing out justice, when delinquents consider they have established a justice which was previously lacking. They do not believe what other people claim : victims' suffering can only have been exaggerated ; witnesses' attitudes are not impartial.

(3) Social factors

In many cases, the difficulties persistent delinquents encounter in terms of their integration in society and their social environment contributes to establishing their delinquent behaviour.

In a case where delinquent behaviour stops, it is often linked to affective relationships that have made it possible to leave delinquency behind. Certain social factors play a significant role in positive change. They are involved in persistent delinquency as an element of reinforcement (Blatier, 2004) :

- the age at which the person is placed in an institution, or prison, and at which they are released
- previous criminal record
- psychoactive substance abuse
- unemployment and unstable housing conditions.

Conclusions

To assess the delinquent behaviour and repeated offences of adolescents, it is important to frame their acts within the context of their individual and social case history. General conduct, behaviours, and clinical symptoms are taken into account to develop an operant contextual analysis of the adolescent's delinquent acts over time. A delinquent act or offence can be analysed in relation to four factors : (a) behaviour ; (b) *modus operandi* or way of doing things ; (c) environment and history ; as well as, (d) a framework of opportunities to put actions into practice, while accounting for these factors according to the individual's *"psyche"* (Harrati, Vavassori & Villerbu, 2006).

Given these facts, it is clear that explanations of delinquency and aggressive acts that rely solely on the analysis of an individual's psyche are no longer sufficient. In order to better conceptualise the factors associated with the aggressive acts and delinquency of adolescents, an interdisciplinary examination of research is needed to provide a richer source of data and theories. In addition to clinical psychology and psychopathology, research and applied areas that may provide invaluable insights in this field include : criminology, forensic psychology, sociology, social psychology, social cognition, social work, and neurobiology.

Selective references for further reading

Blatier, C. (2002). *La Délinquance des mineurs. L'enfant, le psychologue, le droit.* Grenoble : Presses Universitaire de Grenoble.

Fréchette, M. & Leblanc, M., (1987). *Délinquances et délinquants*. Chicoutimi : Gaëtan Morin.

Harrati S., Vavassori D., & Villerbu L. (2009). *Délinquance et violence*. Armand Colin : Paris, coll. « 128 ».

Marty, F. (2002). *Le jeune délinquant*. Paris : Payot.

Exercise 11

Match the terms below with the definition that is most appropriate.

Terms

1. acting-out
2. juvenile delinquency
3. offence
4. young offender
5. self-mutilation

Definitions

a. refers to an individual who repeatedly engages in delinquent acts and criminal offenses in childhood and adolescence.
b. engaging in acts that cause damage to the body, such as cutting oneself with a knife.

c. a modern term used to refer to a juvenile delinquent (the most common and politically correct term).
d. refers to an act that is destructive and generally involves a violation of the law.
e. acting out conflictual emotions through disordered conduct and aggressive behaviour.

23 AN INTRODUCTION TO BASIC CONCEPTS IN PSYCHOANALYSIS

A SHORT DEFINITION

Psychoanalysis contains a body of ideas developed by Sigmund Freud (1856-1939) and continued or developed by others such as Alfred Adler (1870-1937), Sandor Ferenczi (1873-1933), Carl Gustav Jung (1875-1961), Melanie Klein (1882-1960), Otto Rank (1884-1939) and Anna Freud (1895-1982). It is primarily devoted to the study of human psychological functioning and behavior, although it can also be applied to groups and to cultural phenomena such as societies and art (especially literature, cinema, sculpture and painting). According to its groundbreaking inventor, psychoanalysis has the following three aims :

- investigating the human mind,
- systematizing theory about human functioning and behavior,
- treating psychological or emotional illness.

The main Freudian theoretical statements are :

(1) sexuality in children and adults is important for an understanding of human behavior,
(2) symptoms are failed attempts at self-healing,
(3) the patient history – past experience, especially in childhood – is essential for an understanding of current problems,
(4) the unconscious can be encountered via dreams, "Freudian slips", symptoms and mistakes.

MAIN CONCEPTS (IN ALPHABETICAL, NOT CHRONOLOGICAL ORDER)

Defense mechanisms

In Freudian psychoanalytical theory, defense mechanisms are unconscious psychological strategies brought into play to cope with reality and to maintain self-image. Their purpose is to protect the ego from anxiety or social sanctions, or to provide refuge from a situation it cannot currently cope with. Defenses are not pathological in themselves, but may become pathological if they are persistent, frequent or overgeneralized. According to Vaillant (1977), there are four levels of defense : pathological, immature, neurotic, and mature.

Primitive defense mecanisms include denial, dissociation or projection, all of them are common features of psychosis. Idealization is considered immature, more often found during adolescence and in borderline patients. Repression is more typical for neurotic functioning, whereas humour and sublimation are considered mature, more highly-developed defenses. Freud believed that seeking relief and protection, many people bury painful memories deep in their unconscious, and that repression is therefore one key factor in the operation of the unconscious and its defense mechanisms. In his dynamic model, dreams, symptoms, and slips of the tongue break through the barrier of censorship and repression and open access to the unconscious.

Drive

Freud stated that humans are driven by two conflicting central desires : the life drive (libido/Eros) (survival, procreation, hunger, thirst, and sex) and the death drive (Thanatos). Freud's description of Cathexis, whose energy is known as libido, included all creative, life-producing drives. The death drive (or death instinct), whose energy is known as anticathexis, represented an urge inherent in all living things to return to a state of calm : in other words, an inorganic or dead state.

Confronted with clinical and political evidence – the First World War brought unequalled horror to Europe and many soldiers developed shell-shock and traumatic neurosis – Freud acknowledged the tendency for the unconscious to repeat unpleasant experiences in order to desensitize the body. This tendency explains why traumatic nightmares occur, as nightmares seem to contradict Freud's earlier conception of dreams as purely a site of pleasure, fantasy, and desire. The life-drive/death-drive tension represented a revolution in Freud's thinking.

Fantasy

Desire and fantasy are closely related. Desire has its origin in the experience and anticipation of satisfaction. For Freud, if desire is articulated through fantasy, then fantasy itself is a mediator between individuals and their wishes, anxieties, and the difficulty of acting on desires in reality. Thus, daydreams and artistic activity have a protective function for an individual confronted with harsh, mostly frustrating, and sometimes unbearable, reality. For Freud, every fantasy and dream is to be interpreted as a wish-fulfillment.

Oedipus complex

Considered universal by Freud, this complex is based on Sophocles' tragedy *Oedipus Rex*, where Oedipus kills his father and marries his mother. Freud states that during their psychosexual development, children who have successfully gone through the oral and anal stages will have to go through the phallic stage. This stage involves intense love for the parent of the opposite sex and hatred and rejection of the same-sex parental figure. Crucial for the individual's libidinal development, the process unfolds differently if the child is a boy or a girl. The boy, primarily attached to his mother, perceives his father as a rival to be suppressed. His fear of being castrated helps him to overcome this complex that achieves resolution when he identifies with the feared/admired father and fully recognizes his mother's sexual inaccessibility.

For the little girl, things are even more complex. She first has to detach from the primary love object, her mother, to turn to her father in order to ask him for completeness. After being disappointed in her demand for a baby, she is supposed to identify with the mother who was already her first love object. This double movement and object change makes the development and clinical treatment of women especially complicated. It is very important to understand that, in the girl's Oedipus complex, it is castration anxiety that leads her *into* the complex ; whereas for the boy it is the same anxiety that leads him *out* of it. Many obstacles may render the resolution of this complex incomplete and are held responsible for suffering in the professional and the love lives of future adults, both men and women.

Resistance

Resistance, as initially used by Freud, referred to patients blocking memories from their consciousness. This was a key concept, since the primary treatment method of Freud's *"talking cure"* required making these memories available to the patient's consciousness. Later, Freud described five different forms of resistance :

- repression, *e.g.*, reaction-formation, obsession, phobia (denial or avoidance) ;
- transference (projection) ;
- gain from illness (secondary gain) ;
- compulsion to repeat (acting out) ;
- sense of guilt or need for punishment (self-sabotage).

They became associated with various clinical structures such as psychosis and neurosis. Over time, resistance came to mean anything a patient did to make therapy, or a particular intervention, less effective.

Structural theory

In *Beyond the pleasure principle* (1920), Freud proposed his structural theory (Id, Ego, Super ego) according to which the Id is the impulsive, child-like portion of the psyche that operates on the pleasure principle and only takes into account what it wants, disregarding the consequences. The Ego has to reconcile pressures from the Id, on the one hand, and the Super ego on the other. The Super ego is the moral component of the psyche, stemming from internalized societal prohibitions and identifications with the parents' Super egos. Trying to follow the reality principle, the rational Ego attempts a balance between the impractical hedonism of the Id and the equally impractical moralism of the Super ego ; it is the part of the psyche that is usually reflected in a person's actions. When overburdened or threatened by its multiple inner and outer tasks, the Ego may employ defense mechanisms including denial, repression, and displacement, or develop symptoms aiming – but unfortunately without success – at self-healing, or at least withdrawing from the unpleasant situation. The symptom's adaptative and homeostatic functions have to be fully recognized by the clinician before intervening.

Symptoms

Symptom formation is connected with Freud's theory of neurosis, in which there is a conflict around sexual drives, repression, and the return of repressed material in distorted form. He developed his groundbreaking theory mainly in *Inhibition, symptoms and anxiety* (1926). The central idea is that the symptom expresses a compromise between instinctual satisfaction and defense, fuelled by a dynamic that always seeks homeostasis and self-healing.

How are we to analyze the formation and specific form of the symptom ? Both clearly depend on the nature of the conflict : are we dealing with the threat of castration, the loss of the object, narcissism at risk, or alienation ? Is it a case of neurosis, depression, a borderline state, or psychosis ? It has rightly been pointed out that, in this account, no symptom can exist independently of a corresponding clinical entity and underlying structure.

Even when it is fully recognizable as a source of pain, the symptom is not a problem in itself for the individual who has gradually adapted to it, and sometimes even clings to it for its primary and secondary benefits and the reassuring continuity, solidity, and durability it offers. This complexity helps us to understand why the symptom is so stable, as well as the fact that it enabled the temporary resolution of a conflict.

The first and second topologies

Perhaps the most significant contribution Freud made to Western thought was his argument concerning the impact of the unconscious on understanding conscious thought and behavior. Contrary to popular belief, Freud did not actually discover the unconscious – already present in various theories – but found a genuine method to study it. The unconscious can be revealed by analyzing dreams (which he called the *"royal road to the unconscious"*), Freudian slips, errors and mistakes – and art, which for Freud was the product of sublimation. To illustrate the latent logic of the unconscious mind, Freud developed his first topology of the psyche in *The interpretation of dreams* (1900). He proposed that the unconscious truly exists and functions according to strict and intelligible mechanisms, accessible through interpretation. The preconscious was described as a layer, an interface between conscious and unconscious thought ; its contents could be accessed with a little effort. Eventually, Freud completed the idea of the system unconscious (Preconscious, Conscious, Unconscious) by the concepts of the ego, superego, and id.

Transference and counter-transference

As a key concept, **transference** refers to the redirection of a patient's feelings for a significant person towards the therapist. Transference is often manifested as an erotic attraction towards the therapist, but can be seen in many other forms such as rage, hatred, guilt or mistrust.

Countertransference is defined as redirection of the therapist's feelings towards the patient, or more generally, as a therapist's emotional entanglement with the patient's transference. Nowadays we know that therapists' attunement to countertransference is nearly as critical as elaborating transference. Analyzing both transference and contertransference is the crucial issue to reveal unresolved conflicts patients have with figures from their childhood. In supervision, countertransference must be duly analyzed in order to become a technique and not an obstacle in psychoanalytical treatment.

Selective references for further reading

http://www.freud.org.uk : the web-site of the Freud Museum in London, U. K, 20 Maresfield Gardens.

http://www.nyfreudiansociety.org : a glossary of Freudian Terminology elaborated by the New York Freudian Society.

www.freudpage.info : Sigmund Freud, Anna, Biography, Bibliography, Quotes, Glossary, Psychoanalysis (definition, history, theory), Selected Works, FAQ, Museums, Hypnosis.

www.terrapsych.com/freud.html and www.freudfile.org/resources.html : these websites provide resources on Sigmund Freud, psychoanalytic and personal papers, correspondence, photos... Glossary of Freudian terms by Craig Chalquist.

Exercise 12

Questions

1. What methods do psychoanalysts use to discover the contents of the unconscious ?
2. Which of Freud's concepts is closest to that of *conscience* ?
3. During which stage of psychosexual development does the Oedipal conflict take place ?
4. Give three examples of defense mechanisms.
5. What name did Freud give to all life-producing drives ?

24 PSYCHOPATHOLOGY OF DRUG ADDICTION : SUBSTANCE ABUSE AND DEPENDENCE ♫ (AUDIO 9)

DEFINITIONS

The DSM-IV-R classifies substance-related disorders into two major categories : substance *use* disorders and substance-*induced* disorders.

Substance use disorders induce substance abuse and substance dependence. Substance abuse is a pattern of recurrent use that leads to damaging consequences (*i.e.*, social and interpersonal problems). Substance abuse may continue for a long period of time or progress to substance dependence, a more severe disorder associated with physiological signs of dependence (*e.g.*, *tolerance*, a state of physical habituation to a drug resulting from frequent use, such that higher doses are needed to achieve the same effect) and/or psychological dependence (compulsive use of a psychoactive substance).

Substance-induced disorders are disorders induced by using psychoactive substances, such as intoxication, withdrawal syndromes, mood disorders, anxiety, delirium, amnesia and psychotic disorders. However, different substances have different effects, so some of these disorders may be induced by one, a few, or all the substances. The DSM does not use the term addiction to describe these problems. We lack any universally accepted definition of addiction. For us, drug addiction is characterized by its action on the brain, which thus modifies feelings and behaviors. Addiction is the compulsive use of a drug, accompanied by signs of physiological and psychological dependence. The functions of drug addiction include obtaining pleasure, increasing interest and relieving undesirable sensations. Drug addiction behaviours are also characterized by repeated failure to control them, and persistence in spite of negative consequences. Unlike simple habits or consuming interests, the consequences of addictions can seriously impair, negatively affect, or destroy relationships, health (both physical and mental) and the capacity to function effectively. Our conception of drug addiction is based on the interaction of personal vulnerability, a particular context, and the substance used.

Types of drug

Drugs are generally classified within three major groupings : depressants, stimulants, and hallucinogens.

(1) **A depressant** is a drug that slows down or curbs the activity of the central nervous system. It reduces feelings of tension and anxiety, slows movement, and impairs cognitive processes. The most widely used depressants are alcohol, barbiturates and opioids (*e.g.*, morphine, heroin).

(2) **Stimulants** are psychoactive substances that increase the activity of the central nervous system. They thus enhance states of alertness and can produce feelings of pleasure or even euphoric highs. Effects vary with the particular drug. The most widely used stimulants are cocaine, nicotine, amphetamines, and ecstasy.

(3) **Hallucinogens** are in a class of drugs that produce sensory distortions or hallucinations, including alterations in perception and hearing. The most widely used hallucinogens are LSD *(Lysergic acid diethylamide)*, mushrooms, and cannabis.

Main theoretical approaches

Addictions have been studied and written about by many researchers and there are many different ways to understand and make sense of addictive behaviours. The following list describes the main theoretical approaches :

(a) The biological approach : researchers have focused on neurotransmitters (especially dopamine) and on the role of genetic factors.

(b) The cognitive approach : drug use may become habitual because of the pleasure (positive reinforcement) or temporary relief (negative reinforcement) it provides from negative emotions such as anxiety, and from depression which may itself be drug-induced. Different studies show the role of cognitive factors in substance abuse and dependence, especially the role of expectations : expectations about the perceived benefits of using drugs influence the decision to use them. Expectations are strongly influenced by beliefs.

(c) The psychodynamic approach : drug use reflects an oral-dependent personality and traces the origins to fixation in the oral stage of psychosexual development.

(d) The sociocultural approach : cultural attitudes can encourage or discourage drug use. Peer pressure and exposure to a drug subculture are important influences in determining substance use among adolescents and young adults.

Vulnerability and protective factors

Several vulnerability factors have been identified in different theoretical perspectives and various disciplinary fields. It is not possible to isolate a single risk factor which would have a predictive value of substance abuse or dependence ; the whole context created by associated factors constitutes a vulnerability factor in terms of becoming drug-dependent.

Three types of vulnerability factors have been found : individual, environmental, and those related to properties of the substances themselves. Most theories of addictive behaviour acknowledge that there are two major sources of reinforcement for substance use and misuse : positive reinforcement, linked to the positive hedonic effects of many abused substances ; and negative reinforcement, linked to the ability of some substances to relieve negative affective states. Several personality factors have been shown to be associated with risk for substance use disorders, and differentiate substance abusers on the basis of clinical profiles, treatment responses, and susceptibility to other forms of co-morbid psychopathology. Personality factors, such as a tendency to anxiety or depression, impulsiveness, reward-dependence and sensation-seeking, have all been shown to be associated with elevated and problematic substance use patterns.

On the other hand, there are certain factors that have been advanced as increasing resistance to drug use, such as being a highly-involved and well-supported family member. The people who are the best protected from drug use would appear to be those who have :

- well-settled ideas they can express well ;
- a sense of spiritual direction and community involvement, with goals, a role, and a feeling of membership in the community and identification with its values ;
- an attachment with someone who is not a drug user ;
- a high level of intelligence.

Other publications emphasize intrapersonal resources like self-esteem, self-confidence, self-defined fields of excellence, social coping skills, capacity to choose, good behavioral self-regulation, good problem-solving ability, and effective coping strategies. A growing body of research on how adolescents and young adults negotiate environmental risks provides evidence of the protective factors that influence positive development and protect young people from involvement in behaviours that present a health risk. Protective factors are part of the process of resilience. Some studies have demonstrated that resilience factors are also referred to as protective factors or developmental assets that can predict change in young people's health-related behaviours over time. This research makes it possible to locate individuals' capacities to face difficult situations in life without using substances. The notion of protective factors also allows us to understand the mechanisms which make it possible to come out of drug-addiction.

Selective references for further reading

American Psychiatric Association (2000). *Diagnostic and Statistical Manual of Mental Disorders* (4th ed., text rev.). (DSM-IV-TR), American Psychiatric Association. Washington, D.C. : Author.

Nevid, J., Rathus, S., & Greene, B. (2008) *Abnormal Psychology in a Changing World*. Person Edition, 7e éd. Adaptation française dirigée M. Bertrand, M.-C. Gely-Nargeot et M. Siksou.

Varescon, I. (2005). *Psychopathologie des conduites addictives : alcoolisme et toxicomanie*. Paris : Belin.

Varescon, I. (2008). Les addictions. In S. Ionescu et A. Blanchet (dir.), *Nouveau Cours de psychologie. Psychologie clinique, psychopathologie et psychothérapie*. Paris : PUF, p. 159-167.

Exercise 13

Questions

1. What does *tolerance* mean in relation to drug use ?
2. What drug types are : cocaine, cannabis, alcohol ?
3. Which approach to substance use suggests that it may be the result of peer pressure ?
4. What is *negative reinforcement* and how does it relate to substance use ?
5. What personality factors have been linked to drug use ?

Pour en savoir plus sur le DSM *(Manuel diagnostique et statistique des troubles mentaux)*, ses avantages et inconvénients, reportez-vous au DVD contenant le film intitulé :

Film 15 : The diagnostic and statistical manual of mental disorders (dsm) : advantages and disadvantages

Après avoir vu le film sur le DSM, si vous vous posez encore d'autres questions, vous suivrez avec intérêt l'échange entre **Wendy Pullin,** Professeur de psychologie clinique et **Agathe Brochard,** une étudiante en psychologie de l'Université Paris 8 dans le film intitulé :

Film 16 : Discussion of the advantages and disadvantages of the dsm

25 THE TRANSITION TO PARENTHOOD IN WOMEN WITH BORDERLINE PERSONALITY DISORDERS

Borderline personality disorder (BPD), one of the most severe and perplexing of mental disorders, is characterized by persistent and pervasive cognitive, emotional, and behavioral dysfunction. BPD is a heterogeneous phenotype and results from a multiple criterion set ; five of nine behavioral features are required for a diagnosis (DSM-IV-TR). Potentially, two individuals diagnosed with BPD could have only one diagnostic criterion in common. The BPD phenotype is broadly defined by features of emotional dysregulation, poor impulse control, identity disturbance, problematic interpersonal relationships, and suicidal/self-injurious behaviors, among others (APA, 1994). Emotional dysregulation appears to be a core feature of BPD. There is also high comorbidity with other psychiatric illnesses, notably affective disorders, post-traumatic stress disorder (PTSD) and substance abuse.

The prevalence of BPD is estimated to be 2 % in the general population, and 10 % in patients receiving mental health services. Two-thirds of these adults are women. Bearing this in mind, and considering that the transition to parenthood is known as a period of high psychological vulnerability, borderline parents are likely to seek psychological support in perinatal mental health services. The unstable and fragile features of their personalities expose borderline mothers to severe difficulties in the transition to parenthood, infant caregiving and the establishment of healthy interactions in the early years. Perinatal and infant psychologists and psychiatrists are often brought in to cope with complex clinical situations where unresolved traumatic events emerge abruptly from the parent's past, hindering the transition to parenthood. Some of these parents meet the criteria for BPD, particularly the mothers. Therapeutic management of parents with BPD in the perinatal period is often described as hard and challenging, even before the birth (Aidane *et al.*, 2009).

Unlike the extensive literature on the offspring of mothers with other psychiatric disorders, such as depression and anxiety disorders, only a few empirical studies have been conducted in children whose mothers are diagnosed with BPD. Most of the available studies on this population have focused on school-aged children and adolescents. In a recent review of the literature, MacFie (2009) confirms this lack : *"it is unusual in the field of child development to find almost totally uncharted territory"*. However, the high prevalence of social and emotional troubles observed in children and adolescents raised by borderline mothers, including BPD, attention deficit, hyperactivity disorder, and disruptive behavior disorders, may be partly ascribed to early disturbances in the parent-child relationship.

The relationships of individuals exhibiting BPD have often been described as intense, stormy, dependent, and enmeshed. Consistent with this pattern, borderline pathology has been shown to be significantly associated with a preoccupation with relationship concerns and heightened emotionality about relationships (*e.g.*, fear of rejection or abandonment by loved ones, heightened emotional sensitivity to perceived relational difficulties or slights). These problems may reflect prior difficulty acquiring appropriate levels of autonomy and trust within close relationships, a key developmental process that begins in early childhood with the parent-child relationship.

There is considerable evidence to suggest that the development of BPD is associated with early attachment trauma. Individuals diagnosed with BPD are likely to have suffered from maladaptive, neglectful or sexually or emotionally abusive relationships with their parents. When these traumatic experiences remain unresolved, such adults are at risk of re-enacting or replicating these severely distorted interactions with their own children, hindering the development of their own infant's attachment bond. Recent studies have shown that infants of borderline mothers are likely to develop disorganized attachment. When distressed following a brief separation from the mother, these infants (aged 13 months) display simultaneous contradictory behaviors and seem caught between desire to approach the parent and fear of doing so (Hobson *et al.*, 2005).

The transition to parenthood does not seem to significantly modify the usual lifestyle and psychological functioning of borderline mothers. Hence their conflicting relationships, professional and couple instability, impulsive behaviours, and dysphoric mood rapidly become incompatible with the infant's need for emotional security and regular and empathic care. Most of these women, in the first months post-partum, show a state of intense and chronic fatigue, and find it difficult to establish regular rhythms in the infant's daily care. The mother's own personal needs may be prioritized, to the detriment of those of the child (for example, the infant may be fed or put to bed when the mother herself feels hungry or sleepy).

For some women with BPD, pregnancy may be experienced as an idyllic and highly idealized time, with euphoric feelings of plenitude and omnipotence – of having total control over the unborn child. In other cases, physical symptoms of pregnancy may be very intense, and experienced as unbearable. For some mothers, fetal movements, and physical changes brought on by pregnancy, can be difficult to tolerate (they may fear they are going to burst, or suffer persecution fears to do with their "strange" state) or – conversely – may be completely ignored. Attendance at prenatal care is often irregular, and the mother may be ill-prepared to welcome her baby at birth.

Whereas the infant might be strongly idealized during pregnancy, anticipated as filling gaps and solving problems from the mother's past, after birth the little baby is unable to fulfill the mother's narcissistic needs or to dissipate her chronic feelings of emptiness. The baby's existence prompts the mother to relive her own childhood, creating a mirror of her own infantile distress, dependence, and fear of abandonment.

Parenting demands consistent and empathic care, attachment security, physical proximity and a capacity to tolerate dependence and the frustration of one's own desires. Such psychological tasks can be overwhelming for adults with BPD. The few available studies on borderline mothers have shown that these mothers report being less satisfied, less competent, and more distressed in their maternal role (Newman *et al.*, 2007) than other mothers. When interacting with their infants, mothers with BPD were found to be less sensitive, more intrusive, and more inconsistent. They demonstrate less structuring in their interactions with their infants, and may also misinterpret or avoid the infant's attempts at communication.

The lack of studies on mothers with BPD and their children can be seen as both a challenge and an opportunity. Mothers with BPD need to be identified early, if possible during pregnancy, and provided with intervention targeted at the parenthood experience, parenting skills, and infant communication and needs. Further research is clearly needed to understand the transition to parenthood and the parenting difficulties of mothers with BPD, as well as their impact on child outcomes.

Selective references for further reading

Aidane, E., Wendland, J., Rabain, D., & Marie, P. (2009). Un suivi thérapeutique atypique : Co-constructions thérapeutiques de la relation précoce d'une mère borderline et son bébé. *Psychiatrie de l'Enfant*, *52*, 131-166.

Hobson, R.P., Patrick, M., Crandell, L., Garcia-Perez, R. & Lee, A. (2005). Personal relatedness and attachment in infants of mothers with borderline personality disorder. *Development and Psychopathology*, *17*, 329-347.

Macfie, J. (2009). Development in children and adolescents whose mothers have borderline personality disorder. *Child Development Perspectives*, *3*, 66-71.

Newman, L.K., Stevenson, C.S., Bergman, L.R. & Boyce, P. (2007). Borderline personality disorder, mother-infant interaction and parenting perceptions : preliminary findings. *The Royal Australian and New Zealand College of Psychiatrists*, *41*, 598-605.

Exercise 14

Fill in the blanks in the sentences below with the term that best fits the meaning of the text.

List of terms

(a) empathic ; (b) abandonment ; (c) parenthood ; (d) attachment ; (e) narcissistic needs ; (f) parenting ; (g) Post-Traumatic Stress Disorder ; (h) disruptive behaviour.

Sentences with blanks

(1) __________ is a difficult task for anyone. Women who have been diagnosed with Borderline Disorder may face great challenges when they face (2) _________________. Many mothers with borderline disorder have unmet (3) _________________ due to the fact that they were abandoned, neglected, or abused by their own parents in childhood. These early difficulties may lead to the development of (4) _______________. Children need warm and (5) _______________________ care from their caregivers in order to experience a secure (6) ________________. On the mothers' part, if there is (7) _________________ of their children as they cope with their own ongoing psychological concerns, their children, in turn, may develop (8) __________________, attention deficit problems, and hyperactivity.

Pour en savoir plus sur les troubles de la personnalité selon la classification DSM IV-TR, reportez-vous au DVD contenant le film intitulé :

Film 17 : Personality disorders : an example of DSM classification

26 ANXIETY DISORDERS

WHAT IS ANXIETY ?

Defining the term *"anxiety"* is not as straightforward as we might think. It is regularly associated with notions of fear and stress, and the meaning sometimes depends on the language being used. For example, in French, *"angoisse"* and *"anxiété"* are two distinct terms, the first referring to a somatic reaction and the second to thoughts or cognitive manifestations of anxiety, whereas only the term *"anxiety"* is required in English. The word *"anguish"* exists in English, but it is not used as a diagnostic term.

Although considerable attention has been directed to defining anxiety, it still appears difficult to find a consensus. Lewis (1970) defines anxiety as *"an emotional state, with the subjectively experienced quality of fear as a closely related emotion"*. Today we may think of of anxiety as any or all of : a trait, a state, a stimulus, a response, a drive, and a motivation.

One famous author who worked on anxiety is Freud. Anxiety is one of the foundations of Freud's theory, and has three major aspects. First there is overt anxiety, due to fear of a real object, and the desire to flee an objectively dangerous stimulus. Second, there is a more subjective kind of anxiety (neurotic anxiety) where perceived threats intrude on the field of consciousness. Finally there is moral anxiety, created by conflicts between the Id's desires and the superego's prohibitions. As shown by Banovic and Pédinielli (listen to the audio version of the text on the DVD called, "*A psychiatric and psychopathological approach to delirium and hallucinations*"), this older view has been replaced by approaches that describe symptoms or classify clusters of symptoms as syndromes.

At present, the chances of experiencing neurotic anxiety (as Freud calls it) are commonly seen as linked to a high predisposition to develop long-term anxiety states. This directly parallels the view of Spielberger and colleagues (1966), who are frequently cited for their multidimensional definition of anxiety in terms of trait-anxiety and state-anxiety. Spielberger defined trait-anxiety as an individual's predisposition to respond in an anxious way, and state-anxiety as a transitory emotion characterized by physiological arousal and consciously perceived feelings of apprehension, dread, and tension. Reiss (1997) compared anxiety sensitivity with trait-anxiety. Anxiety sensitivity is defined as *"a specific propensity to respond fearfully to the sensations of anxiety"*.

What are anxiety disorders ?

Usually anxiety is a normal reaction, part of normal functioning which makes it possible to deal with stressful situations. However, anxiety can also become excessive and disabling. Anxiety disorders are among the most common psychiatric disorders. They have high rates of comorbidity with other psychiatric disorders and result in significant disability and decreased quality of life.

According to the DSM-IV-TR (Diagnostic and Statistical Manual, Fourth Edition, Text Revision, APA, 2003), there are several disorders in the class of anxiety disorders :

(1) **Panic Disorder** : Like many people with anxiety disorders, individuals with panic disorder usually adapt their lives to avoid experiencing high anxiety levels. Meetings, travel, hobbies, pastimes, etc. are all arranged in such a way as to avoid any recurrence of panic attacks. Lives become organized around the perceived likelihood of another attack. People do

not generally consult a doctor or a psychologist when attacks occur – either because they are worried about the stigma attached to a diagnosis, or because they attribute the attack to something else, possibly another major physical or mental disorder.

Panic disorder is characterized by sudden attacks of terror, with somatic manifestations like rapid heartbeat, sweating, weakness, dizziness, fear of losing control and fear of dying. People who experience panic attacks often have a sense of unreality, lose control of their breathing, and fear they will die from lack of air. Panic attacks become panic disorder when they are repeated. The duration of an attack is normally short, with symptoms peaking within the first ten minutes. It is common for people with panic disorder to experience other serious difficulties (*e.g.*, depression, or other anxiety disorders, such as social phobia or generalized anxiety disorder). In an attempt to cope with fear and anxiety, drug or alcohol abuse is common, making the earliest possible treatment a priority.

(2) **Social Phobia** consists of being excessively self-conscious, with a fear of social rejection when observed and judged by others. Individuals with social phobia are also embarrassed by situations where their performance is evaluated (*e.g.*, exams, sports competitions). When a forthcoming event is experienced as threatening, people feel nervous and the autonomic nervous system is activated, accelerating all the physiological processes associated with the *"fight/flight"* response (sweating, increased pulse, shaking, etc). People cognitively interpret their professional and personal experiences as distressing and difficult. Fear of social situations can also cause panic attacks.

(3) **Obsessive Compulsive Disorder** (OCD) is defined by the intrusion of recurring obtrusive thoughts (obsessions), which lead to repetitive, unnecessary actions (compulsions) that often become rituals, to regulate the anxiety induced by the thoughts. People with this disorder may engage in a variety of behaviors to reduce obsessive thoughts and anxiety. Some people are obsessed by the thought of germs, and tend to engage in excessive cleaning or grooming compulsions, showering for many hours a day or repetitively washing their hands. Others may engage in hoarding or counting rituals.

(4) **A Specific Phobia** is an acute fear of an object. People with this disorder may live quite functional lives, in spite of their fear of the target object. Someone with a cat phobia may simply avoid cats or phone ahead when invited to someone's home to make sure that all pet cats are safely placed somewhere where they will not arouse fear.

There is an endless number of objects in everyday life that can be a source of phobias (see for example http://phobialist.com). The following adapted chart (Bourdon, 1988, *Journal of Anxiety Disorders*, 2, 227-241) shows the main phobias encountered and how they rank in women and men. Among these, ordinary or simple phobias are the most frequent. Specific phobias are found in 6-7 % of the general population.

Table 2

Different types and names for phobias

Women	Men	Phobias	Name
1	2	a. Insects b. Mice c. Snakes	a. Acarophobia or Entomophobia or Insectophobia b. Musophobia, Murophobia or Suriphobia c. Ophidiophobia or Snakephobia
2	1	Height	Acrophobia, Altophobia, Batophobia, Hypsiphobia or Hyposophobia
3	5	Public transport	Agoraphobia
4	6	Water	Hydrophobia
5	11	Storm, thunder	Brontophobia
6	3	Crowded public places	Agoraphobia
7	4	Other fears	
8	8	Enclosed spaces	Claustrophobia
9	10	Tunnels, bridges or crossing them	Gephyrophobia, Agoraphobia
10	9	To talk in front of a familiar audience	Social phobia
11	14	To go out alone	Agoraphobia
12	13	To stay alone, isolated	Autophobia or Monophobia or Isolophobia
13	15	To keep at a safe distance from dangerous animal	
14	7	To talk with strangers	Social phobia
15	12	To eat with familiar persons	Social phobia

(1) **Generalized Anxiety Disorder** (GAD) is an expanded state of anxiety that impacts a person's life almost totally. The main features of this disorder are excessive worry, the tendency to anticipate a lot of things and to see everything from a defeatist point of view.

(2) **Post-Traumatic Stress Disorder** (PTSD) is a particular disorder caused by a stressful situation, *e.g.*, an event which endangered a person's life. People relive the trauma in their thoughts, day and night, during flashbacks consisting of powerful emotions, images, etc., and feel very anxious for some months, or even years, after the event.

Anxiety is generally treated using both medication and psychotherapy, depending on the kind of disorder. Different types of antidepressants (selective serotonin reuptake inhibitors – SSRIs, tricyclics, monoamine oxidase inhibitors – MAOIs), anti-anxiety drugs (benzodiazepines, azapirone, benzoxazine. etc.), and beta-blockers (propanolol, etc.) are used for the medical part of the treatment. In terms of psychotherapy, cognitive-behavorial therapy has been found very useful. Individuals are encouraged to cope with their anxiety-provoking thoughts by modifying their attitudes or thoughts. Psychoanalysis could also be prescribed to help understand the *reasons* underlying anxiety.

Selective references for further reading

American Psychiatric Association (2003). *DSM-IV-TR. Critères diagnostiques*. Washington DC. Traduction française par Guelfi J.-D. *et al.*, Paris : Masson.

Debray, Q., Granger, B., & Azaïs, F. (2005). *Psychopathologie de l'adulte*. Paris : Masson, coll. « Les âges de la vie ».

Endler, N.S., & Kocovki, N.L. (2001). State and trait anxiety revisited. *Journal of Anxiety Disorders*, *15* (3), 231-245.

The National Institute of Health, (2009). NIMH. *Topic Anger : Anxiety Disorders*. On line http://www.nimh.nih.gov/health/publications/anxiety-disorders/nimhanxiety.pdf, visited 11/24/2009.

Exercise 15

Questions

1. How is anxiety usually treated ?
2. What might be the diagnosis of someone who is obsessed by thoughts of germs and keeps washing their hands ?
3. What is the difference between a panic attack and panic disorder ?
4. According to Freud, what is the cause of moral anxiety ?
5. Define agoraphobia.

27 BIPOLAR DISORDER

Since descriptions of *"circular madness"* (Falret, 1854) and *"manic depressive illness"* (Kraepelin, 1899), the concept of *bipolar disorder* has been greatly enriched. The term manic-depressive illness has been replaced by a set of bipolar disorders with a wide variety of forms. Thus, treating them all as a single disorder may be misleading (Mirabel-Leygnac-Sarron & Solignac, 2009).

A MOOD DISORDER

Bipolar disorder is a chronic and severe form of mental illness characterized by the occurrence of manic and depressive episodes. Bipolar patients experience mood fluctuations with various degrees of severity, duration and clinical presentation.

The major depressive episode is defined by the presence, every day for at least two weeks, of either : (1) a sad mood ; or (2) a loss of interest or pleasure in activities. This is associated with the following problems : (a) sleep disturbances, including hypersomnia and insomnia ; (b) excessive guilt ; (c) low energy ; (d) psychomotor retardation or agitation ; (e) significant disturbances in appetite and/or weight ; (f) poor concentration ; (g) suicidal ideation or suicide attempts.

The manic episode is characterized by an abnormally elevated mood (euphoria and/or irritable mood) for at least one week, associated with the following problems : (a) pressured speech ; (b) increased self-esteem ; (c) greater communicability ; (d) significant disorganization or distractibility ; (e) increased goal-directed activity ; (f) decreased sleep ; (g) excessive pursuit of high sensation-seeking, including addictive behaviours that put the patient at risk for severe life consequences. The intensity of the symptoms described above allows a distinction between mania and hypomania, which has less disabling symptoms that are often compatible with the maintenance of certain activities and appropriate social functioning.

For a bipolar diagnosis, the symptoms just described must continue for at least four days.

Current classifications (ICD-10, DSM-IV) agree in recognising three types of bipolar disorders : Bipolar Disorder Type I, Bipolar Disorder Type II and Cyclothymia. Alongside these classical forms, there are a great variety of clinical presentations. Thus, the field of bipolar disorder covers all of the following :

(1) Bipolar Disorder Type I (BPI), characterized by manic and major depressive episodes.

(2) Bipolar Disorder Type II (BPII), characterized by spontaneous hypomanic episodes and major depressive episodes ; Bipolar Disorder II ½ (½ BPII),

characterized by the presence of Major Depressive Disorder with Cyclothymia (alternating episodes of hypomania and subsyndromal depressive mood[1]).

(3) Bipolar Disorder Type III (BPIII), characterized by manic or hypomanic episodes induced by treatment, and major depressive episodes.

(4) Bipolar Disorder Type IV (IV BP), characterized by major depressive episodes with hyperthymic temperament ; Bipolar Disorder Type V (V BP), characterized by major depressive episodes with a family history of mania ; Bipolar Disorder Type VI (VI BP), characterized by recurrent episodes of mania without major depressive episodes. Bipolar disorder thus corresponds to a variety of clinical forms that can make diagnosis and treatment difficult.

A PUBLIC HEALTH PROBLEM

Bipolar disorder affects approximately 1.2 % of the general population (Rouillon, 2008), whatever the ethno-cultural profile. This prevalence increases further if we consider milder forms of the disorder, with rates ranging from 3.4 % (Hirshfeld *et al.*, 2003) to 6.4 % (Epidemiological Catchment Area). This disorder is therefore a major public health problem. It is the 6 th cause of disability worldwide (Woods, 2000).

Bipolar disorder affects both men and women. Age of onset is early (around 20). Bipolar disorder is a recurrent disorder, recurring in 60 % of patients within approximately 2 years of an acute episode, and 75 % within 5 years (Gitlin, Swendsen, Heller, & Hammen, 1995), even with prophylactic treatment (medication). The mortality rate is 2 to 3 times higher than the general population. The suicide risk is significant, with a frequency between 10 and 15 %, 15 times higher than the general population (Harris & Barraclough, 1997).

Comorbidities, (*i.e.*, more than one disease in the same patient at the same time) are also common in bipolar disorder. In a study of 288 patients with bipolar disorder, McElroy *et al.* (2001) showed that 65 % of bipolar patients have at least one other psychiatric disorder during their lifetimes. In their sample, 33 % had one concurrent disorder. Among these, the authors found anxiety disorders in 42 % of patients, substance abuse in 42 % to 60 % (especially alcohol – 33 %), 3 to 4 times higher than the general population. These comorbidities can mask the disorders and form factors of resistance. Patients with comorbidities may present more frequent cycles, lower remission rates, and greater difficulties in their work and social adjustment. Bipolar disorder has major quality-of-life consequences : left untreated, it triples the number

1. Intermediate states that have neither the criteria for major depression nor those of a manic episode.

of divorces. One third of these patients are unemployed. Bipolar disorder is a severe disease that has a significant impact on the family, social, and professional lives of patients.

TREATMENTS FOR BIPOLAR DISORDER

In recent years, psychotherapeutic approaches have been added to prophylactic treatments (such as lithium, carbamazepine and derivatives of valproic acid). Although a majority of patients with bipolar I disorder experience significantly improved mood (Gitlin *et al.*, 1995), 75 % relapse within 5 years and 37 % continue to experience mood fluctuations, leading to difficulties in carrying out daily activities, disrupting their relationships and affecting their self-esteem. In the past 10 years, many psychotherapeutic approaches have emerged (*Psychoeducation* : Colom & Vieta, 2008 ; *Cognitive and Behavioral Therapies* : Basco & Rush, 1996 ; Bauer & McBride, 2001 ; Lam, Jones, Hayward & Bright, 1999 ; Newman, Leahy, Beck, Reilly-Harrington, & Gyulai, 2001 ; *Interpersonal Therapy* : Frank *et al.* 1997 ; *Therapy Focuses on the Family* : Miklowitz & Goldstein, 1997).

Most psychotherapeutic modalities for bipolar disorder have been developed as a complement to *prophylactic* treatment, rather than as an alternative treatment. In 1994, a series of guidelines was published for the treatment of bipolar disorder, in which psychotherapy is considered an essential element in managing the disorder.

Bipolar disorder is a severe and recurrent illness associated with high mortality, persistent subsyndromal symptoms in over half the cases, and significant impairment of behaviour and quality of life in general.

Selective references for further reading

Gay, C. (2007). Clinique des troubles bipolaires. In : Guelfi J.-D., Rouillon F. *Manuel de psychiatrie*. Paris, Elsevier Masson, p. 266-278.

Mirabel-Sarron, C., & Leygnac-Solignac, I. (2009). *Les troubles bipolaires : de la cyclothymie au syndrome maniaco-dépressif. Comprendre, traiter, prévenir les rechutes*. Paris : Dunod.

Siobud-Dorocant, E., Mirabel-Sarron, C., Docteur, A., Bachelard, M., Goujon, D., Guelfi, J.-D., & Rouillon, F. (2009). Les thérapies de groupe pour patients bipolaires. *Les Annales Médico-Psychologiques*, *167*, 818-821.

Exercise 16

Match each of the following terms with the most appropriate definition.

List of terms

1. Sleep disturbances
2. Diagnosis
3. Euphoria
4. Comorbidity
5. Sensation-seeking
6. Disability
7. Bipolar disorders
8. Hypersomnia
9. Psychomotor retardation
10. Self-esteem

Definitions

a. Mental disorders that consist of periods of excitability (mania) alternating with periods of depression.
b. An individual who takes risks and constantly seeks sensory stimulation and excitement.
c. A feeling of elevated excitement, elation, and exaggerated well-being.
d. Feeling sleepy and/or sleeping most of the time.
e. Problems with all types of sleep : falling asleep, staying asleep, waking up, or staying awake.
f. A slowdown in initiation and continuation of body movements.
g. A physical or mental impairment that interferes with work or everyday life.
h. More than one medical condition experienced at the same time by an individual.
i. The degree to which you feel confident and satisfied with yourself.
j. The act of identifying a disease from its signs and symptoms.

28 THEORY OF MIND ♫ (AUDIO 10)

Theory of Mind (TOM) is a key element of social intelligence. It is the ability to suppose the existence of mental states, such as intentions, feelings, beliefs or emotions, in other people. It is also what enables us to focus our attention on, and/or predict other people's behaviour. Shamay-Tsoory *et al.* (2007) distinguish cognitive and affective TOM (knowledge, beliefs, and emotions, respectively), with affective TOM particularly associated with the ability to empathize. Adopting appropriate social behaviour therefore requires TOM skills. They involve decoding mental states from perceivable social information, such as tone of voice, body posture, or facial expressions. Another aspect is reasoning about a person's mental states by integrating contextual and background information about them.

A number of interpretations of TOM have been proposed, predominantly stemming from the developmental literature. The *"theory-theory"* argues that our ability to explain and predict behaviour is based on a theory of an innate or acquired structure and functioning of the mind. Another theory put forward to explain TOM is the *"simulation theory"*. Social understanding of mental life is thought to occur through a process of imaginative simulation. This theory postulates that assigning a mental state to somebody else is based on the ability to put oneself in his or her place. The debate between these two theories is ongoing, although nowadays it is more oriented towards the limits of these assumptions, and suggests that mixed theories may be more satisfactory (Perner, 1996). Some contexts may involve theorizing about other people's minds, while others may require us to imagine how we would feel. Modularity theorists suggest that these abilities may lie in a specialized brain area.

The acquisition of TOM may be innate or learned : simulation could be based on an innate genetic ability, or a child could develop and modify TOM in terms of acquired information, or TOM could be an aspect of education and enculturation. Perhaps TOM is acquired organically, through the development of an innate module (a brain area specific to a particular application). Already at 14 months, children develop *joint attention* (they understand when someone points at something) and can see what other people are looking at by following their eyes. An 18-month old child can understand other people's desires, and that they may be in conflict with the child's. Children can understand pretend play, and the notion of cheating. At 3 to 4 years old, children begin to have a representation of other people's intentions. At four, a child acquires the ability to attribute mental states to someone else. Between 3 and 4 years old, s/he begins to understand that others may have a false conception of the world. S/he becomes able to represent someone else's mental states, going beyond his/her own knowledge and perception of the immediate environment.

The famous *"false belief" task* (Wimmer & Perner, 1983) can be successfully completed by a child of this age, who understands that somebody else's mental representation of the situation is different from theirs, and can predict their behaviour accordingly. At age 6, s/he acquires the skill of *"complex mentalisation"* : this has been operationalised in experiments by the *"second-order false belief task"*, where the child has to interpret *"beliefs about beliefs"*. At this age s/he can represent the beliefs of different protagonists, and assess the relevance of one protagonist's beliefs about the state of mind of another.

More subtle interpretations of TOM, like problems solving "faux pas", are acquired at the age of 9 to 11. These tests explore children's ability to understand if someone has said something they should not have said, and whether the person hearing it would be upset or hurt. Differing levels of complexity in these tasks allow for clinical assessment of TOM ability impairment.

A specific deficit in mindreading is a central component of autism (Baron-Cohen, 1995). Autistic children lack the intuitive understanding that others have mental states. Most autistic children are unable to solve false belief tasks, or to understand that someone is pretending or cheating. They cannot use gaze direction to understand what others are looking at. They are also unable to judge emotions or intentions from facial expressions. Autistic children do not represent others as animate beings, or as having intentions. This deficit is constant and unchanging. The central symptoms of autism (anomalies in social interaction, communication and pretence) may perhaps be explained by a specific TOM deficit. Baron-Cohen (1997) suggested that autism is the result of a congenital alteration of an innate module for TOM.

However, children with better verbal skills and no learning difficulties, who fit the diagnostic criteria for Asperger's syndrome, show different abilities from those with more severe forms of autism. They can do the false belief task, but not the more sophisticated tasks. Thus, although TOM problems may explain the socialisation deficits and communication problems seen in autism, it does not explain other aspects. Perhaps TOM research in this area ought to be associated with other mechanisms, such as the executive functions.

Frith and Frith (1988) pointed out that the problems seen in people with autism in terms of social relationships, verbal and nonverbal communication, and imagination, are also present in schizophrenia. Unlike children with autism, schizophrenic patients are able to attribute mental states to others until the onset of schizophrenia during adolescence, when they lose the ability. Autism and schizophrenia may both be related to abnormal development of the frontal lobe ; the frontal lobes are involved in motor function, problem-solving, spontaneity, memory, language, initiation, judgement, impulse control, and social and sexual behaviour. Building on Frith's (1992) model, schizophrenic patients present impairments in their representation of mental states. TOM deficiency is found in schizophrenia, particularly when there is incoherent speech, or a disorganisation syndrome with difficulty taking contextual information into account. However, the link between these disorders and the overall symptomatology of the disease is not established with any certainty. Inability to use intent-attributing TOM is recognized in some, particularly disorganised patients. So some patients interpret others' behaviour without regard for their mental state, and thus inappropriately. TOM deficit may disappear during periods of remission from acute episodes.

Some studies have reported TOM deficiency in mood disorders (Sarfati *et al.*, 1997 ; Kettle *et al.*, 2007), but results are contradictory. The deficiency is not present in the same tasks, so it cannot involve the same processes. The TOM deficiency of depressed patients shows a pattern of dysfunctional interpersonal interactions (fewer social interactions, and negative feelings about them). There is TOM deficiency in acute phases of illness (Kerr *et al.*, 2003) and in periods of symptomatic remission (Inoue *et al.*, 2004). Depressed patients with TOM deficiency may be at high risk of recurrence and inhibited social functioning a year after recovering from a major depressive episode (Inoue *et al.*, 2006). Performance in the *"Eyes Task"* does not vary according to the seriousness of the depression, but is seriously impaired among those with a high score for affective symptoms of depression (Lee *et al.*, 2005).

The concept of TOM has become fundamental in psychopathology to explain certain behavioural symptoms. Although TOM research is controversial, it has contributed to the study of many areas, such as normal and pathological development, communication and frontal lobe function.

Selective references for further reading

Baron-Cohen, S. 1995. *Mindblindness : An essay on autism and theory of mind.* Cambridge, MA : The MIT Press.

Frith, C. D. (1992). *The Cognitive Neuropsychology of Schizophrenia.* LEA : London.

Perner, J. (1996). Simulation as explicitation of predication-implicit knowledge about the mind : arguments for a simulation-theory mix, in Carruthers, P. & Smith, P.K. (eds), *Theories of Theories of Mind*, Cambridge, Cambridge University Press, p. 90-104.

Shamay-Tsoory, S.G., Shur, S., Barcai-Goodman, L., Medlovich, S., Harari, H., & Levkovitz, Y. (2007). Dissociation of cognitive from affective components of theory of mind in schizophrenia. *Psychiatry Research, 149*, 11-23.

Exercise 17

Questions

1. At about what age do children generally begin to understand that other people may not know something that they know ?
2. How is autism relevant to the theory of mind (TOM) ?
3. If you point at something, a dog will look at your finger. What does this show about dogs and TOM ?
4. What is the difference between cognitive and affective TOM ?
5. How does schizophrenia affect TOM ?

D'autres thèmes de la psychologie clinique à découvrir sur le DVD :

Pour en savoir plus sur l'image du corps et l'obésité, reportez-vous au DVD contenant le **texte** et la **version audio 11** intitulés :

📖 ♫ **Obesity and body image**

Pour en savoir plus sur l'approche psychiatrique et psychopathologique du délire et des hallucinations, reportez-vous au DVD contenant le **texte** et la **version audio 12** intitulés :

📖 ♫ **A psychiatric and psychopathological approach to delirium and hallucinations**

Chapitre 4

PSYCHOLOGIE DU DÉVELOPPEMENT/ PSYCHOLOGY OF LIFESPAN DEVELOPMENT

The psychology of lifespan development provides a framework for understanding human aging from infancy and childhood to adolescence and adulthood. Aging is universal. Similar changes (milestones) in human behavior occur at about the same age for all human beings. Paradoxically, even while respecting the common milestones of aging, all individuals progress in their own unique way as a function of the interactive effects of biology, personality, and social context. The main purpose of theory and research in the study of development is to provide a context for the description and explanation of the regular transformations that occur over time. In general, theories contribute to the process of articulating meaningful patterns from observations, while examining issues, such as disciplining and rewarding children, and understanding how cognition changes over time. In this section, a variety of topics related to behavior and development across the lifespan will be covered.

31. REWARDING AND PRAISING CHILDREN ♫ (AUDIO 13)

How many adults best encourage children to engage in more of the activities that will be beneficial to them in the future ? Adults often want to support children in being creative, learning to write, and engaging in altruistic acts, to mention just a few such activities. Psychological theories have more than once inspired people in this endeavor. Behaviorism led to token economy programs where children received rewards such as stickers or tokens when they had completed their homework. In the 1960s and 1970s, the focus on self-esteem led to a popular conception that uncritical praise was the best way to encourage children.

But does reward and praise always have the desired effects ? A number of studies have shown that reward and praise can actually have completely the opposite effect. Children may end up engaging in much less of the desired behavior. In this chapter, we examine positive feedback in the shape of praise through a series of recent studies by Carol Dweck and her colleagues. In the audio version called "*Rewarding and praising children*", we examine material rewards in a behaviorist perspective, taking our point of departure in the now classic study by Mark Lepper and his colleagues from 1973.

Pour la suite de cet article sur le role du conditionnement dans l'éducation des enfants, reportez-vous au DVD contenant le **texte** et la **version audio 13** intitulés :

📖 ♫ **Reward and praising children**

Children's reactions to praise

The classic study by Lepper and his colleagues asked if material rewards would necessarily benefit children in the universe of behaviorism. It inspired research on other forms of positive feedback such as praise, and its significance for intrinsic motivation. Carol Dweck of Stanford University asked the provocative question if uncritical praise is always good for children.

Dweck and her colleagues conducted extensive research into the academic achievement of children, adolescents, and young adults. In one line of research, they investigated the consequences of the feedback that children receive in preschool or grade school (Dweck, 1999). They showed that there is a particular kind of feedback often used by adults that has far more negative consequences than intended. Additionally, this kind of feedback may lead children to develop a negative view of their own ability to master and learn difficult material.

Person-directed praise

Praise such as *"Good girl"*, or *"You're so clever"*, could be characterized as person-directed praise, and at an even more specific level, it could be termed ability-directed or intelligence-directed. Positive feedback of this type should be good for children's self-esteem, from a merely intuitive point of view. When children excitedly show the various things they have done, *e.g.*, drawings, it is difficult not to praise them in this way. This intuition is supported by an informal social movement which could be termed the self-esteem movement. Since the 1960s, this movement has popularized the notion that high self-esteem is important for children and adults alike. That is, everybody should have a positive view of their own abilities, intelligence, looks, and personal qualities.

An informal pedagogical goal for the self-esteem movement is to try to provide children with a sense of high self-esteem. Given this line of reasoning, it seems obvious to praise children's "self". The sense that one can foster high self-esteem in children is so deeply rooted, at least in parents' minds in the US, that 85 % of the people asked by Dweck indicated that praise of children's abilities is necessary to achieve this goal.

There may be less of a tradition of praising children in strong and effusive terms in northern than in southern Europe, but nevertheless it is not uncommon to hear this type of praise. At the weekend soccer game, parents on the sidelines are busy praising their children's soccer abilities. At the Exploradome, adults do not hold back with praise of their children's intelligence when they solve scientific puzzles. Even computer games for children have built-in feedback such as, *"You're so smart"*, when the children score points. This sense is backed up by research. Existing research supports the notion that praise of children's intelligence and abilities leads to better performance, exactly as behaviorism would predict – at least, as long as the tasks remain manageable for them.

Children, however, are apt to think further about the feedback they receive, and this is where Dweck and her colleagues made a novel contribution. Perhaps children reason that if a good drawing leads to them being called good and smart, would a less successful drawing not lead to the opposite ? Even if children are never called things such as stupid when the paint runs or they are slow to get dressed, they might still form an informal theory that the quality of their performances is linked to their worth as a person. Once children have formed such a *"self-theory"* they may believe that a less successful performance makes adults think of them as of lesser worth, if not downright stupid. Nobody likes the idea that they are stupid, and so children reason that they had better stay on the safe side and avoid difficult tasks. Playing it safe means that nothing can go wrong ; one is sure to receive praise. However, always playing it safe entails avoiding challenging tasks. To the extent that one learns from mastering difficult problems, the consequence may be that children do not learn as much as they should.

PROCESS-DIRECTED PRAISE

Not all forms of praise are directed at children's selves, or intelligence or abilities. Adults may praise the process that went into a certain product in many ways, *e.g.*, *"I can see that you worked hard on this drawing"*. In Dweck's theoretical framework, the assumption here is that children do not link their self-esteem directly with the quality of a performance. Rather, this kind of praise entails an attitude, or theory, that even difficult problems are solvable as long as one tries hard enough. Finally, there is a third type of praise which is a combination of the two and which could be termed product-directed praise, *e.g.*, *"What a nice drawing"*. While this kind of praise may evaluate the quality of the product, the evaluation is not directly coupled with the person but rather with the result of the effort that went into the product. However, for research purposes, Dweck and her colleagues focused on the types at each end of the spectrum of praise.

Comparing Person and Process-directed Praise

Dweck and her colleagues investigated the consequences of the type of person-directed praise that they term *"intelligence-directed"*, with process-directed praise in a series of studies with children in 5th grade. The studies typically followed an identical setup : All children were first given some easy tasks to solve. They were then divided into two experimental groups which were given different kinds of praise. One group received intelligence-directed praise such as, *"You are really smart"*, and the other group received process-directed praise such as, *"You have worked hard on this"*. Then followed the crucial test of the studies. All children were given challenging tasks and their work process and their reactions to the tasks were recorded on video. The researchers then judged from the tapes whether children's reactions to challenges depended on the type of praise they had received for the easy tasks.

Results from the 5th graders showed that everybody was equally engaged in and equally successful at the easy tasks. Thus, there were no differences between the groups before they received the two types of feedback. However, when they were facing challenges, there were considerable differences between the groups. Children who had received intelligence-directed praise quickly gave up, were not successful at solving the tasks, and expressed that they did not enjoy doing the tasks. The children who had received process-directed praise spent more time on the tasks, were more successful at solving them, and even expressed that they enjoyed working on the challenges.

The results thus showed that intelligence-directed praise led to giving up, if not outright helplessness, when faced with challenges, whereas process-directed praise led to behaviors characterized by an *"I can do it !"* attitude and a sense of mastery. In the follow-up studies, Dweck and her colleagues showed that the phenomenon applies across genders, ethnic groups, geographical regions such as rural versus city area, and across different types of tasks.

Even down to preschool age, Dweck showed that person-directed praise led children to give up sooner when faced with challenging tasks. In contrast, process-directed praise led children to want to persevere and spontaneously provide suggestions for how to solve the challenging tasks.

Two types of criticism

What about the other side of the coin, that is, when feedback consists of criticism rather than praise ? Dweck and her colleagues also investigated preschool children's reaction to negative feedback. Criticism, in fact, can be conveyed in a constructive manner, for example by embedding it in a process-directed frame, such as : *"This didn't seem to work. Perhaps you could think of a different way to do it ?"* But criticism can also be directed at the person, such as, *"I'm disappointed in you !"* Or, *"I don't think you are able to do this"*. According to Dweck's theory, this latter form of person-directed criticism does not make children want to try harder. On the contrary, it leads to a sense of helplessness.

In their actual studies, Dweck and her colleagues did not wish children of preschool age to hear criticism aimed directly at their person. It would not be ethical to use statements such as, *"You are no good at this"*. Instead, the study cleverly set up a situation where children where asked about the reactions of puppets who had been criticized. The procedure otherwise remained the same as in the above studies. Children first witnessed that the puppets solved some easy tasks. Then the puppets received the two different kinds of criticism for their performance on the easy tasks. And then the puppets were given the difficult tasks. Children were asked how the puppets dealt with the challenges and were asked to report the reactions of the puppets.

As predicted, the results showed that process-directed criticism made children report that the puppets wanted to overcome the challenges. In other words, their attitudes were a constructive consequence of the criticism. In contrast, person-directed criticism made children attribute a helpless attitude to the puppets. Dweck concludes that just as was the case for praise, criticism works best when children do not feel that their self-esteem is being questioned. This is an important point, but not nearly as paradoxical as Dweck's groundbreaking insight that praise may have unintended consequences.

DISCUSSION OF THE RESULTS

The studies on feedback must be discussed in a behaviorist perspective. Existing studies do show that material rewards may increase motivation. Similarly, studies also show that positive feedback such as praise may increase children's motivation to solve tasks. When this is the case, why is it that Dweck and her colleagues could show that praise may lead to diminished motivation ? Dweck provides a more high-resolution way of thinking about positive feedback. She proposes that it is only when tasks are too challenging for children to master right away that they give up after person-directed feedback. Past research has not distinguished between attitudes to easy and difficult tasks. The effects of different types of praise have probably gone unnoticed. The paradox that praise can lead to diminished motivation in the face of particularly challenging tasks further corroborates Dweck's proposition that it is the threat to self-esteem, in the shape of fear of failure, that explains her findings.

Dweck focused on two clear types of positive feedback, *i.e.*, person- and process-directed praise. However, one can also identify combinations of the two, such as product-directed praise. Are children in real life ever exclusively exposed to person-directed praise which leads them to feel that they risk their sense of self-worth when engaging in challenges that are too difficult ? This is unlikely, but it is equally unlikely that children dissect in detail which impression to take way away from all the kinds of praise they receive. It is more likely that praise from key persons such as parents or one's favorite teacher has a higher impact than praise from more peripheral people. It may also be the case that there are singular episodes of challenge and feedback that stand out and cause children to form a particular view of praise, or in Dweck's terms, a particular *self-theory*.

IMPLICATIONS OF THE RESULTS

When one is around children of preschool and early grade school age, an obvious implication of Dweck's research is to cut back on person-directed praise and instead provide process-directed praise along the lines of, *"I can see that you put a lot of work into combining the yellow and the blue paint so that it became green"*. But providing process-directed praise is easier said than done. While doing research at Bing Nursery School on Stanford campus, the present author found that observing the local ethos of not providing person-directed feedback was in itself a challenge. Such an ethos certainly makes sense because of Lepper's original findings, but it is also sensible from a didactic point of view. If a preschool teacher starts praising children in a person-directed way, one may quickly end up with a group of children on the playground who are all shouting, *"Look at me, look at me"*. This, of course, is not a way to encourage children to engage in productive play on their own.

Despite the good reasons to provide process-directed praise, the present author nevertheless found it difficult to wean himself from person-directed praise. It actually requires effort and time on the part of the adult to visualize the process the child undertook to arrive at a certain product and then comment on it. It is much easier to utter the more automatic, *"Good girl"*. Additionally, one has the feeling of trying to suppress one's immediate sense of awe as one is often truly impressed by children's productions. So by providing process-directed feedback, one may feel a little less spontaneous than one would otherwise be. In turn, children's reaction to process-directed feedback may even be one of disappointment, partly because they expect something else, and partly because they already know how they mixed the colors for the painting. In fact, they may look surprised not to be met with, *"Good girl"*. However, even in the short term, there are advantages to cutting back on person-directed praise. The atmosphere becomes much more relaxed when one is less evaluative towards the children. And in the long term, Dweck's results indicate that one avoids promoting an atmosphere where children are afraid to invest themselves in unknown and challenging tasks.

CONCLUSION

Children are probably exposed to much worse things than reward and praise, if we look at Dweck's results in a larger perspective. Nevertheless, her well-documented theoretical and empirical work may draw our attention to the fact that the self-esteem movement's effusive praise of children's self and abilities may not prepare them well for future challenges. In contrast, comments about the process and effort behind children's performances, *e.g.*, during the visit to the Exploradome or at the soccer match, may build resilience to adversity.

Selective references for further reading

Dweck, C. S. (1999). *Self-Theories : Their Role in Motivation, Personality, and Development*. Philadelphia : Psychology Press.

Henderlong, J. & Lepper, M. R. (2002). The effects of praise on children's intrinsic motivation : A review and synthesis. *Psychological Bulletin, 128*, 774-795.

Lepper, M. R., Greene, D., & Nisbett, R. E. (1973). Undermining children's intrinsic motivation with extrinsic reward : A test of the "overjustification" hypothesis. *Journal of Personality and Social Psychology*, *28*, 129-137.

Thorndike, E. L. (1911). *Animal Intelligence*, Macmillan.

Warneken, F., & Tomasello, M. (2008). Extrinsic rewards undermine altruistic tendencies in 20-month-olds. *Developmental Psychology*, *44*, 1785-1788.

Exercise 18

Fill in the blanks with the best term from the choice of terms given.

List of terms

(a) self-esteem ; (b) process-directed praise ; (c) helplessness ; (d) person-directed criticism ; (e) product-directed praise ; (f) token economy ; (g) person-directed praise ; (h) process-directed criticism. *(Note : two terms are used twice).*

Sentences with blanks

A (1) ________________________ program is used to give children rewards such as stickers or tokens for completing tasks or homework. A focus on (2) ____________________ in the 1960s and 70s led to the idea that uncritical praise promoted self-esteem. Studies have shown that uncritical reward and praise can actually have a negative impact on self-esteem.

Praise such as *"Good boy"*, or *"You're so smart"*, could be characterized as (3) ____________________. When children constantly hear this type of praise they may come to believe that a less successful performance makes adults think of them as not "good" or "smart". They may avoid taking risks and not attempt to master difficult challenges. Children can also receive (4) ________________________ such as, *"You worked hard on that problem"*. An example of the combination of the two types of praise, called (5) ____________________ would be, *"What a nice drawing"*. Different types of praise were directed at children facing challenges. Children who had received (6) ______________________ quickly gave up, were not successful at solving tasks, and expressed that they did not enjoy doing the tasks. Children who had received (7) ______________________ spent more time on tasks, were more successful at solving them, and even expressed that they enjoyed working on the challenges. Similarily, according to Dweck's theory, (8) __________________ such as, *"That solution does not seem to work, can you try another one ?"* led to continuing to try hard to master challenging tasks while (9) _________________________did not make children want to try harder. On the contrary, it led to a sense of (10) ________________.

32 THE IMPACT OF EARLY MOTHER-INFANT INTERACTION ON THE DEVELOPMENT OF INFANT ATTACHMENT 🎬 ♫ (AUDIO 14)

The role of early mother-infant interaction and its influence on later social and emotional child development has received increasing attention over the past thirty years. The discovery of the infant's early communication competencies gave great impetus to studies in this domain. Results of these studies have revealed an active and intentional role of infants in interactions with their adult partners. As a result, early interactions are now seen as bi-directional processes in which synchrony, reciprocity, and mutual attunement play important roles. In parallel with these findings, a series of studies has begun to show that early interactions are a core aspect of the development of the infant's affective bond to its parents. The most significant contributions in this area come from attachment theory (Bowlby, 1969).

A central premise of attachment theory is that the development of attachment depends upon the quality of the interaction, and, in particular, that differences in attachment patterns can be partly attributed to the quality of caregiving. The nature and delay of the primary caregiver's (usually the mother's) responses to infant behavior throughout the first year are believed to be among major contributing factors to infant behavioral organization, including attachment behavior. Through interactive contingencies, infants build expectations regarding maternal behavior in different situations, and learn to organize their own adaptive behavior in a way that is coherent with their expectations.

Attachment theory posits that the infant in a healthy mother-infant dyad uses its mother as a safety haven, and a secure base for exploration. This means that the infant is enabled both to explore independently and to connect with the parent for interaction when it needs to (for example when distressed, in perceived danger or needing support for exploration or play). Such moving away from, then back toward, the parent indicates that the parent is being used as a secure base for emotional refueling, protection, and encouragement for exploration. Moving away is possible because the child has confidence in the parent's availability, while moving toward means that the child is sure of the parent's acceptance and welcome.

The ***Strange Situation*** (Ainsworth *et al.*, 1978) is a paradigmatic observational measure of infant attachment behavior, which includes eight brief episodes of interaction, separation, and reunion, involving the infant, the parent, and a stranger. Within this stressful procedure, it is inferred that infant behavioral organization, especially during reunion episodes, is a reflection of his or her expectations regarding parental behavior, learned from interaction in more habitual settings.

Secure attachment

Infants classified as having a secure attachment pattern show protest behaviors during separation, but welcome the parent when she or he comes back and seeks proximity with the caregiver for awhile. This contact then allows the infant to return to exploration. The parent typically serves as a secure base for reassurance and exploration. These parents are portrayed as sensitive, responding promptly and appropriately to their child's signals and behaviors, and providing a supportive, predictable, and coherent context for infants to develop.

Insecure-avoidant attachment

Insecure-avoidant infants appear less disturbed by the separation, and behave as if they have no need for comfort after the separation. These infants appear more independent and explore the new environment without using the parent as a secure base. They ignore or avoid the parent at reunion, as they do not expect soothing and reassurance from the parent. These infants tend to focus their attention on toys and play activity. If distressed by the separation, they may accept being soothed by the stranger. Parents of avoidant infants are generally perceived as being predictably insensitive, and perhaps stressful to their child because of their intrusive or rejecting behaviors.

INSECURE-AMBIVALENT ATTACHMENT

Conversely, insecure-ambivalent infants are highly disturbed by the procedure, and show anxious and distressed behavior during separation. At reunion, these infants seek the parent for soothing but in a manner that reflects their uncertainty concerning the parent's reaction and availability. These infants may then display fussy, immature, or infantilized behavior. They may seek physical proximity but simultaneously show rejection and anger towards the parent. Their parents have mostly been described as lacking in appropriateness and consistency in their caregiving behaviors.

DISORGANIZED ATTACHMENT

Lastly, some infants do not show any organized attachment pattern in the Strange Situation, and display contradictory or atypical behaviors, including simultaneous proximity seeking and avoidance, remaining still, freezing, or engaging in odd behavior at reunion. Rather than being distressed by the procedure, the infant seems to be afraid of the parent. Some authors contend that when the potentially protective parent is also a source of fear, a disorganized attachment relationship may ensue. Under these circumstances (*i.e.*, fright without solution), the child is faced with an insoluble dilemma that prevents the development of an organized strategy. Disorganized attachment has been linked to child maltreatment, neglect, trauma, and role reversal in the relationship with the parent. In turn, parents of disorganized infants have been found to suffer from unresolved trauma and loss, and to display insensitive, odd, abdicating, role reversal, frightening or frightened behavior in the relationship with the child.

During infancy, the interaction between the youngster and his or her attachment figure compensate for, and complement, the lack of motor, communication, affective and social skills on the youngster's part, such that the infant will always be protected while being afforded as much independence as possible in order to acquire these skills. Bowlby describes the parent's role as being available, ready to respond when called upon to encourage and perhaps to assist, but to intervene only when clearly necessary. As for affective development, it has been shown that the primary caregiver's sensitivity and responsiveness to the infant's signals provide the context in which the infant's experiences and feelings of security will be organized. There is ample evidence that parental sensitivity and responsiveness play an important role in the formation of secure attachment. Sensitive and responsive parents are more likely to notice their baby's signals and use those to guide their own behavior, and also are more knowledgeable about their infant. In turn, infants of sensitive parents have been shown to respond more positively to physical contact, to cry less, and to vocalize more to their parents compared to infants of less sensitive parents.

Bearing this in mind, a significant body of studies has shown that increasing parental awareness of the infant's competencies can enhance parent-infant interaction, and promote infant attachment. Mothers who have been familiarized with the newborn's capacities are more likely to spend time stimulating the infant, to pay more attention to the infant, and to be more responsive to the infant's signals (Cooper *et al.*, 2009 ; Wendland-Carro *et al.*, 1999). The perinatal period has been described as a sensitive period for the parents and the newborn, and therefore suitable for early intervention. Improvements in mother-infant interaction and infant attachment may be linked to long-term positive child outcomes. This should encourage further research in this promising field.

Exercise 19

Questions

1. What are the four attachment patterns identified in the text ?
2. Who is usually the *"primary caregiver"* ?
3. Which researcher developed the *"Strange Situation"* technique ?
4. Which attachment style is associated with inconsistent parenting ?
5. According to attachment theory, what is the role of the primary caregiver in a healthy relationship ?

Selective references for further reading

Ainsworth, M.D., Blehar, M.C., Waters, E., & Wall, S. (1978). *Patterns of Attachment : A Psychological Study of the Strange Situation.* Hillsdale, NJ : Lawrence Earlbaum Associated.

Bowlby, J. (1969). *Attachment and Loss.* London : Hogarth Press and Institute of Psycho-Analysis.

Cooper, P. J., Tomlinson, M., Swartz, L., Landman, M. Molteno, C., Stein, A., McPherson, K., & Murray, L. (2009). Improving quality of mother-infant relationship and infant attachment in socioeconomically deprived community in South Africa : Randomized controlled trial. *British Medical Journal, 338*, 1-11.

Wendland-Carrro, J., Piccinini, C. A. & Millar, S. (1999). The role of an early intervention on enhancing the quality of motherinfant interaction. *Child Development, 70*, 713-721.

Pour en savoir plus sur les types d'attachement et leur lien avec les relations amoureuses développées dans la vie adulte, reportez-vous au DVD contenant le film intitulé :

Film 18 : Early attachment in childhood : links with adult relationship patterns

Pour en savoir plus sur la théorie de l'attachement et ses origines, reportez-vous au DVD contenant le **texte** et la **version audio 7** intitulés :

Introduction to attachment theory

33 ARE MACRO-DEVELOPMENTAL PIAGETIAN CONCEPTS RELEVANT TO DESCRIBE MICRO-DEVELOPMENT ?

Piaget's genetic epistemology describes how human knowledge arises and develops. The constructivist epistemology of Piaget, applied to cognitive psychology, leads to two assumptions :

(1) Humans generate knowledge and meaning from their experiences (which for Piaget means that knowledge is rooted in actions)

(2) Knowledge is not the *"internal mirror"* of the world, but a real construction/edification requiring complex mental processes.

Through observations of children solving problems, and clinical-critical interviews, Piaget elucidated the core processes of individual development as well as the logic and order with which cognitive structures are built, thereby creating a model of macro-development (lifespan development) which describes a series of stages.

It was not Piaget's intention to be exhaustive. This is understandable if we take into account that, for Piaget, a stage is described according to its own structure, and one of its essential properties is that it subsumes the previous ones. For any given stage, what must be understood in its structure is whether the child has assimilated adequately the *logical system* sustaining the skills, thereby becoming able to move on to a new stage. This does not mean that the skills themselves are fully formed ; they continue to be improved and sustain the development of new ones. Because the concept of *"stage"* is often wrongly associated with what the child can and cannot do depending on her/his age, this concept, although linked to Piaget's fundamental constructivist approach, is not the most informative aspect of his theory. We will focus instead on some important psychological processes and show how they are involved in learning at any age, and can even be decisive at certain points in an individual's development.

Along with some of Piaget's followers who applied his model to analysing how new knowledge emerges from a single activity (how learning occurs, in other words), we will illustrate the use of some Piagetian concepts to describe aspects of micro-development.

We will illustrate the theoretical explanations using Piaget's classical experiments and two cases showing the usefulness of the Piagetian concepts introduced. One concerns vocational training : a group of teachers involved in practice analysis (collective analysis of a situation experienced by one of the participants). The other concerns ten-year-old pupils who individually perform a task consisting of classifying various kinds of thermometers.

Reflecting abstraction, and the concrete/abstract issue

In the widest sense of the word, to abstract is to neglect certain aspects of the object or situation and to concentrate on those which become meaningful in the context of the task and its aim. First, we would like to clarify the confusion between *"abstract thinking"* and *"abstraction"*. Abstraction is a lifelong process which enables us to interact effectively with our environment, whereas abstract thinking is the ability to think beyond the domain of concrete objects, and to hypothesize.

From a very early age, babies make abstractions-in-action, by adapting motor schemes to the particularities of the objects they manipulate (smooth ones, ones with holes, etc.). When assimilating new objects into one of the schemes of her/his repertory, the baby demonstrates abstraction. Later on, classifications made using properties such as colour or shape will reveal abstraction processes expressed in an explicit way (a baby would not create groups of objects based on the properties implicitly used to adapt his motor schemes). *Reflecting abstraction*, instead of relying on an object's properties, relies on an action's coordination, and is described by Piaget as having two components :

(1) *re-description* : properties of an action are linked to properties of an object, constituting a new representation of the situation

(2) *synthesis* : a logical deduction from the items re-described leads to a more economical representation of the situation

> *"Each act of reflecting abstraction involves displacing and using coordinations already at work at the previous level, but adds new characteristics which result from a construction that is creative in this regard"* (Piaget, 2000, p. 312).

As an example, conservation is the awareness that altering a substance's appearance does not change its basic properties. In one conservation experiment, equal amounts of liquid are poured into two identical containers. The liquid in one container is then poured into a different shaped cup, such as a tall thin cup, or a short wide cup. Children are asked which cup holds the most liquid. Non-conservant children choose the cup that appears fuller according to their own perception *("the level is higher", "it is larger")*. Abstracting conservation includes representation of the concepts of *"reversibility"* (a transformation can be reversed), *"compensation"* (a change in one dimension can be compensated in another dimension) and *"no changes"* (nothing was added or removed). The synthesis process leads to the principle that changing the appearance of an object does not change its basic identity (*e.g.* quantity of matter, weight, volume).

EGOCENTRISM/DECENTERING

Egocentrism refers to a child's inability to view a situation from any other perspective than her/his own and the belief that her/his perspective is the only one possible. Piaget initially explored spatial egocentrism : three differently coloured mountains are shown and the child is asked what a travelling hand puppet would see at the various angles ; the egocentric children pick their own view compared to what the puppet actually "sees".

Egocentrism also concerns relationships. A child will assume that the person s/he is talking to has the same perspective and knowledge that s/he does and will therefore leave out specific details that are needed in order to be understood. Moreover, egocentric communication becomes more an issue of agreement/disagreement than an exchange and analysis of different points of view. Progressively, children can decentre – that is, come to the realization that other people's thoughts and perspectives differ from their own. As mentioned earlier with regard to conservation, children's decentring makes them able to think about two or more aspects of a problem simultaneously.

The *"practice analysis"* group we observed had to deal with decentering and reflecting abstraction (Nadot & Bruno, 2008). It was the role of the group facilitator to establish a framework (limits and rules) involving the participants in decentering and abstracting. Even adults continue to encounter difficulties with this, especially when dealing with complex situations such as teaching. *Decentering* : when giving an interpretation of the situation, each participant is supposed to consider it as an element adding meaning to the group's shared understanding of the situation, rather than considering their proposed interpretation as a total explanation, something like a truth. *Abstracting* : when working on a decentered approach to the situation, the group progressively takes into account more and more of its parameters. At a certain point, the group combines them in a new picture of the situation, which was not previously in any of the participant's minds.

Symbolic thinking and imitation

Imitation permeates children's lives ; it is a way for them to discover their own bodies, by imitating others' movements, and to discover social conventions (*e.g.*, saying goodbye by waving). As well as imitating social conventions, children progressively become familiar with the use of symbolic function – *i.e.*, representing a class of things (a concept) or a specific thing. This may be done either with the child's own body (*e.g.*, imitating a cat sleeping) or with an object chosen in a more or less personal way (*e.g.*, using a match box as a car), or with conventional toys (*e.g.*, a teddy bear or a doll's house).

Imitation, like drawing and other kinds of representational activity, helps children transform non-conventional ways of expressing themselves (babbling, making sounds, using idiosyncratic symbols while playing, etc.) into social language.

Piaget showed how symbolic activities participate in developing language skills. With Ray, an 11-year-old pupil, we see how symbols can be a means to classify, and to develop conceptualisation (Decaudin & Bruno, 2009). During a task which consisted of classifying thermometers, Ray started his grouping with the thermometers that were familiar to him. Then he continued to categorize the objects by looking for symbolic indications printed on the others, using two kinds of symbols appearing on the objects to group them : scientific symbols (*e.g.*, "C"), and analogues (drawings of suns and snow flakes, etc). In this short report, we have tried to illustrate how particular short term activities can be described using piagetian macro-genetic concepts.

Selective references for further reading

Decaudin, M. & Bruno, S. (2009). *L'abstraction au regard de la culture. In* Actes du Symposium International « Ecole (s) et Culture (s). Quels savoirs ? Quelles pratiques », Lille, 12-13 novembre 2009, CD-Rom.

Nadot, S. Bruno, S. (2008). Pourquoi superviser l'analyse de pratiques ? *La Nouvelle Revue de l'Adaptation et de la Scolarisation*, *41*, 183-199.

Piaget, J. (2000). *Studies in Reflecting Abstraction* (edited and translated by Robert L. Campbell). Hove : Psychology Press.

Exercise 20

Questions

1. What process consists of concentrating only on certain aspects of an object ?
2. What is egocentrism ?

3. What processes help children to learn social conventions ?
4. What is *"decentering"* ?
5. What term refers to the awareness that differently shaped containers may have the same volume ?

34 NON-MEDICAL TREATMENTS AND INTERVENTIONS FOR ALZHEIMER'S DISEASE

DEFINITION

Alzheimer's disease is the most common form of dementia. It is a progressive neurodegenerative disease that gradually destroys brain cells, spreading to all parts of the brain that deal with intellectual and behavioral functions. At the first stage of the illness, the regions of the brain that enable memorization of new information are weakened. The damage caused by the illness in the brain progressively diminishes the patient's autonomy. It therefore represents an enormous burden on patients and their families.

The disease was named after German psychiatrist Alois Alzheimer who was the first to describe it in 1906. It usually affects people over 65 years old but the less common early-onset disease can occur at a very early age.

STATISTICS

According to a study carried out by the French research organization Inserm, 850,000 people suffer from Alzheimer's disease in France, that is 5 % of the population over 65 and 15 % of the population over 85. With the aging population, it is predicted that two million people might suffer from this illness in France in 2040.

TREATMENT

Given the number of people concerned by the illness, much attention is being paid to medical and non-medical treatments and interventions that can slow or prevent the losses it causes. These interventions are part of the French Government's "Alzheimer Plan" which is to be carried out between 2008 and 2012.

Currently, medication can slow the progress of Alzheimer's disease but cannot cure it, nor restore impaired functions. This explains a growing interest in the use of methods that do not involve medication, used nonetheless in combination with medication.

These interventions have different objectives :

- Improving cognitive functions ;
- Reducing behavior problems, emotional symptoms, and stress ;
- Maintaining patient autonomy as long as possible ;
- Maintaining positive interactions and communication with the environment ;
- Maintaining and improving quality of life ;
- Postponing placement in a nursing home ;
- Helping the helpers.

In France, such therapies for dementia, and more specifically Alzheimer's, are spreading. The Second International Colloquium on non-medical interventions for Alzheimer's disease took place at the "Cité des Sciences et de l'Industrie" in Paris in November 2009. Recent studies have shown that these interventions can have an effect on symptoms such as memory loss, behavior problems (confusion and agitation), language and speech symptoms, disturbed visuo-spatial orientation.

A SHORT REVIEW OF NON-MEDICAL INTERVENTIONS THAT ARE SPREADING IN FRANCE

(1) Reality Orientation Therapy

Reality Orientation Therapy was developed in America in 1958. The patient's environment is organized so that he or she will find information to enable reorientation. It also provides intensive reeducation groups. Orientation into reality is encouraged though repetition (of the date or of the name of the nursing home for example) and through visual marks.

(2) Sensory Capture and **Feedback** in the management of behavioral disturbances in demented elder patients during basic care – Yves Gineste and Rosette Marescotti

This method, developed in 1996, helps **health-care workers** deal with aggressive behavior from patients who suffer from dementia, particularly during nursing care (screaming, care refusal, hitting, biting, insulting, etc). It recommends approaching the patient through visual contact, then touching the patient on a neutral part of the body such as the forearm and creating serene conditions through gentle words before a nursing intervention. Recent studies have shown that this method diminishes behavioral problems in 90 % of the cases.

(3) The Validation Method

This method has been developed in America by Naomi Feil since 1963. Validation is a theory that very old people are trying to resolve unfinished life issues before death and that helping them express these issues will soothe them. The method provides verbal and non-verbal techniques to communicate with and help disoriented people. In some cases, it can be used with people who suffer from Alzheimer's disease. It consists of an empathic attitude, encouraging helpers to put themselves in the patient's place to try to understand the meaning of strange or repetitive behavior. It can be used with individuals or with groups.

(4) Behavioral Stimulation

It is important to note that before any intervention on problem behavior, one should always make sure that there are no underlying medical causes for this (such as a chronic infection, intoxication from medication, thyroid disease, etc.).

There are many ways of intervening in problem behavior. One of these was developed by Cameron Camp, director of the Myers Research Institute. He looked into the Montessori method as a way of helping people who suffer from Alzheimer's disease. (This method was initially developed for children.) Cameron Camp adapted these activities and suggests stimulating the patients by taking their background and interests into consideration.

(5) Design of the Environment

More effort is being put into architecture and the environment for people who suffer from Alzheimer's disease. Wandering and behavior problems can be limited by changes in the environment such as the creation of distinctive visual marks (different colors for each door/room). Contrasts are exaggerated so that the patients can clearly notice the differences.

(6) Sensory Stimulation

Different stimulations are used such as music, colors in the environment as mentioned previously, aromas and massages. Art and animals are also used.

(7) Family support groups

Alzheimer's family support groups seek to provide enhanced community education, support, and services for families dealing with Alzheimer's Disease and other forms of dementia.

Non-medical interventions for Alzheimer's disease to help prevent myths/misconceptions/stereotypes about people who suffer from the illness

It is often said that there is nothing much to be done for people who suffer from Alzheimer's disease. There are many myths and misconceptions about the illness. These can be very harmful and they can lead to misconceptions being projected onto the patients. These attitudes are then in danger of becoming self-perpetuating and preventing the person from communicating and participating.

The now famous *"Carpe Diem"* home in Quebec for people who suffer from Alzheimer's disease bases its work on *"the conviction that the evolution of a person depends to a great extent on how the person is viewed, managed or perceived"* and *belief* in *"the great resources of all human beings and everyone's right to live his or her life fully up until the end"*.

Conclusion

Working as a psychologist in a day center for people who suffer from Alzheimer's disease and other neurodegenerative diseases, I am keenly interested in these new issues. A study published in the *American Journal of Psychiatry* in 2007 shows that adult day care can protect patients who suffer from Alzheimer's disease against accelerated cognitive decline in nursing homes : *"higher level of day care use substantially reduced association of placement with accelerated cognitive decline"*.

Selective references for further reading

Dartigues, J.-F. (2007). Efficacity assessment of three non-pharmacological therapies in Alzheimer's disease (ETNA3). http://clinicaltrials.gov/ct2:show/NCT00646269.

Wadelmat, G., *et al.* (2007). Recommendations for the diagnosis and management of Alzheimer's disease and other disorders associated with dementia : EFNS guideline. *European Journal of Neurology*, *14*, 1-26.

Wilson, R. S. (2007). Nursing home placement, day care use, and cognitive decline in Alzheimer's disease. *American Journal of Psychiatry*, *164*, 910-915.

Woodrow, P. (1998). Interventions for confusion and dementia, Part 4 : Alternative approaches. *British Journal of Nursing*, *7*, 1247-1250.

Exercise 21

Questions

1. A nurse takes care to make eye contact with a patient and talks gently before treatment. What technique is being used ?
2. Which method, usually used with children, might also be helpful with Alzheimer's patients ?
3. What sort of disease is Alzheimer's ?
4. Give the main symptoms of Alzheimer's.
5. What method involves frequent repetition of factual information ?

Chapitre 5

PSYCHOLOGIE DE LA SANTÉ/ HEALTH PSYCHOLOGY

Health psychology is focused on understanding how to assist individuals to prevent and manage health problems such as chronic illnesses. Specifically, research topics are centred on the interrelationships between social factors, biological factors, and behaviour. Thus, health psychologists are interested in the psychological and behavioural aspects of physical and mental health. They develop methods to assist patients in maintaining healthy lifestyles. They also help patients manage chronic disease and avoid preventable diseases. They provide rehabilitative services to individuals with chronic diseases. Health psychologists examine behaviours that might influence disease development such as compliance with taking medication. Their research and interventions are intended to assist patients with chronic illnesses as they deal with daily challenges, and to help all members of a given society to maintain healthy lifestyles and/or to take preventative measures to avoid health problems. A number of related topics will be covered in this section.

36 FACTORS DETERMINING FOOD PRACTICES

What factors determine food practices ? Food choices would seem to depend on our biological and cultural heritage : biologically, humans are omnivorous, *i.e.*, obliged to have a varied diet (unlike specialized herbivores), but specific traits are also determined individually (for example, our metabolism and links to sensory perception). Our cultural heritage includes knowledge, customs, habits, and beliefs about food. These are transmitted through education, and involve implicit and explicit behaviors, but they are also largely contingent on differences between individuals or particular social groups (dancers, swimmers, or religious communities may have very different beliefs about food).

With regard to cultural factors, social groups provide individuals with a food repertoire among which they establish their preferences. Social groups influence individual food preferences by assigning a symbolic value system to food. Thus, each group defines food practices with regard to the following : rules of hygiene, table manners, life events, symbolic food systems, and food typologies that reserve certain foods for children, women, men, the elderly, or medical patients such as anorexic women (Urdapilleta *et al.*, 2005). The social group determines norms about what is "edible". Twenty-first-century French people do not eat insects, larvae, dogs, foxes, swans, peacocks, other big birds, or whales – all of which are, or have been, enjoyed in other times and places. In contrast, raw shellfish (especially live oysters), snails, frogs, calves' heads and pigs' trotters are highly popular in France today. Each social group and culture has its own definition of what is edible and what is not.

The cultural aspect of food is also expressed through the rites surrounding it. In many countries, certain foods carry connotations of virility and are reserved for men (*e.g.*, snakes in Asia). In France, drinking alcohol for the first time often marks the passage from childhood to adolescence. Culinary practices are systematic markers of social rites. This cultural heritage is transmitted by learning. As Rozin and Schiller (1980) showed, if Mexican children eat peppers (although the first time they taste it, they usually hate it), it is because if you like peppers you have "become a man" and thus part of the group. These are cases of cultural learning in which the hedonic value of stimulation is understood by reference to group standards.

How we acquire preferences is also determined by the environment, particularly the emotional context that accompanies food consumption (Puhl & Schwartz, 2003). When positive personal interactions are associated with food, children appreciate it better than when the context is emotionally neutral. *"You did well at school ! Have a candy !"* provides a positive emotional context ; *"Finish what's on your plate before going out to play"* creates a coercive context – and the two are likely to generate a positive or negative taste for the food concerned. In the same way, forcing children to eat something *("Finish your soup if you want dessert")* will reduce their appreciation of it (Bastell *et al.*, 2002). Through this traditional, Pavlovian conditioning, the individual learns to associate an initially neutral food with the properties of another event (unconditional stimulus).

Pleasure-judgments about food also involve memories of earlier pleasant experiences. They integrate the experience gained in connection with food and the expected effects of eating. Recollections of consuming a particular food generate expectations about the future, for example, *"I expect not to like oysters, because I once ate oysters that made me sick"*. An individual's appreciation of a food increases when eating it is accompanied by positive consequences (such as feelings of satisfaction or satiety) ; conversely, it decreases when accompanied by negative consequences (such as discomfort or nausea). These conditioned aversions result in rejection of a food, if a person thinks that food made him or her sick. Conditioning is powerful and long-lasting : a single bad experience can create aversive conditioning. Individuals' experiences with various foods can determine their food tastes through a continuous training process. In this training, a food's sensory characteristics are associated in memory with the physiological consequences of eating it.

Food preferences involve many factors that lie beyond simple sensory pleasure. Eating for pleasure involves not just nourishment, but also entails a range of symbolic rituals and cognitive acts. Food is part of a symbolic value system, reflecting a belief that, *"to incorporate a food is to incorporate all or part of its properties"* (Fischler, 2001). These cognitions, or *"magic thinking"*, are controlled by our food choices and our perceptions. The way we talk about food shows this way of thinking, a kind of 'magical' logic ; a belief that by incorporating food we assimilate certain virtues of the thing we eat. So a tomato from the South or an orange from Morocco can make us *"drink in the Mediterranean sun"* ; someone who eats red meat is *"vigorous or violent"*. The incorporated object can transform us invisibly from the inside.

Selective references for further reading

Bastell, J., Brown, A. S., Ansfield, M., & Paashall, G. Y. (2002). "You will eat all of that" : A retrospective analysis of forced consumption episodes. *Appetite*, *28*, 211-219.

Fischler, C. (2001). *L'homnivore*. Paris : Odile Jacob.

Puhl, R. M., & Schwartz, M. B. (2003). If you are good you can have a cookie : How memories of childhood food rules link to adult eating behaviors. *Eating Behaviors*, *4*, 283-293.

Rozin, P., & Schiller, D. (1980). The nature and acquisition of a preference for chili pepper by humans. *Motivation and Emotion*, *4*, 77-101.

Urdapilleta, I., Mirabel-Sarron, C., Eiber, R., & Richard, J.-F. (2005). What categorization tells us about food representation ? *Current Psychology Letters, Behaviour, Brain and Cognition*, *17*. Available on line at cpl. revues. org.

Exercise 22

Questions

1. A child is conditioned to associate a particular food with an unpleasant event. Which is the unconditional stimulus ?
2. What are the two factors identified as determining human practices to do with food ?

3. Which two foods are associated with virility, and in which parts of the world?
4. *"Conditioning related to food has to be repeated many times to be effective"*. True or false ?

37 RELATIONSHIP BETWEEN SMOKING AND PERCEIVED RISK OF LUNG CANCER

Most people agree that smoking is dangerous to their health, even though the nature of the risk may not be formulated accurately. When a sample of Americans was asked, thirty years ago, about the lethal risk associated with smoking, it was already found that the mean rating for this item was roughly 68 on a severity scale ranging from 0 to 100. This value placed smoking in ninth place on a list of extremely heterogeneous items after warfare, nuclear weapons, DDT, crime, nuclear power, pesticides, and herbicides. This mean rating is one of the most stable across different countries. Smoking was rated 67 in France, 70 in Portugal, 64 in Burkina Faso, and 61 in Hungary when comparable material was subsequently used in each of these countries. This awareness of health risks has also been observed in smokers and even in children as young as six. It appears not to be very dependent on social class.

Epidemiologists are concerned with the relationship between the amount of exposure to a risk factor and the incidence of disease. Usually they portray the relationship graphically and attempt to derive a mathematical function from the observed data that best describes this relationship. They conclude, for example, that the dose-response relationship between cigarettes smoked per day and annual incidence of lung cancer could be expressed as a second order polynomial equation. Compared to a nonsmoker, the risk of developing lung cancer may be increased 10 times for someone who smokes one pack a day, and more than 25 times for someone who smokes two packs a day. Most smokers and nonsmokers are aware, not only that smoking is a health risk, but also that this risk increases with greater exposure. This appreciation of a dose-response effect is implied by the manufacture, advertisement, and sales of cigarettes with filters and with lower tar and nicotine content, by public concern with passive smoking, and by patients' frequent efforts to decrease their smoking rather than to stop entirely.

Researchers in public health and preventive medicine have, at the same time, studied people's perceptions of their own risks from such exposure ; particularly with the aim of discovering how best to get people to reduce this exposure. These researchers have not, however, attempted to describe people's conception of the precise relationship between amount of smoking and degree of health risk - the exact form of the function linking tobacco consumption and perceived risk. The importance of this issue was, however, demonstrated in several studies on the cognitive processes involved in judging the effect of alcohol on one's own ability to drive safely. It was shown that judged drunkenness was not conceived as a linear function of the number of drinks. Participants in these studies failed to understand that the impact of increasing by one drink remains approximately the same, whether the number of drinks is increased from two to three, or from three to four drinks. In other words, the effect on drunkenness of the last drink was incorrectly viewed as less than the effect of the first drink. Other studies showed a similar pattern for the risks associated with smoking. In one of these studies, estimated risk increased about six points from no consumption to one pack of cigarettes and only six points more from one pack to three packs.

The issue of the form of the function governing the relationship between sensation (in this case, number of cigarettes) and perception (estimated risk of ill-health) is a very old one in psychophysics and in psychology. Since Fechner's work, it is well known that the function form is logarithmic. It is still important, however, to study precisely the extent to which the relationship between substance consumption level and judged health risk departs from linearity within current consumption ranges. If a «trier» (someone starting to smoke) tends to think that the risk associated with high levels of tobacco consumption is not much greater than the risk associated with his or her current consumption level, he or she may not find much incentive to try to maintain a moderate level of tobacco intake. Symmetrically, if a heavy smoker tends to think that the risk associated with high levels of consumption is not much greater than the risk associated with moderate levels, he or she may not find sufficient incentive to start trying to reduce his or her daily tobacco intake.

Our study was specifically aimed at delineating the precise relationship between tobacco intake and perceived risk of lung cancer. The participants in this study were a convenience sample of 155 French adults aged 15 to 79. The material was made up of 25 scenarios. Each of the scenarios described the smoking habits of a person. Twenty-four scenarios were devised as a function of an orthogonal factorial design with two factors : number of cigarettes (daily intake) and type of tobacco.

The first factor had eight levels, each of which was five cigarettes more than the previous level : 0 cigarettes, 5 cigarettes, 10 cigarettes, up to 35 cigarettes a day. The second factor had three levels : normal tobacco, light tobacco, and normal and light tobacco, depending on circumstances. The twenty-fifth scenario - labeled *"two packs of cigarettes (normal tobacco) daily"* - corresponded to an "extreme" stimulus.

Each scenario was printed on a separate sheet of paper. The same question appeared below each text : *"In your opinion, what level of risk of developing a lung cancer is she (or he) taking ?"* A scale appeared beneath this question. The left-hand anchor was labeled *"No risk"*, the right-hand anchor *"Very high risk"*.

THE EXPERIMENTAL PROCEDURE CONSISTED OF TWO PHASES :

The first phase familiarized the participants with the material. The 25 scenarios were presented in random order ; the 25 th was presented three times. The participants were asked to read each scenario aloud and place an X on the response scale at what they believed to be the appropriate point. At the end of this phase, the participants were allowed to compare their responses and change their ratings until they were satisfied with the entire set of ratings.

The second phase was the test phase proper. It was identical to the first phase, in that the participants were again instructed to read each scenario and place an X on the response scale. They were, however, no longer allowed to compare their responses. After completing the ratings, they were asked to indicate their sex, age, and current smoking status. The participants worked individually at their own pace.

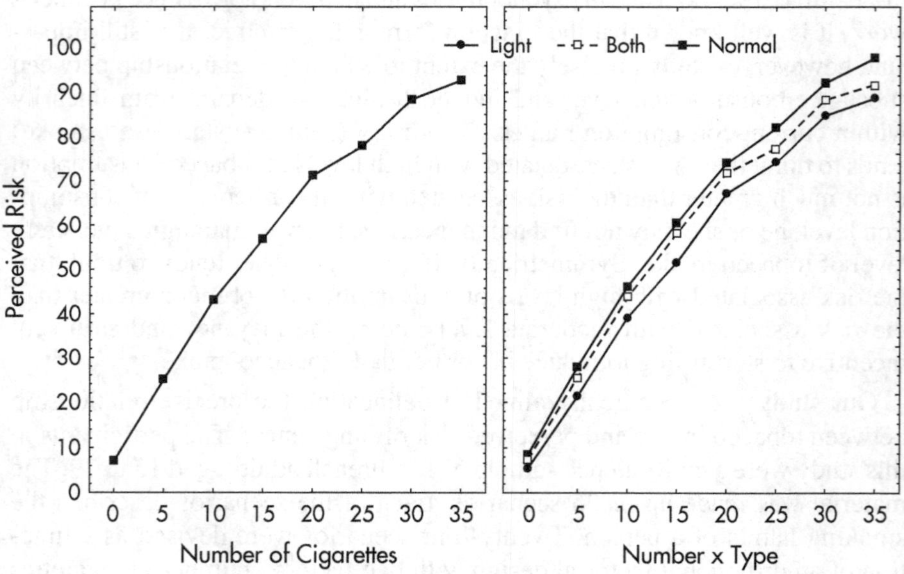

Figure 3

Mean risk estimations as a function of daily intake (left panel) and as a function of daily intake and nicotine concentration (right panel).

The means for the distances of the perceived risk from the *"No risk"* anchor for the different levels of cigarette consumption (number of cigarettes smoked) appear in Figure 3.

The subjects used the entire range of the response scale to rate the 24 scenarios. The left-hand panel shows the means for all three levels of nicotine combined (light tobacco, normal tobacco, and normal or light depending on circumstances). The highest mean was still distant from the maximum, which suggests that there was no ceiling effect. The left-hand panel also shows that, from the zero consumption level to the fourth level (15 cigarettes per day), the curve ascends steeply. It flattens out from the fifth to the eighth consumption levels. The function governing the relationship between daily intake and estimated risk was thus a negatively accelerated one. In the right-hand panel, the means are plotted according to the main design : number x type of tobacco. The three curves are clearly separated but close together ; the effect of the type of tobacco is, at best, small compared to the effect of the number of cigarettes. The curves are slightly divergent, so that the effect of the type of tobacco appears greater at higher levels of smoking than at lower levels.

In this study, the form of the function linking the number of cigarettes smoked daily to the perceived health risk (namely, the risk of developing cancer) was not linear. Instead, the additional risk was judged to diminish as the amount of smoking increased, especially after passing a threshold of 15 cigarettes per day. This result was not affected by the nicotine concentration of the tobacco nor by the sex, age, and smoking status of the participants (as was shown through additional comparisons). This result was in line with previous findings regarding the perceived effect of the number of drinks on drunkenness. Overall, the study confirmed that smokers and nonsmokers of all ages are aware that greater exposure to cigarette smoke increases their risk of ill health (in particular of cancer). They think, however, that additional cigarette consumption adds a diminishing rather than an increasing, amount of risk. This health belief must be taken into account in designing interventions to change people's health-related ideas and behavior.

Selective reference for further reading

Muñoz Sastre, M. T., Mullet, E. & Sorum, P. C. (1999). Relationship between cigarette dose and perceived risk of lung cancer. *Preventive Medicine*, *28*, 566-571.

Bonnin-Scaon, S., Lafon, P., Chasseigne, G., Mullet, E., & Sorum, P. C. (2002). Learning the relationship between smoking, drinking alcohol, and the risk of esophagal cancer. *Health Education Research*, *17*, 415-424.

Exercise 23

Complete each sentence with the best ending.

Sentences

1. Scientists who study the amount of exposure to a risk factor and the incidence of disease…
2. The risk of developing lung cancer may be increased…

3. The dose-response effect refers to the fact that…
4. The non-smoking public is very concerned about…
5. Heavy smokers might not experience enough incentive to reduce the number of cigarettes smoked per day if…
6. One false health belief held by the public…

Sentence endings

a. they think that high levels of consumption do not produce greater risk than moderate levels.
b. greater exposure to cigarette smoke increases one's risk of ill health (in particular of cancer).
c. 10 times for someone who smokes one pack a day, and more than 25 times for someone who smokes two packs a day.
d. are called epidemiologists.
e. is that additional cigarette consumption adds a diminishing, rather than an increasing, amount of risk.
f. the risk to their health due to passive smoking.

38 HEALTH PSYCHOLOGY ♫ (AUDIO 16)

WHAT IS HEALTH PSYCHOLOGY ?

Health psychology is a relatively young subdiscipline within psychology which emerged in the 1970s and is rapidly expanding in many directions : teaching, research and practice. The term designates a field of research and practice devoted to understanding psychological influences on health-related processes, such as why people become ill, how they respond to illness, how they recover from a disease or adjust to chronic illness or how they stay healthy in the first place. It was described by Matarazzo (1980) as the aggregate of the specific educational, scientific and professional contributions of the discipline of psychology to the promotion and maintenance of health, the promotion and treatment of illness, the identification of etiologic and diagnostic correlates of health, illness, and related dysfunction and the improvement of the health care system and health policy formation.

The primary focus is on physical rather than mental health, although these are not easily separable in practice. This design is congruent with the definition of health proposed by the World Health Organisation (WHO, 1946) which emphasizes the existence of a state of complete physical, mental and social well-being and not merely the absence of disease or infirmity.

THE HISTORY OF HEALTH PSYCHOLOGY

In 1969, William Schofield, from the University of Minnesota, wrote an *American Psychologist* article on the role of psychologists in medical settings, in which he deplored their lack of involvement in both research and healthcare. In 1973, the Board of Scientific Affairs of the American Psychological Association (APA) appointed Schofield to identify contributions of psychology in health research and, in 1978, a formal section on health psychology was created : Division 38. From this period onward, health psychology has grown rapidly, as evidenced by the large number of scientific journals devoted to the subject. For example, Division 38 publishes the bimonthly journal, *Health Psychology*, and the quarterly newsletter, *The Health Psychologist*.

In France, the discipline began to develop later than in English-speaking countries. *The Association Francophone de Psychologie de la Santé* (AFPSa[1]) was created in 2001 and several textbooks have been published since then (see references). At present, nearly a dozen universities offer a Professional Master's degree in Health Psychology. The growing enthusiasm for Health Psychology can currently be attributed to four factors in Western countries : (a) increasing disenchantment with the biomedical model and its dominance in healthcare ; (b) increasing evidence that much illness and mortality is caused by health-damaging behaviours and lifestyles ; (c) escalating costs of medical care ; and (d) the growing belief in western societies that individuals are responsible for their own health.

WHAT DO HEALTH PSYCHOLOGISTS STUDY ?

Health psychologists study the origins and correlates of several common chronic diseases or severe states, including cardiovascular disease, cancer, diabetes and HIV/AIDS. They perform a variety of tasks aimed at identifying and evaluating the myriad of factors that undermine health. They first seek to understand the links between our psychological and physical health, in order to promote and maintain physical health. Their findings lead them to develop theories which they test by putting them into practice. In this way, they try to prevent the onset of somatic diseases, or alternatively, to facilitate their management. They also aspire to improve the health care system and help in determining health policies.

In this way, pre-morbid personalities and dysfunctional coping strategies that may negatively affect physical health and lead to deteriorating quality of life have been studied. Two major lifestyle risks are more specifically described in the literature : the A style, characterized by an attraction towards competition and challenges, as well as impatience and hostility, which may predispose an individual to the emergence of cardiovascular problems ; the

1. http://www.afpsa.fr.

C style, which is characterized by low distress expression suggesting the existence of a suppression of negative emotions and which was believed to promote carcinogenesis.

The deleterious effects of stress on somatic health have also been much studied by health psychologists. Stress is defined as a particular relationship between a person and the environment that the person perceives as taking or exceeding his or her resources and endangering his or her well-being (Lazarus & Folkman, 1984). In this perspective, research on stressful life events indicates that their impact on health depends on how they are interpreted. It is assumed to be the consequence of a double appraisal process that involves specifying the adaptive challenges (Is it a harming, threatening, or challenging situation ?) and resources available to address them (Is it possible to control the situation and/or to be helped ?).

Health psychologists are not just interested in what people think, but also what they do to manage as much as possible what happens to them. They refer to the concept of coping which describes the set of cognitive and behavioural attempts aimed at managing the external and/or internal demands perceived by the individuals as using up or exceeding their resources and threatening their well-being (Lazarus & Folkman, 1984). The research literature shows that cognitive and behavioural efforts to directly manage a stressful event (active efforts such as problem-solving coping) ensure a better adjustment to illness than attempts to regulate the emotional consequences of this potentially stressful event (emotion-focused coping) or a strong propensity for emotional, cognitive and behavioural avoidance.

Other roles and functions of health psychologists

Health psychologists may also examine the adoption of unhealthy behaviours (*e.g.*, smoking, drinking alcohol, high risk sexual behaviours, a sedentary lifestyle), as well as analysing the development of healthy habits (*e.g.*, balanced diet, exercising). They also try to identify and evaluate factors of non-adherence to medical treatments and seek to discover the key factors of behavioural change (*e.g.*, stopping smoking, diet compliance). They rely on these types of research results for patient treatment programs or for broader health recommendations. Specifically, these investigations lead them to focus on prophylactic measures that are divided into *primary prevention* (to prevent the development of a disease), *secondary prevention* (to promote early disease detection or reduce its progression) and *tertiary prevention* (to avoid relapses). They test the effectiveness of their programs tailored to specific needs and psychosocial characteristics of individuals. For example, they can take into account anxiety levels, their coping styles and current openness to change. These customized clinical trials allow them to target their interventions better and, thus, increase their beneficial effects.

The ultimate aim of health psychologists is actually to help people to stay well by taking better care of themselves. To achieve this goal, practitioners participate in healthcare in a multitude of contexts, including inpatient medical units, primary care programs for preventable disorders and specialized healthcare interventions such as stopping smoking, preparation for stressful medical procedures, physical rehabilitation or pain management. Chronic disease self-management programs that they offer frequently have a cognitive-behavioural orientation. They often include a psycho-educational phase, a skills learning phase (stress management, problem-solving) and terminal work focused on the maintenance of therapeutic gains (relapse prevention).

Most of the time, clinical health psychologists focus on buffering the effects of (di)stress on health by promoting adequate coping strategies or improving the use of social support. Some other proactive approaches are specifically designed to induce the sustainable development of a sense of well-being that helps to cope with any somatic health problems that arise. In addition, innovative forms of treatment have recently been gaining attention and empirical support, particularly mindfulness approaches and acceptance-based therapies to promote insight and beneficial changes in attitudes towards health. It is essential to consider not only the short-term effects of interventions designed to modify health habits, but also their long-range effectiveness.

The biopsychosocial model of health (Engel 1977, 1980) encourages the integration of biomedical information about health and illness with current psychological knowledge in order to transcend Cartesian mind-body dualism. It guides health psychologists in their practice and research efforts to uncover factors that predict states of health and illness. For example, they try to specify links between indicators of immune functioning (*e.g.*, lymphocyte rates) and psychological criteria (*e.g.*, self-efficacy, perceived social support). Such investigations lead them to develop complex explanatory models of health and disease, highlighting the existence of reciprocal influences between psychological attitudes and somatic phenomena. Accordingly, Health Psychology must be considered as a field of research and practice at the crossroads of several fields that require interdisciplinary collaboration.

Selective references for further reading

Bruchon-Schweitzer, M. (2002). *Psychologie de la santé : modèles, concepts et méthodes*. Paris : Dunod.

Fischer, G. N., & Tarquinio, C. (2006). *Les Concepts fondamentaux de la psychologie de la santé*. Paris : Dunod.

Ogden, J. (2008). *Psychologie de la santé*. Bruxelles : De Boeck.

Santiago-Delefosse, M. (2002). *Psychologie de la santé. Perspectives qualitatives et cliniques*. Paris, Bruxelles : Mardaga.

Exercise 24

Match the definition with the term that is most appropriate.

List of terms

1. Mindfulness approaches :
2. Cartesian mind-body dualism :
3. Compliance :
4. Relapse prevention :
5. Social support :

Definitions

a. Methods used to prevent individuals from re-engaging in unhealthy practices such as smoking or eating foods that damage health.
b. Engaging in practices that have been prescribed by a health practitioner (*e.g.*, taking the pills that have been prescribed).
c. A meditative focus on present awareness with an attitude of acceptance, based on Zen or Bhuddist practices.
d. Emotional, physical, and material support received from family, friends, and community.
e. This incorporates the idea that the body and mind function independently of one another.

39 HEALTH AND COGNITION

Health psychology is the latest development in the process of including psychology in our understanding of health. It emphasizes the role played by psychological factors in the causes, development and consequences of health, illness and death. Illness can be caused by a combination of biological factors (*e.g.*, genetics, viruses), psychological factors (behavior, beliefs, emotions) and social factors (employment/unemployment, social norms, peer pressure). Changes in causes of death over the twentieth and twenty-first centuries suggest an increasing role for beliefs and behaviors. Changes in behavior-related illnesses, such as coronary heart disease, cancers and HIV may partly explain changes in causes of death. Coronary heart disease, for example, is related to behaviors such as smoking and lack of exercise. Many cancers are related to behaviors such as diet, smoking, alcohol consumption and failure to attend for screening or health check-ups. Understanding the role of psychological factors and behaviors in illness can allow unhealthy behavior to be targeted. In this chapter, the author will examine theories of health behaviors, and provide a comprehensive introduction to the main models that have been developed to try to understand relationships between behavior and health.

A brief definition of health behaviors

Health psychologists define three types of health behaviors. They can be aimed at preventing disease (*e.g.*, eating a healthy diet), seeking a remedy (*e.g.*, going to the doctor) and getting well (*e.g.*, taking prescribed medication or resting). Health behaviors are also defined in terms of either health-impairing habits (smoking, eating a high fat diet) or health protective behaviors (attending a health check). Behaviors can have negative or positive effects, and play an increasingly important role in health and illness.

Belloc and Breslow (1972) examined the relationship between mortality rates and behaviors among 7,000 people. They concluded from this correlational analysis that several behaviors were related to health status (sleeping 7-8 hours a day ; having breakfast every day ; not smoking ; rarely eating between meals ; being near or at prescribed weight ; moderate or no alcohol use ; taking regular exercise).

Research on the relationship between different health behaviors has produced weak correlations. People who take precautions (such as limiting the intake of foods like coffee or sugar) may also take risks, like driving too fast. Health behaviors are frequently undertaken for reasons unrelated to health. For example, people often diet to improve their looks, rather than for health reasons. Health behavior can, therefore, be considered in terms of its actual, rather than intended, consequences. It is also important to try to understand and predict health-related behaviors.

Predictors of health behaviors

Beliefs about causes of health and illness

Health behaviors are related to people's beliefs about the general causes of health and illness. For example, Bradley (1985) showed that patients' attributions about responsibility and perceived control over illness influenced their choice of treatment *("Can I – or someone else with more power – control diabetes ?")*. Patients who believed their illness was not controllable, and that they were not personally responsible for it, were more likely to choose an insulin pump (a small mechanical device attached to the skin, which provides a continuous flow of insulin) rather than other methods of injection (the conventional treatment of daily injections) – and they were also more likely to hand over responsibility to doctors. Another study (King, 1982) examined the relationship between attributions for an illness and attendance at a hypertension screening clinic. If patients considered their hypertension controllable, they were more likely to attend the screening clinic. In other words, perceived lack of control over health influences the extent to which people adopt preventive behavior (*e.g.*, give up smoking).

Individuals differ also as to whether they feel they can control events, according to whether their locus of control is more internal *("I am responsible for my health")* or external *("Whether I am well or not is a matter of luck")*. Locus of control in health matters is related to whether people change behavior (*e.g.*, give up smoking) and the kind of communication style they need from health professionals. People who feel they are not responsible for their health are less likely to comply with doctors who encourage them to make lifestyle changes.

Beliefs about susceptibility to health problems : unrealistic optimism

One of the reasons people continue to adopt unhealthy behaviors is their inaccurate perceptions of risk and susceptibility. Unrealistic optimism refers to the fact that most people believe they are less likely to have health problems than other people of the same age and sex (Weinstein, 1983, 1984). At a general level, or in multiple health behaviors, unrealistic optimism is most often linked to unhealthy or downright risky behaviors. Some factors contribute to unrealistic optimism, like :

(1) lack of personal experience of a particular health problem ; (2) the belief that the health problem can be prevented by individual action ; (3) the belief that if a health problem has not yet appeared, it will not appear in the future ; and (4) the belief that the health problem is infrequent. People show selective focus, ignoring their own risk-increasing behavior *("I may not always practice safe sex...")*, and focus primarily on their risk-reducing behavior *("...but at least I don't inject drugs")*. This selectiveness is also characterized by people's tendency to ignore others' risk-decreasing behavior, or to underestimate other people's ability to control their own health risks. People who are focused on *risk-decreasing factors* (*e.g.*, questions phrased in the form *"since becoming sexually active, how often have you tried to select your partner carefully ?"*) show more optimism, rating themselves as less at-risk than those who are focused on risk-increasing factors (questions like *"since becoming sexually active, how often have you asked about your partner's HIV status ?"*).

Structured models of health have integrated beliefs about causes and control of health, and susceptibility to health problems. In these models, cognition is regarded as being shared by members of a given society, and predictors and precursors of health behaviors are examined.

Exercise 25

Match the first half of each sentence with the best second half.

First half of sentences

1. Not smoking, being at or near prescribed weight, rarely eating between meals, and sleeping 7-8 hours per day…
2. Research has demonstrated that individuals who choose to inject their own insulin…
3. Individuals with diabetes who do not feel they have control over their illness…
4. Individuals who feel they are responsible for their own health…
5. Individuals who feel whether or not they are healthy is a matter of luck…
6. The majority of people feel that they are less likely to have health problems…

Second half of sentences

a. have an internal locus of control.
b. are more likely to feel they can exercise some control over their illness.
c. may opt to use an automatic continuous flow insulin pump.
d. when compared to people of the same sex and age due to their unrealistic optimism.
e. are predictors of positive health status.
f. have an external locus of control.

Pour en savoir plus sur l'importance de la notion de contrôle et ses limites dans le champ de la santé, mais aussi dans d'autres domaines, reportez-vous au DVD contenant le **texte** et la **version audio 17** intitulés :

The locus of control : Contributions and limits

41 CHANGES IN FRENCH PEOPLE'S MISCONCEPTIONS ABOUT HEPATITIS C

Hepatitis C (HC) is quite prevalent in France, the most recent estimate being 1,26 %, *i.e.*, about 760,000 people. French lay people's perceptions of HC were examined in 1997, when it was found that they had multiple misconceptions about HC. On January 22 1999 the French health ministry launched a multi-faceted plan of attack against hepatitis C. The government and health insurance funds began a campaign to alert health care providers, drug addicts, and the general public to the danger of infection with HC and to urge people at risk to be tested for it. Posters and pamphlets were displayed in local health insurance offices, in doctors' offices, and in schools. The major themes of the campaign were the mode of transmission, the risk factors for HC (listing which took up the most space), the high prevalence of HC, the nature and consequences of HC, the way to get tested for it, and the value of getting tested. Starting in 2000, the unions of medical laboratories sponsored annual screening days for the general public. Facts about HC and calls for screening were diffused via regional and national daily newspapers and radio.

The purpose of our study was to examine the change in people's knowledge about HC between 1997 and 2003. We expected for several reasons that people would become more knowledgeable about HC : the impact of the information campaigns, the public's increasing contact in daily life with people infected with HC, and education in school.

The lay sample consisted of 706 (415 female and 291 males) French adults aged 18 to 87 years (*M.* = 36.66 years). Two hundred and eighty-two had not completed secondary education, 318 had completed secondary school, and 106 had a university degree. The experts were 14 hepatologists (2 female and 12 male) working in a gastroenterology service. The material was a questionnaire, designed as a general instrument for the study of knowledge and misconceptions related to AIDS. A typical knowledge item was *"Hepatitis C is caused by a virus"*. An 11-point scale followed each item. The two extremes of the scales were labeled *"Completely sure that it is false"* (0) and *"Completely sure that it is true"* (10).

Table 3 shows the mean responses in 2003 of the experts, and the mean responses in 1997 and 2003 of the lay participants to the items for which clear misperceptions were evidenced. In 23 cases (see column 5), the participants' mean response in 2003 was closer to the experts' response than the participants' mean response in 1997. In the remaining 3 cases, they were farther. The differences ranged from – 1.12 to 1.02 (see column 6). It was significant in 16 cases. The sign test showed that the change was significantly more positive than negative. An index of change was computed by (a) summing the absolute values of the "positive" differences (+ sign on column 5), (b) summing the absolute values of the "negative" differences, (c) subtracting b from a, and (d) averaging the total. The value of this index was 0.42 ; that is, the improvement in knowledge over the items in Table 3 was about half a point on a 10-point scale.

The study demonstrated an evolution in knowledge about hepatitis C between 1997 and 2003. Improvements in lay persons' knowledge took place in all of the themes of the public education campaign, including the key theme of risk factors. The participants were more aware, for example, that HC is

Table 3

Responses in 1997 and 2003 on the 26 key items in 1997

1	2	3	4	5	6	7
Items	Experts	Lay People				
	Mean 2003	Mean 1997	Mean 2003	Direction	Dif	p
1 - HC weakens the body's ability to fight infections	2.29	7.03	7.48	-	0.45	.01
2 - Everyone who tests positive for the HC infectious agent has HC	1.43	5.38	4.55	+	– 0.83	.001
3 - At the present time, the group which is most at risk is drug addicts	10.00	4.90	5.64	+	0.74	.001
4 - A vaccine has been developed to treat HC	0.00	5.08	4.49	+	– 0.59	.01
5 - At the present time, there is no known cure for HC	0.00	5.19	5.03	+	– 0.16	.42
6 - HC can produce carcinoma in people	10.00	5.42	6.29	+	0.87	.001
7 - HC can be spread by using someone's personal belongings (*e.g.*, toothbrush, nail clippers)	9.07	3.64	4.17	+	0.53	.02
8 - Drinking a lot of alcohol can enhance the risk associated with having the HC infectious agent	10.00	3.39	4.21	+	0.82	.001
9 - HC can be cured	10.00	5.41	5.61	+	0.20	.29
10 - HC can be cured if treated early	10.00	5.06	5.07	+	0.01	.98
11 - HC can be caused by the same infectious agent that causes venereal diseases	0.00	3.86	3.54	+	– 0.32	.07
12 - Most people who get HC usually die from this disease	0.14	5.61	4.91	+	– 0.70	.001
13 - HC is caused by a bacteria	0.00	3.66	3.11	+	– 0.55	.01
14 - The cause of HC is unknown	0.00	3.62	3.38	+	– 0.24	.20
15 - You can get HC from saliva	0.00	4.33	3.69	+	– 0.64	.01
16 - People can get the HC infectious agent by blood donation	0.00	3.48	4.15	-	0.67	.001

Table 3 *(suite)*

Responses in 1997 and 2003 on the 26 key items in 1997

1	2	3	4	5	6	7
17 - Currently, a medication is available that would prevent people from getting HC	0.00	4.09	2.97	+	– 1.12	.001
18 - You can get the HC infectious agent from public toilets	0.00	3.30	3.17	+	– 0.13	.50
19 - You can get HC by sharing a cup or glass with a person who has HC	0.00	3.36	2.80	+	– 0.56	.01
20 - Female homosexuals (lesbians) are at risk for HC	2.50	5.50	5.37	+	– 0.13	.53
21 - You can get the HC infectious agent from semen	4.29	6.24	5.77	+	– 0.47	.04
22 - Thanks to a blood test, it is possible to determine whether you have been in contact with the infectious agent	10.00	6.98	8.00	+	1.02	.001
23 - You can get HC from someone who is infected but doesn't have any symptoms	9.00	7.04	7.64	+	0.60	.001
24 - A mode of transmission of the HC infectious agent is mosquito bites	0.00	2.93	3.51	-	0.58	.001
25 - HC is caused by a virus	10.00	7.32	7.69	+	0.37	.05
26 - Almost all homosexual men are positive for the HC infectious agent	0.00	2.48	1.51	+	– 0.97	.001

Column 1 = Questions for which the difference in 1997 between the mean responses of lay persons and experts was large (> 2 points) and significant (p < .01).

Column 2 = Experts' mean responses in 2003.

Column 3-4 = Lay people's mean responses in 1997 and 2003.

Columns 5 = Direction of the change from 1997 to 2003, + means that the change was in the direction of the expert's responses and - means that the change was not in the direction of the expert's responses.

Column 6-7 = Differences between the lay people's mean responses in 1997 and 2003, significance of these differences.

transmitted in blood, that people with HC can be asymptomatic, that HC can be diagnosed by a blood test, and that HC is treatable. This increase in knowledge should have benefits. It should, in theory, translate into more screening, particularly among those with risk factors. In fact, the percentage of French people who have been screened has risen in the last few years (although not necessarily as a consequence of people's increased awareness and knowledge of HC). In addition, the increase in knowledge should reduce people's fear of those who are infected. Participants in 2003 felt less risk of getting infected through personal contact with someone with HC. This change should in turn facilitate the normalization of social relations between those with and those without the disease.

Yet the picture is not actually so optimistic : the magnitudes of positive change were small (even if statistically significant), and some changes were negative. Much education of the high risk groups and the general public is left to do. This same conclusion has been reached after studies of high school students in Australia, of intravenous (IV) drug users in U.S. cities, of internal medicine residents in Michigan, and of orthopedic surgeons in Maine. The French campaign against HC must be evaluated in the context of other public health initiatives aiming to educate people and change their health-related behaviour. These are most successful when they are multi-modal and aim simultaneously at a variety of relevant audiences – as the French authorities did in their efforts to educate physicians, people at risk, and the general public. Even then they can expect to make only gradual and modest impacts.

This study has several limitations. First, the sample of experts was small in number. Second, the lay participants were convenience samples of people living in two cities in France. Generalizations to other people in France and elsewhere must, therefore, be done with care. Third, since the lay participants were not the same people as those surveyed in 1997, their state of knowledge before the information campaign is unknown. Fourth, it is well known that increases in knowledge do not always lead to improvements in behavior. We did not examine this issue : not only were the 2003 participants different from those in 1997, but also we did not ask participants about their own risky behaviour and use of screening tests.

Selective reference for further reading

Kpanake, L., Muñoz Sastre, M. T., Mullet, E., & Sorum, P. C. (2009). Misconceptions regarding Hepatitis C in the Togolese public. *Preventive Medicine*, *49*, 269-271.

Munoz Sastre, M. T., Bacq, Y., Mullet, E., & Sorum, P. (2002). Misconceptions as Regards Hepatitis C in the French Public. *Preventive Medicine*, *34*, 596-599.

Muñoz Sastre, M. T., Monsirmen, S., Morin, G., Presutto, E., Séguéla, L., Vinel, J.-P., Mullet, E., & Sorum, P. C. (2006). Changes in French People's Misconceptions about Hepatitis C, 1997-2003. *Preventive Medicine*, *42*, 150-153.

Exercise 26

Questions

1. What two populations did this study compare ?
2. What was the objective of the study ?
3. Give an example of a statement the experts were completely sure was true.
4. Can hepatitis C be transmitted by mosquitoes ?
5. What reservations are expressed about the conclusions of this study ?

Chapitre 6

PSYCHOLOGIE DES ORGANISATIONS ET ERGONOMIE/ ORGANISATIONAL PSYCHOLOGY AND ERGONOMICS

Ergonomics is the science designed to make work processes and work environments healthy and productive. Psychologists working in ergonomics contribute to the analysis and improvement of work processes and systems so that workers experience favourable work conditions, satisfaction in their work, and better health. For example, an ergonomic psychologist might improve office furniture placement so that employees are more comfortable and sustain less work-related strain.

Industrial-organisational psychologists contribute to an organisation's success by improving the performance and well-being of its people. An organisational psychologist might develop better communication systems within an organisation to improve the flow of essential information and allow employees to spend less time responding to email. The texts in this section will cover a variety of topics related to human well-being and adaptation of work environments.

42 ORGANIZATIONAL STRESS AND BURNOUT

Stress at work has become the subject of considerable public debate in recent years. Stress refers to the emotional and physiological reactions to stressors, that is, the demands, situations or circumstances that disrupt a person's equilibrium. At work, as in ordinary life, we can experience three type of stress : acute, post-traumatic, and chronic stress. A special form of chronic stress at work that impairs many people is called *"burnout"*.

ACUTE STRESS, POST-TRAUMATIC STRESS AND CHRONIC STRESS (OR BURNOUT)

An acute stress reaction may develop after exposure to a traumatic event, for instance, a physical aggression or an accident. However, following the sudden arousal state, a return to "normal" can be expected within a fairly short period of time. When people face a life-threatening event, they first experience acute stress. Nevertheless, following such an event, a delayed response can also develop : the post-traumatic stress reaction. In that case, the onset of symptoms ranges from immediate to delayed, sometimes 6 months following the event. People suffering from post-traumatic stress re-experience the traumatic event, that is, recurrent and distressing memories of the trauma. Symptoms include intrusive memories of the event, avoidance of places or things that remind them of the event, withdrawal, and psychological and physiological reactivity to cues that trigger those recollections.

Unlike acute and post-traumatic stress, which are responses to abrupt, easily identified major events, burnout, a form of chronic stress, doesn't occur overnight. It is a cumulative process, beginning with little warning, and developing gradually. Its causes are more difficult to identify. Burnout can be conceptualized as the final stage in the rupture of adaptation resulting from the long term disequilibrium between work demands and work resources.

To date, scholars consider that burnout is a three stage process.

- The first stage, emotional exhaustion, refers to feelings of being overextended and depleted of one's emotional and physical resources, resulting in loss of energy and chronic fatigue. Workers feel they are no longer able to give of themselves at a psychological level.
- With the second stage, cynicism, people respond to persistent stress (or emotional exhaustion) by developing cynical attitude towards their work, their colleagues, or by putting a distance between themselves and service recipients (clients, pupils, etc.). We also name this second stage *"depersonalization of relationships"*. Through cynicism or depersonalization, employees attempt to distance themselves emotionally from their job, colleagues, recipients, as a way of coping with emotional exhaustion and job demands.
- The third stage of the burnout syndrome is reduced personal accomplishment. It refers to the fact that employees evaluate their work and themselves negatively and feel dissatisfied with their work accomplishments.

Symptoms and consequences of burnout

It is of great importance to recognize the signs of burnout in order to prevent or treat its harmful effects. Of course, as burnout develops gradually, its symptoms and consequences develop accordingly. As a consequence, people may not pay attention to warning signals.

At the physical level, depleted energy or chronic fatigue is the most typical symptom of burnout. Various psychosomatic disorders such as ulcers or gastro-intestinal problems can develop. Often people who suffer from burnout report physical complaints such as headaches and musculoskeletal disorders. Prolonged colds and flu, and, more generally, an increased susceptibility to viral infection, are frequently reported. Actually, when stress level is high for a long period of time, the immune system is impaired due to a reduced level of hormones such as ACTH or cortisol. Sleep disturbances also frequently occur.

At the psychological level, when they are burned out, people feel impatient, moody, and get frustrated more easily that they normally would. Relationships with colleagues, patients, pupils or clients are disturbed. Emotional control decreases, which can lead to outbursts of crying, irritable and oversensitive attitudes, and aggressive behaviors. As emotional resources are depleted, because they have been overused for too long a time, social isolation and withdrawal occur. For instance, we demonstrated that general practitioners with a high degree of burnout develop attitudes of withdrawal towards their patients (Truchot, Roncari & Bantegnie, 2010). Burnout is also associated with addictive behaviors and eating disorders. Cognitive skills might be impaired : concentration becomes difficult and thinking becomes more rigid.

At the organizational level, with burnout there is also an increased rate of absenteeism, staff turnover, and sick leave. People suffering from burnout tend to be less effective at work.

Etiology of burnout

As stated above, burnout results from a rupture of equilibrium between work demands and work resources. Job demands include work stimuli that require sustained physical, cognitive, and emotional efforts on the part of the employee, and that lead to negative consequences if the efforts required go beyond the usual. Note that job demands can be proximal or distal. When proximal, they may be associated with the content of the job : time pressure, work overload, task complexity, variety of task performed, problem with equipment (*e.g.*, computers), shift work, exposure to risk and hazards, etc. Proximal demands may also be associated with the immediate work environment : lack of participation in decisions, role conflict and role ambiguity, poor career development perspectives, quality of supervision, etc. When distal, job demands include characteristics like job instability or insecurity, involuntary termination (*i.e.*, reducing the size of the workforce, and all the pressures due to the global economy (merger, downsizing, etc.).

Job resources refer to those psychological, social, or organizational characteristics that reduce job demands, stimulate personal growth and engagement, and that are functional in achieving work goals. Not only may job resources have a direct positive effect on employees well-being, they may also reduce the impact of job demands, *i.e.*, buffer the effects of stress. These resources can be situated and analysed at the level of the task (*e.g.*, skill variety, autonomy), at the level of the organization of work and supervison (*e.g.*, role clarity), at the level of social relationships (supervisory style, coworker support), or at the level of the global organization (*e.g.*, salary). If resources are lacking, therefore, the employee is at risk of experiencing burnout, not only because work is less rewarding, but also because it is more difficult, even impossible, to face job demands.

A good example of resources at work is *social support*. This refers to the belief that one is cared for, esteemed, valued, and that one belongs to a network of mutual obligations (Cobb, 1976). House (1981) differentiated between four main categories of social support. Emotional support takes the form of empathy, concern, trust, or sympathy with a person's difficulty. Informational support occurs when the person is given advice, suggestions that give her or him assistance in facing situational demands. Appraisal support involves information, especially feedback, concerning the person's functioning. Instrumental support includes concrete behaviors such as giving direct help, money, and practical interventions on the person's behalf. It is comprehensible that these several functions of support are rewarding and help to treat problems at work. Of course, social support is not the only resource potentially available. For example, feelings of control and mastery and perceptions of justice and fairness are also basic requirements that, if lacking, impinge on employee burnout.

Nevertheless, we must keep in mind that work is not necessarily always boring, stressful, or physically dangerous. Work is part of the development of self esteem and social identity. It provides the opportunity to develop one's skills and social engagement. Loss of work is associated with a myriad of negative reactions ranging from loss of social contact to chronic illness and suicide.

Selective references for further reading

Truchot, D. (2004). *Épuisement professionnel et burnout : concepts, modèles, interventions*. Paris : Dunod.

Truchot, D., Bantégnie, D., & Roncari, N. (à paraître, 2010). Burnout, compliance du patient et retrait psychologique chez les médecins généralistes : Une étude exploratoire. *L'Encéphale, Revue de psychiatrie clinique biologique et thérapeutique*.

Exercise 27

Questions

1. What is the onset period for symptoms of post-traumatic stress ?
2. Is burnout easy to identify when it first appears ?
3. A teacher makes dismissive remarks to colleagues about students. What symptom, characteristic of the second phase of burnout, might this be ?

4. Is the risk of losing one's job as a result of downsizing a proximal or a distal job demand ?
5. What are the four categories of social support referred to in the text ?

43 ROLE AMBIGUITY, ROLE CONFLICT, AND ORGANIZATIONAL STRESS

SOCIAL ROLE AND ROLE CONFLICT

A *role*, or *social role*, refers to the set of expected behaviors, rights, and obligations associated with a particular social status or social position. Within a social role, appropriate and expected behaviors are dictated by social norms, that is to say, organizational rules and regulations supposed to be known by the individuals playing the role and by those who interact with them.

To perform a role, an individual has to know the expectations of the role set (*e.g.*, duties, responsibilities), the activities required to perform the role adequately, and the consequences of the role performance for self, others, and the organization (Kahn, Wolfe, Quinn, Snoek, & Rosenthal, 1964). According to Katz and Kahn (1978, p. 197), *"The process of organizational role-taking is simplest when a role consists of only one activity, is located in a single subsystem of the organization, and relates to a role-set all of whose members are in the same organizational subsystem"*. Nevertheless, when there is uncertainty about work requirements or when individuals engage in multiple incompatible roles, psychological tensions will arise due to role ambiguity and role conflict.

ROLE AMBIGUITY

Role ambiguity refers to a lack of information about the requirements of one's role, a lack of clarity about expected behaviors in one's work activity, or to the unpredictability of the consequences of one's role performance. In either case, what is expected is vague, unclear, and ill-defined, and employees do not know how their role requirements are to be met. Additionally, in work environments where there is work ambiguity, people are obviously uncertain about the evaluative procedures that will ensure that the role was performed successfully. Role ambiguity can concern the task itself : in that case, it refers to uncertainty about work requirements. It can also concern the way employees are evaluated by another person.

Role ambiguity could occur, for instance, in a newly-created job, or when there are continuous organizational changes, or when the work entails crossing organizational boundaries. In some professions, work assignements are particularly broad, leaving much to the judgement of the professionals. This is particularly true for social workers, for whom the scope of the job and the expectations of others are broad and ill-defined.

Since role ambiguity implies a lack of information about the way to perform a job, it reduces the links between effort and performance, as well as the links between performance and rewards. This, in turn, will lower motivation and performance at work.

Role conflict

In the organizational literature, role conflict is often associated with role ambiguity. Role conflict arises when a person faces pressures to comply with inconsistent demands. For instance, a nurse may have to deal with contradictory expectations from doctors and patients. Another example of role conflict occurs when organizational expectations conflict with one's own beliefs or values.

Rizzo *et al.* (1970, p. 155) identify four principal types of role conflict :

(1) **Person-Role conflict** : *"Conflict between the focal person's internal standards or values and the defined role"*. A person-role conflict occurs when an employee perceives a conflict between his or her values and expectations on the one hand, and those of the organization or the supervisors on the other. For instance, the organizational pressure to discharge patients or clients quickly, the lack of time to provide emotional support, may be at odds with the professional ideals of nurses or social workers. Therefore, the employee will experience an internal conflict : either s/he acts according to his or her values, or consistently with the role expectations defined by the organization – or fruitlessly seek a compromise between the two.

(2) **Intra-sender conflict** refers to an incompatibility among various demands placed on the employee. It also includes conflicts between the time and resources at the disposal of the employee and the defined role behavior. This is the case when a supervisor expresses expectations that are mutually incompatible, when the employee does not have the skills needed to perform his or her role, or when resources are insufficient. This sort of role conflict may generate role overload. In that case, the individual perceives that the cumulative role demand exceeds his or her ability to perform a task.

(3) **Inter-role conflict** : *"Conflict between several roles for the same person which require different or incompatible behaviors"*. Inter-role conflict occurs when the demands associated with one role are incompatible with the demands stemming from another role. Role-family conflict is a special case of inter-role conflict (Greenhaus & Beutell, 1985). It can be time-based, for instance, when role pressures from two domains compete for the individual's time (*e.g.*, between having to work late and picking up a

child from school). It can be strain-based when the stress arising from one role interferes with the performance of another role (*e.g.*, it is difficult for parents who are anxious about a sick child to concentrate at work). It is behavior-based when two different roles imply incompatible behaviors ; when a behavior required in one role is inappropriate in another role. For instance, the authoritarian interaction style of a police officer is inappropriate when at home. Of course, the conflict is bi-directional. Work can interfere with family (work-to-family conflict) and family can interfere with work (family-to-work conflict).

(4) **Inter-sender conflict is defined as** *"Conflicting expectations and organizational demands in the form of incompatible policies"*. This is the case when two or more people (supervisors, colleagues, clients) express expectations that are incompatible.

Measuring role conflict and role ambiguity

The scale developped by Rizzo, House, and Lirtzman (1970) is the most popular measure of role conflict and role ambiguity. The assessment of role conflict consists of eight items referring to job requirement compatibility (*e.g.*, *"I receive assignments without the manpower to complete them"*, *"I have to do things that should be done differently"*, *"I receive incompatible requests from two or more people"*). The assessment of role ambiguity consists of six items referring to the clarity or existence of guidelines and requirements, and to the predictability of outcomes (*e.g.*, *"I know exactly what is expected of me"*, *"There are clear explanations of what has to be done"*, *"I clearly know what my responsibilities are"*).

Role conflict, role ambiguity and work outcomes.

Empirical evidence demonstrates that role conflict and role ambiguity have detrimental effects on the well-being of workers. They are corrrelated with job dissatisfaction, tension, anxiety, stress, low commitment to the organization, reduced performance, and/or propensity to leave.

Selective references for further reading

Greenhaus, J. H., & Beutell, N. J. (1985). Sources of conflict between work and family roles. *Academy of Management Review*, *10*, 76-88.

Greenhaus, J. H., Allen, T. D., & Spector, P. E. (2006). Health consequences of work-family conflict : The dark side of the work-family interface. In P.L. Perrewe & D.C. Ganster (Eds.). *Research in occupational stress and well-being : Vol. 5.* (p. 61-98). Amsterdam : JAI Press/Elsevier.

Katz, D., & Kahn, R. L. (1978). *The social psychology of organizations*, 2nd ed. New York : John Wiley and Sons.

Exercise 28

Questions

1. Why do social workers suffer from role ambiguity ?
2. Someone's job requires them to do something they believe to be morally wrong. What sort of role conflict is this ?
3. I find I cannot do what my boss wants and what my customer wants. What sort of conflict is this ?
4. What is *"role overload"* ?
5. Why is it in the interests of organisations to reduce role ambiguity ?

Pour en savoir plus sur le domaine de la didactique professionnelle, reportez-vous au DVD contenant le **texte** et la **version audio 18** intitulés :

📖 ♫ **Learning to work : an introduction to professional didactics**

45 ACTIVITY AND LEARNING : RESEARCH IN PROFESSIONAL DIDACTICS

Professional didactics is a recent field of research founded in the 1990's by Vergnaud, Pastré and Mayen (2006). The objectives of this field include analyzing what people do when they work, and how they learn to work. This field of research has been developed in France and other French-speaking countries, with only a few publications in English. An association founded in 2006[1] publishes a peer-reviewed journal : *Work and Learning* (*Travail et apprentissages*).

The approach is based on certain principles : adults are continuous learners ; they can learn in workplaces *by* doing and *while* doing – and they develop specific knowledge (also called *"practical knowledge"* or *"know-how"* in common language). It is possible to study this knowledge systematically through the way people act and think – or reason – in real situations, through their activity. Activity can be defined as a stream of actions and thoughts. It takes place in situations (which surround and influence people's activity), and aims at transforming certain dimensions of those situations. It is possible to study the cognitive part of activity, *i.e.*, what organizes people's choices in action, using the *"scheme"* model developed by Piaget.

1. www.didactiqueprofessionnelle.org.

The practical objective is to improve professional training processes. The main idea is that training can be improved if you look at work activities in real contexts (for instance, to create simulators and other teaching tools, to identify key conceptual fields in a domain, and to evaluate skills).

Researchers in professional didactics not only refer to activity theories (Vygotsky, Leontiev) and developmental psychology (Piaget, Bruner), but also to the psychology of work (or ergonomics studies in the French tradition) and philosophy of action (James, Dewey). They have studied different professional activities in various fields (first manual activities, then service and creative activities).

To analyse people's activity, researchers in this field use a mix of qualitative methods developed in work analysis (in the French ergonomics tradition). They observe people in their workplaces, they question them on what they are doing and the meaning they give their actions. They carry out :

- prescription analysis,
- field observations (recorded and transcribed),
- interviews with professionals (based on work records, or oriented by the *explicitation* framework developed by Vermersch),
- clinical interviews based on case studies.

Researchers generally study a few professionals, and try to compare experienced people with beginners, or experienced people with different profiles. The aim is to highlight the complexity of the activity in real situations, to explore reasons for choices, to underline all the dimensions the professionals have to deal with, and all the compromises they make to "get by" and cope with difficulties. The researchers try to identify the key conceptual fields people use.

A FEW RESEARCH RESULTS

Different kinds of activities

Observing people working first leads us to identify visible differences in their activities. Here we refer to the first sense of *"activity"*, that is, the stream of actions that can be observed, or the way people "get by" in real complex work situations. Different choices are made to achieve different results and performances. People's activities are more or less adapted to situational variations and complexity[1].

1. This has been observed and explored in other psychology research, especially differences related to the level of experience or expertise.

Examples :

- Mayen observed garage mechanics receiving customers who wanted their cars repaired. They spent different amounts of time talking to them, and had different ways of questioning and listening to them.
- Caens-Martin (2005) observed trainee winegrowers, and found that some pruned the vines in the wrong place, putting the crop at risk.

Different ways of interpreting a situation

Differences in activity can be related to differences in the way people reason in action. Activity in a larger sense of the word is therefore understood as a partly conscious stream of thought (reasoning, in particular) before, during, and after action. People take different situational indications into account, and reason differently about them (making different interpretations of an actual situation and its expected development). Differences can also be related to people's different intentions, different goals (both prescribed and personal) and different compromises they make in a situation.

Different conceptual resources used in action

Why do people reason in a certain way ? According to these models, reasoning in action depends on mobilising a set of conceptual resources. It can be described as a dynamic unit made of goals, action rules (conditional reasoning *"if... then..."*)[1] and pragmatic knowledge (*"pragmatic concepts"* and *"propositions believed to be true in the world"*, see Vergnaud, 2001). We recently introduced the concept of *beliefs* to describe what Vergnaud designates as "propositions believed to be true in the world". Beliefs refer to any kind of assertive proposition describing a state of the world and used in action, for example, the way customers usually act, what they usually expect, etc. This is what *"pragmatic knowledge"* consists of. These representations are believed to be true by those who use them in action, even if they are not fully conscious or easy to express.

To return to our examples :

- The garage mechanics have different representations of the situation related to the concept of client-feeling (*"client-ressenti"*) (Mayen) among other things. For instance, some of them think that *"women don't know anything about mechanics"*. As a consequence, they do not listen to women's information about the breakdown (when it occurred, etc.), information which is nonetheless potentially useful to determine the repairs to

1. "If I observe this, then the situation is like this; If the situation is like this, then I'd better do that; If I do that, then this will happen". These are expert forms of reasoning in action, also called "action rules" when they are generalized to a class of situations.

be done. This assertion (a *"proposition believed to be true in the world"* or a *"belief"*) orients certain people's activity.

– When experienced wine growers prune grape vines, they use the pragmatic concepts of *load* and *balance* to diagnose the situation (taking account of the number of grapes, the vigour of the plant, and so on) and then decide where to cut (Caens-Martin, 2005). Trainees, on the other hand, have not yet built such concepts to help them decide where to prune.

Concepts – and associated beliefs – help us to reduce information to what is necessary and sufficient for our actions ; they help us to interpret a particular situation, make a hypothesis about how it will develop, and decide what action to take. This research also shows that certain conceptual fields are essential to dealing with a certain class of professional situations (Mayen, 1999).

How is activity learned ?

Early research put the emphasis on the key role of experience. Vergnaud named it the process of *"conceptualisation in action"* (2001), not unlike a process of *"learning by doing"*. People learn by being confronted with the world and work situations, and from both the repeated and varied experiences that result. People may develop action rules and *"propositions believed to be true in the world"* through a process of generalisation.

However, learning can also be seen as a socio-historical process, in the tradition of Vygotsky's works. Work situations are fully social. In other words, the world is full of potential resources for activity, full of artefacts (cognitive and material tools), rules, procedures and prescriptions, other people working and having experience, attributed roles and goals, written and oral knowledge on work processes and situations, instituted ways and means to work in an organisation or a work team. Development can therefore be thought of as an *"appropriation process"* (Clot, 1999) of what is already there, *"re-creating"* it through activity – with the possibility of transforming it at the same time.

Selective references for further reading

Caens-Martin, S. (1999). Une approche de la structure conceptuelle d'une activité agricole : La taille de la vigne. *Éducation Permanente*, *139*, 99-114.

Clot, Y. (dir.) (1999). *Avec Vygotski*. Paris : La Dispute.

Mayen, P. (1999). Des situations potentielles de développement. *Éducation permanente*, *139*, 65-86.

Pastré, P., Mayen, P. & Vergnaud, G. (2006). Note de synthèse sur la didactique professionnelle. *Revue Française de Pédagogie*, *154*, 145-198.

Vergnaud, G. (2001). *Forme prédicative et forme opératoire de la connaissance.* Actes du Colloque GDM 2001 « La notion de compétence en enseignement des mathématiques, analyse didactique des effets de son introduction sur les pratiques de la formation », Jean Portugais (Ed), Montréal, mai 2001. Disponible sur : http://www.didactiqueprofessionnelle.org

Exercise 29

Fill in the blanks in the sentences below with the most appropriate term from the following list.

List of terms

(a) compare experienced people with beginners ; (b) observing people working ; (c) professional didactics ; (d) how they learn to work ; (e) work activities in real contexts ; (f) the stream of actions that can be observed ; (g) reasoning in action ; (h) be thought of as an *"appropriation process"* ; (i) confronted with the world and work situations.

Sentences with blanks

(1) ________________ is the science of what people do when they work, and (2) ____________________. The main idea is that training can be improved if you look at (3) ___________________. Researchers generally study a few professionals, and try to (4) ______________________, or experienced people with different profiles. (5) _______________________ first leads us to identify visible differences in their activities. Activity is (6) ________________________, or the way people "get by" in real complex work situations. (7)____________________ can be described as a dynamic unit made up of goals, action rules (conditional reasoning *"if... then..."*) and pragmatic knowledge *("pragmatic concepts' and 'propositions believed to be true in the world")*. People learn by being (8) ________________________, and from both the repeated and varied experiences that result. Development can therefore (9) _______________________ what is already there, *"re-creating"* it through activity – with the possibility of transforming it at the same time.

Chapitre 7

NEUROPSYCHOLOGIE/ NEUROPSYCHOLOGY

Neuropsychology is both a scientific discipline and an area of applied clinical practice. Neuropsychologists examine the structure and function of the brain and nervous system. They are also particularly concerned with specific psychological processes and overt behaviours that are related to brain structures or functions. One major applied practice is neuropsychological testing conducted in multiple clinical settings, including rehabilitation hospitals that treat patients with brain injuries or cognitive and/or behavioural disorders. Some neuropsychologists are both academics and clinicians. They may work in industry using their knowledge in the management of pharmaceuticals or clinical trials for drugs that might impact the brain and subsequent cognitive functions and behaviours. When neuropsychologists work in forensic settings, they assess people for legal reasons. For example, as expert witnesses, they might determine whether individuals have the necessary cognitive capacity to appreciate the impact of their criminal behaviours. A variety of neuroscientific topics, of interest to those who study and practice neuropsychology, will be covered in this section.

46. NEUROPSYCHOLOGICAL TESTS ASSESSING CONSTRUCTIONAL ABILITIES : CONCEPTUAL AND EXECUTIVE FUNCTIONS

(1) Construction

Constructional abilities include both drawing and combining objects or parts of objects. A full-scale assessment will examine each aspect of construction in several ways.

Internationally, the most common technique for examining the ability to draw a copy of a visual stimulus is the copy trial of the Complex Figure Test (Rey, 1941 ; Osterrieth, 1944). The popularity of this test has encouraged the development of alternate forms which reduce the likelihood of practice effects (higher scores as a result of familiarity with the test format) contaminating a drawing on a second or third examination. Distortions in the copy of a complex geometric design can provide information concerning the presence of a spatial dysfunction (*e.g.*, incorrect placement of internal details) as well as the probable location of a lateralized lesion (*e.g.*, a noticeable shift in the midline of the figure).

To examine the ability to make free drawings, the subject is typically instructed to draw a person or some common object (usually a bicycle or a house). Patients' bicycle drawings provide information about their ability to maintain size relationships within a drawing, and to appreciate the interrelationship of relevant parts ; house drawings can elicit distortions in perspective and spatial orientation, as well as in size relationships. A skilled examiner can learn much about a subject's practical reasoning as well as visuospatial functioning by means of these drawing techniques.

The different aspects of abilities to assemble objects can also be measured by tests that require a copy of a stimulus and by those presenting cut-up pieces that can be put together into something meaningful. The Wechsler battery (Wechsler, 1997) contains examples of both kinds of construction. Copying printed designs with blocks has both visuospatial and analytical components. Completing jigsaw puzzle pictures (*e.g.*, a jigsaw of a hand or an elephant) requires an appreciation of details and the ability for conceptual synthesis. Other kinds of assembling tasks used to assess neuropsychological functioning include copying shapes made with sticks and 3-dimensional block construction (Benton *et al.*, 1994). Each of these may bring to light a different aspect of constructional dysfunction.

(2) Conceptual functions

These include aspects of thinking such as abstract reasoning, generalization, hypothesis testing, and problem-solving. Tests have been developed to examine each dimension. The most useful ones assess several aspects of concept formation and reasoning. The kinds of errors that occur provide information regarding the nature of the conceptual disorder.

Three of the tests in the Wechsler battery focus on specific conceptual functions. In the comprehension task, most of the comprehension items assess practical reasoning ; the two items asking for interpretation of proverbs require verbal abstraction. Similarities call for concept formation based on verbal abstraction. Verbal skills can significantly contribute to success on these tests. Arithmetic tests mathematical reasoning in subjects whose attention and verbal functions are fairly intact. Because the questions are read to the subject, who has to mentally solve these more or less lengthy and complex problems, it becomes an attention test for many subjects with an attentional disorder (Lezak *et al.*, 2004).

Many tests of conceptual functions use visual, rather than verbal stimuli ; however, like other tests with non-verbal stimuli, they vary in the degree to which verbalization plays a part. For example, Raven's Progressive Matrices (Raven, 1996) asks the subject to identify which of several designs or puzzle parts would complete a given visual pattern, thus calling on abilities for hypothesis testing, concept formation, and generalization. However, this is not a test of non-verbal reasoning alone since, of the 60 items, 36 have a significant verbal reasoning component. The Category Test (Halstead, 1947) requires the subject to develop and test hypotheses about the internal organization of sets of visual stimuli, based on processes of abstraction and generalization. This format has a predominantly visuospatial component. Some of these tests focus especially on hypothesis-testing and good judgment (*e.g.*, Identification of Common Objects) ; others primarily test abstraction and the ability to discern shifting concepts, for example, the Wisconsin Sorting Test. These tests tend to be so sensitive to brain dysfunction that none are useful for lesion localisation, although the types of errors elicited by them may relate to specific areas of structural damage.

(3) Executive functions

The four major components of the executive functions are the abilities to formulate a goal, to plan, to carry out purposive activities effectively, and for self-regulation, *i.e.*, to self-monitor and self-correct spontaneously and reliably (Lezak, 2004). Open-ended tests which require patients to decide how to perform the task, and when to stop, can elicit important information about executive functioning. However, much can be learned by close observation of how the patient proceeds and the kinds of errors made on the different tests given in an examination.

The ability to formulate a goal can be tested by an open-ended task such as the Tinker Toy Test. The subject is given 50 pieces of a children's construction set with instructions to *"make whatever you like"*. Some patients simply put pieces together with no idea that something nameable can be made with them. When goal formulation is intact, the subject typically quickly has an idea and proceeds to attempt to realize it (for example, to build a plane). Success will depend on whether other executive functions are operative, such as the ability to plan what parts are needed, or the ability to identify and correct errors.

The classical test for planning is the Porteus Mazes (Porteus, 1950) as it requires the subject to search alternative possibilities to reach an already identified goal. More recently developed maze formats are also graded in difficulty but take less time (*e.g.*, see some tests in the Wechsler). The Tower of London test gives the subject three small poles, connected to a small wooden platform, on which three wooden balls are arranged with instructions to rearrange the balls on the poles in a given pattern with the fewest possible moves (Culbertson & Zillmer, 2001). This test and its many variants are sensitive to even the early effects of many degenerative brain diseases.

To examine the ability for purposive activity, almost any open-ended task can be useful. Bicycle drawings, for instance, show whether the subject can carry out a project effectively, as many patients with executive disorders omit the pedals, or the chain linking pedals to the wheel ; occasionally one of these patients will link the chain to both wheels. Other children's construction kits, besides the Tinker Toy Test, also permit the subject to demonstrate how effectively s/he can work. Some neuropsychologists give their patients parts of a wheelbarrow to assemble, evaluating their performances on the basis of how well they stay focused on the job, and how long they take to finish.

Many aspects of self-regulation can be assessed in the course of test-taking generally : the examiner notes whether the subject is aware of mistakes, and if so, whether s/he attempts to correct them. Other signs of impaired self-regulation that can show up on the usual tests of cognitive functions are impulsiveness, diminished productivity, and carelessness.

Specific tests are available for some aspects of self-regulation, such as flexibility and the capacity to shift. Some verbal fluency tests have a built-in shifting component (*e.g.*, giving men and women's names alternately in alphabetical order). Two graphic fluency formats require shifting responses. The Ruff Figural Fluency Test (Ruff *et al.*, 1987) provides 40 dotted squares on each of five pages with instructions to make different designs in as many squares as possible within a one-minute time limit for each page. An impaired ability to shift can show up on these tests as perseverance such that the subject repeats the same response despite instructions to give different ones.

Selective references for further reading

Montreuil, M., Lezak, M. D. (2006). La neuropsychologie clinique. In Ionescu, S., Blanchet, A., Montreuil, M., Doron, J. *Nouveau cours de psychologie, psychologie clinique et psychopathologie*. Paris : PUF.

The tests described in this paper are detailed in the following handbook :

Lezak, M.D., Howieson, D.B., & Loring, D. W. (2004). *Neuropsychological assessment (4th ed.)*. New York : Oxford University Press.

Exercise 30

Find the best description to match the test named.

Tests

1. Porteus Maze :
2. Tinker Toy Test :
3. A full-scale assessment (of constructional abilities) :
4. The Wechsler battery :
5. Raven's Progressive Matrices :
6. Wisconsin Card Sorting Test :

Descriptions

a. Instruction : "*Make whatever you like*". This open-ended instruction tests the ability to formulate a goal.

b. Contains examples of both kinds of construction tasks. Examples of tasks include : (a) copying printed designs with blocks to test both visuospatial and analytical abilities ; (b) completing jigsaw puzzles to reflect an appreciation of details and the ability for conceptual synthesis.

c. Requires the subject to search alternative possibilities to reach an already identified goal.

d. Aspects of constructional abilities are examined in several ways, including both drawing and combining objects or parts of objects.

e. Primarily tests abstraction and the ability to discern shifting concepts.

f. Asks the subject to identify which of several designs or puzzle parts would complete a given visual pattern, thus calling on abilities for hypothesis-testing, concept formation, and generalization.

Pour en savoir plus sur les examens neuropsychologiques, reportez-vous au DVD contenant le **texte** et la **version audio 19** intitulés :

📖 ♫ **The neuropsychological examination**

48 PSYCHOPATHOLOGY AND NEUROLOGICAL DISEASES

For a long time, the psychopathological aspects of patients with neurological diseases (Alzheimer's disease, Parkinson's disease, Multiple Sclerosis[1] (MS), etc.) were seriously neglected. It is only recently that the psychopathology, psychological adaptation, and quality of life of these patients have been taken into account.

All neurological diseases present an impairment of the nervous system or the central nervous system. They are considered chronic diseases since no curative treatments exist. However, the way they develop varies greatly, not only from disease to disease, but also from patient to patient. A medical team cannot predict when symptoms will appear, how fast they will develop, or how long the disease will last. In Multiple Sclerosis, for example, some patients will need a wheelchair within five years ; others may still be walking unaided after twenty years living with the disease.

Psychological reactions

Even if there is great variation between neurological diseases and between patients, there are still some common aspects. Being diagnosed with a neurological disease is a great shock ; it generates strong psychological reactions, as well as psychic processes needed to come to terms with the disease, learn to live with it, and accept that it will last a lifetime.

The psychological process which leads the patient to acceptance of the diagnosis is long and difficult. The different stages that the patient must go through were first described in cancer patients by Kübler-Ross (1976). They have been observed and described in various chronic diseases. At the time of diagnosis, the patient is in a state of shock and usually unable to understand what is happening to him/her.

The first stage is a period of denial, where the patient refuses to admit the diagnosis and lives as if nothing has happened. S/he often wants to undertake more medical examinations and see other physicians. Then, progressively, after a few days or weeks, the patient becomes aggressive and irritable.

1. Multiple Sclerosis is a chronic, unpredictable, progressive, disabling disease, generally diagnosed in young adults between the ages of 20 and 40 ; symptoms of MS may include profound fatigue, depression, gait disorder, spasticity, blurred vision, bladder and bowel problems.

This aggressiveness can be directed towards healthy family members or friends (in the form of the question *"Why me ?"*), or towards the medical staff – who gave the diagnosis, but who have neither any treatment to offer, nor any forecast about the development or duration of symptoms. This stage usually lasts about six months, after which patients gradually enter the acceptance stage. They can either accept the disease and become able to live with it, or fail to do so. The aim of the medical team, especially the psychologist, is to help the patients towards this acceptance stage. However, as soon as there are new symptoms or increased impairment, denial or aggressiveness are likely to reappear for a while. Patients have to accept each new stage of their disease gradually, in order to be psychologically able to return to the acceptance stage.

Patients with a neurological disease are also confronted with their mortality. They constantly have to readjust their life objectives, as well as their professional, social and leisure activities. For the youngest patients, the questions raised may include whether or not they can find a life partner, have children, and do the job they always wanted to do. Older patients will have to question whether they can continue the same job and live in the same place, as well as who will take care of them.

Psychopathological Disturbances

Among the various psychopathological disturbances observed, the most frequent is depression. Usually there is mild or moderate depression ; major depressive episodes are less frequent. These symptoms are very common during the first six months following diagnostic disclosure and tend to diminish thereafter. Depressive symptoms can also be considered adaptive troubles, since most often they do not persist. They reappear when the disease develops and new symptoms or impairments appear. Depressive symptoms can lead to suicidal ideation, and suicides are always more frequent in chronic diseases than in the general population. Anxiety is also frequent, and can take on many forms.

In some patients, anxiety-manifestations are essentially physical (tension, pain, sleep disturbance) ; in others, they are more psychological (irritability, aggressiveness, rumination, difficulty concentrating). The unpredictability of the way these diseases develop reinforces anxiety symptoms.

Some studies have observed a specific emotional profile in these patients. Most of the time, patients present an emotional deficit which can be observed through their monotonous mood or anhedonia. Some, on the contrary, show loss of emotional control. Usually these psychopathological disturbances are not correlated with the length of the disease, nor with functional impairment, but they have a great impact on the patients' quality of life.

It is often difficult to determine the origin of the symptoms observed. In fact, there is an important overlap between psychopathology and neurology. For example, a patient who is tired, apathetic, anxious, with disturbed sleep patterns and impaired concentration, may be seen as mildly depressed ; but all these symptoms can also be related to the neurological disease itself. The same goes for loss of emotional control, which can also be related to depression, or to the disease itself. It seems reasonable to suppose an interaction between neurological and psychological factors.

Coping strategies

When a patient encounters an event that threatens his/her psychological balance such as a chronic disabling disease, s/he resorts to coping strategies to deal with the situation.

The concept of coping, proposed by Lazarus in the 1960s, was defined as *"the overall cognitive and behavioral efforts to master, reduce or tolerate inside or outside demands, which threaten or surpass personal resources"*. Two coping strategies have been identified : problem-focused coping, the effort made to overcome difficulty, and emotion-focused strategies, which are associated with regulating emotions.

There are no inherently "good" or "bad" coping strategies ; rather, there are responses that are more or less adapted to the circumstances. However, most authors consider avoidance or emotion-focused strategies to have a significant positive association with depression and poor physical and mental quality of life ; and problem-focused strategies are generally considered more effective in avoiding depression and anxiety.

Patients with a neurological disease should be evaluated from diagnosis to the late stages of the disease. These evaluations should include neurological, psychological, psychopathological and cognitive assessments. The psychological evaluation should focus on adaptive mechanisms and coping strategies, on depression, anxiety and emotional status, and also on evaluating beliefs and representations about the illness. More accurate knowledge of psychological and emotional aspects, as well as adaptive patterns observed in patients, allow us to provide better clinical treatments and to tailor the psychological interventions to patients and their families at the different stages of the disease. Different studies have also reported the importance of including the patient's caregiver, who plays a highly significant role in his/her well-being.

Selective references for further reading

Bungener, C., Jouvent R., & Derouesné, C. (1996). Affective disturbances in Alzheimer's disease. *Journal of American Geriatrics Society*, *44*, 1-6.

Montel S, & Bungener, C. (2007). Coping and quality of life in 135 subjects with multiple sclerosis. *Multiple Sclerosis*, *13*, 393-401.

Montel, S., Bonnet, A. M., & Bungener, C. (2009). Quality of life in relation to mood, coping strategies and dyskinesia in Parkinson's disease. *Journal of Geriatric Psychiatry and Neurology*, *22*, 95-102.

Exercise 31

Fill in the blanks. Choose the most appropriate term from the list below.

List of terms

(a) avoidance, (b) caregiver, (c) chronic diseases, (d) diagnostic disclosure, (e) emotion-focused strategies, (f) medical team, (g) Multiple Sclerosis, (h) problem-focused strategies.

Sentences with blanks

All neurological diseases, including (1) ______________, present an impairment of the nervous system or the central nervous system. They are considered (2) ______________ since no curative treatments exist. A (3) ______________ cannot predict when symptoms will appear, how fast they will develop, or how long the disease will last. Mild or moderate depression commonly occurs during the first six months following (4) ______________ and tends to diminish thereafter. Two coping strategies have been identified. (5) ______________ are generally considered most effective to prevent depression and anxiety. (6) ______________, including denial and (7) ______________, are associated with more depression and poor quality of life. The patient's (8) ______________ plays a significant role in promoting his/her well-being.

Pour en savoir plus sur la qualité de vie et le mécanisme de coping dans la dépression et la maladie de Parkinson, reportez-vous au DVD contenant le **texte** et la **version audio 20** intitulés :

Coping and quality of life in relation to depression and anxiety in Parkinson's disease

50 THE RELATION BETWEEN COGNITION AND BRAIN FUNCTIONING : AN INTRODUCTION TO NEUROSCIENCE ♫ (AUDIO 21)

The nervous system is at the origin of cognitive functions, such as thoughts, actions, feelings, memories, etc. It is composed of the brain, the spinal cord, and nerves. The aim of neuroscience is to understand the nervous system and the pathologies that might affect it (Purves & Augustine, 2003). Important advances were made in this discipline during the 20th century, providing a better understanding of brain function. Two examples of these major discoveries will be considered here, illustrated by three recent findings that have revealed some dysfunctions of the nervous system.

Luigi Galvani (1737-1798) was the first to observe "animal" electricity while working on muscle contractions in frogs' legs. He observed accidentally that hanging frogs' legs on a metal balcony provoked a contraction. This muscle contraction is initiated by an electrical current called the nervous influx. Herman von Hemholtz (1821-1894) measured the speed of this nervous influx flow ; it is slower than the speed of light. At present, we know that the nervous influx is an electrical current that is conveyed by neurons, cells that are part of the nervous system. Neurons can communicate with each other and the rest of the organism by means of this nervous influx. This activity is at the root of our behavior.

A question frequently asked of researchers in neuroscience is what a memory is, or, more precisely, how memories are encoded in the brain. At first sight, this question seems trivial, but a better understanding of what a memory trace in the brain is will help us find ways to get rid of traumatic memories that can cause problems in everyday life. Recent investigations on rodents have led researchers to identify the chain of neurons responsible for a specific fear memory, also called a neuronal network (Han *et al.*, 2009). Rodents can acquire fear memories during an experimental procedure called fear conditioning. The rodents are subjected once to small electric shocks in the paws while an auditory signal sounds. When the animals are moved to a new place and hear the special signal again, they freeze. A frozen mouse is one that stops moving for few seconds : this specific behavior corresponds to a behavioral fear response that can be quantified. During the acquisition of this fear memory, researchers have identified a few neurons, located in a cerebral area called the amygdalae, that are selectively activated, *i.e.*, they produce electrical nervous influx specifically when a mouse hears the fear-inducing tone. Biological and genetic manipulations allow us to target these special neurons for selective erasure. Once these neurons are specifically deleted, the rodents lose this specific fear behavior : when they hear the sound that previously induced freezing, they no longer present any freezing behavior.

Researchers thus succeeded in erasing a specific fear memory. These findings do not mean that we can erase specific memories in humans, but they provide strong evidence of the composition of a memory trace in the brain. These approaches have launched new ways to investigate how a memory is encoded in the human brain and give new clues to psychologists and neuroscientists as to how to develop future techniques to overcome the dramatic effects of traumatic memories on everyday life.

A second important finding for neuroscience was made during the First World War. Surgeons had to heal many soldiers with head injuries, removing part of the skull and leaving the brain unprotected. Although a head injury is lethal most of the time, some people can survive. Surgeons observed that touching this exposed brain does not induce any pain in the patients. Benefiting from the observations of brain insensitivity, Wilder Penfield (1891-1976) discovered that electrical stimulation of a specific cortical area can induce movement or sensation in some body parts. More precisely, he identified that stimulating a specific area called the precentral gyrus (located in the frontal lobe, the anterior part of the brain) induces movements of the body : stimulation of the upper part of this cerebral area produces movements in the lower part of the body (feet and legs), while movement of the tongue follows stimulation of the most inferior part of the precentral gyrus. These observations allow us to draw up a motor representation of the body on the surface of the brain : this schematic representation is called the motor homunculus. Similar findings were made for the cerebral area just posterior to the precentral gyrus, the postcentral gyrus ; stimulating this area induces sensations in the corresponding body part. In the same way, a sensory representation of the body is present on the surface of the brain, leading Penfield to build the sensory homunculus.

Besides identifying the function of these brain areas, these findings led to the conclusion that the brain does not have any pain receptors like the rest of the body, allowing the investigation of its function in conscious patients. This is specifically important for patients suffering from brain tumors or who present brain tissue that does not function normally – for example patients with epilepsy, an incapacitating disease caused by sudden and massive electrical activity of some neurons in a specific part of the brain. Normally, when surgeons have to remove some body tissue, they remove a large piece, including healthy tissue, to be sure that the tumors or the malfunctioning cells are removed. This large resection is possible because all the cells of the body can be replaced. But it is different for neurons, as they cannot regenerate. So when brain tissue has to be removed, it is most important to cut out the malfunctioning tissue and leave the healthy tissue intact. If healthy tissue is removed, cerebral activity can be irremediably lost. During surgical resection of tumors or epileptic foci in the postcentral gyrus, the neurosurgeon can stimulate the surrounding tissues while the neuropsychologist questions the patient about what he feels (Desmurget *et al.*, 2009). If the patient expresses that he has a special sensation like tingling, the neuropsychologist indicates to the neurosurgeon that the stimulated cerebral area is functioning well. If no sensation is perceived by the patient, this indicates that a non-functioning area is being stimulated, and that it has to be removed. This procedure leads to better post-surgery recovery.

Observing the brain's insensitivity has also enabled French researchers to develop a new technique to reduce or completely stop trembling in patients suffering from Parkinson's disease, which is characterized by a progressive loss of neurons in the basal ganglia of the brain, leading to motor dysfunction. By introducing electrodes in this particular region, without any pain for the patients, a small amount of current raised the activity of the remaining intact neurons to replace the activity of the dead neurons (Drouot *et al.*, 2004). This technique improves the quality of life of patients by completely stopping trembling – yet, unfortunately, it cannot cure them.

Understanding the relation between the brain and cognition has led to major discoveries that have improved the quality of life of numerous patients. Nonetheless, further investigations are important to find new ways of curing the diseases that affect the nervous system.

Selective references for further reading

Desmurget, M., Reilly, K. T., Richard, N., Szathmari, A., Mottolese, C., & Sirigu, A., (2009). Movement intention after parietal cortex stimulation in humans. *Science*, *324*, 811-813.

Drouot, X., Oshino, S., Jarraya, B., Besret, L., Kishima, H., Remy, P., Dauguet, J., Lefaucheur, J.-P., Dollé, F., Condé, F., Bottlaender, M., Peschanski, M., Kéravel, Y., Hantraye, P., Palfi & S. (2004). Functional recovery in a primate model of Parkinson's disease following motor cortex stimulation. *Neuron*, *44*, 769-778.

Han, J. H., Kushner, S. A., Yiu, A. P., Hsiang, H. L., Buch, T., Waisman, A., Bontempi, B., Neve, R. L., Frankland, P. W., & Josselyn, S.A., (2009). Selective erasure of a fear memory. *Science*, *323*, 1492-1496.

Purves, D., & Augustine, G., (2003). *Neuroscience*. Bruxelles : De Boeck University.

Exercise 32

Questions

1. What are the three components of the nervous system ?
2. What is the quantifiable behaviour in a mouse which demonstrates fear ?
3. Which part of the body moves if the lowest part of the precentral gyrus is stimulated ?
4. What distinctive feature of the brain makes it possible to study its function in conscious subjects ?
5. How has it been possible to stop trembling in Parkinson's patients ?

Pour en savoir plus sur les différents types de mémoire et leur rôle, reportez-vous au DVD contenant le film intitulé :

Film 19 : Neurocognitive psychology : memory

51 DRUG ADDICTION : NEUROBIOLOGICAL BASIS OF DEPENDENCE

Alcohol dependence and other drug addictions are characterized by criteria such as tolerance development, withdrawal symptoms, drug craving and reduced control of drug intake. According to the DSM-IV-TR, substance dependence is a maladaptive pattern of substance use, as manifested by at least three of the following characteristics, occurring at any time in the same 12-month period :

(1) Tolerance, as defined by either of the following :
   a. a need for markedly increased amounts of the substance to achieve intoxication or desired effect ;
   b. markedly diminished effect with continued use of the same amount of the substance.

(2) Withdrawal, as manifested by either of the following :
   a. the characteristic withdrawal syndrome for the substance ;
   b. the same (or closely related) substance is taken to relieve or avoid withdrawal symptoms.

(3) The substance is often taken in larger amounts or over a longer period than was intended.

(4) There is a persistent desire or unsuccessful efforts to cut down or control substance use.

(5) A great deal of time is spent in activities necessary to obtain the substance, use the substance, or recover from its effects.

(6) Important social, occupational, or recreational activities are given up or reduced because of substance use.

(7) The substance use is continued despite knowledge of having a persistent or recurrent physical or psychological problem that is likely to have been caused or exacerbated by the substance.

Whatever the psychoactive substance used, the withdrawal syndrome is due to the cessation of (or reduction in) heavy and prolonged substance use. It causes significant physical and psychological distress or impairment in social, occupational, or other important areas of functioning. Withdrawal symptoms can vary significantly among individuals, but there are some commonalities (table 4).

Table 4

Withdrawal symptoms, according to psychoactive substances

Withdrawal symptom	Alcohol	Amphetamines	Cocaine	Nicotine	Opiates	Anxiolytics	Cannabis
Autonomic hyperactivity (sweating, pulse rate > 100)	X				X	X	X
Decreased heart rate				X			
Increased hand tremor	X					X	
Insomnia	X	X	X	X	X	X	
Nausea or vomiting	X				X	X	
Transient visual, tactile or auditory hallucinations or illusions	X					X	
Psychomotor agitation	X	X	X			X	
Psychomotor retardation	X	X	X				
Anxiety	X			X	X	X	X
Grand mal seizure	X					X	
Fatigue		X	X				
Vivid, unpleasant dreams		X	X				X
Hypersomnia		X	X				
Increased appetite		X	X	X			
Decreased appetite							X
Dysphoria/depression				X	X		X
Irritability, frustration, anger				X	X		X
Difficulty concentrating				X			
Restlessness				X	X		X
Weigh gain				X			
Weigh loss					X		X
Muscle aches					X		
Lacrimation or rhinorrhea					X		
Diarrhea					X		
Yawning					X		
Fever					X		
Stomach pain					X		X

Physical dependence	⟷	Withdrawal syndrome
Psychological dependence	⟷	Craving/Reduced control of drug intake Positive reinforcement

Neurobiological basis of drug use disorders

Use of ethanol (alcohol), nicotine (tobacco), delta – 9-tetrahydrocannabinol (cannabis), heroin and opiates, cocaine, amphetamines or ecstasy (MDMA) leads to the activation of the reward system, located in the brain and involving the following anatomical structures :

- *Ventral Tegmental Area* (VTA), populated with dopamine neurons, and 4 efferent fiber projections : mesocortical, mesolimbic, mesostriatal and tuberoinfundibular pathways,
- *Nucleus Accumbens* (NAc), with dopamine neuron projections from VTA,
- *Prefrontal Cortex* (involved in executive functions and behavioral control), and *Orbito-frontal Cortex* (involved in cognitive processes such as decision-making), with dopamine neuron projections from VTA,
- *Amygdala* and *hippocampus*, involved in explicit and implicit memorization, conditioned response, learned associations and reinforcement processes,
- *Substantia Nigra* (a part of the basal ganglia, including the striatum), with dopamine neuron projections from VTA.

Dopamine is one of the neurotransmitters involved in the process of reward and reinforcement. Like other drugs, alcohol initially increases dopamine release in the mesocorticolimbic system, which is mediated through interactions with other signaling systems and neurotransmitters, such as the following :

- glutamate (primary excitatory neurotransmitter in the central nervous system), with its N-methyl-D-aspartate (NMDA) receptors,
- gamma aminobutyric acid (GABA),
- serotonin, with receptors for activation (5-HT1B) and inhibition (5-HT1A, 5-HT2C and 5-HT3) when alcohol is used,
- endogenous opioids, such as beta-endorphins, pro-enkaphalins and dynorphins (with opioid receptors),
- cannabinoids, with its CB1 receptors,
- norepinephrine (involved with serotonin in nicotine dependence).

Dopamine is a key element in identifying natural rewards for the organism. These natural stimuli such as food and water cause individuals to engage in approach behaviors. Dopamine is also involved in unconscious memorization of signs associated with these rewards. The assessment of satisfaction of needs (hunger, thirst, sex, friendship), *i.e.*, natural signals, leads to the activation of the VTA first and NA second. But psychoactive substances short-circuit this system by activating the pleasure circuits directly. The drug is used for its pleasant effects : well-being and pleasure sensations (reward).

In the work of American psychologist Burrhus Frederic Skinner, operant conditioning is the use of consequences to modify the occurrence and form of behaviour. *Positive reinforcement* occurs when a behavior (response) is followed by a favorable stimulus (commonly seen as pleasant) that increases the frequency of the behaviour. So the psychoactive substance is used again and again, leading to dependence. But during the dependence period, in order to avoid the withdrawal syndrome, people need to use their drug : this is *negative reinforcement*. It occurs when a behavior (response) is followed by the removal of an aversive stimulus (commonly seen as unpleasant) thereby increasing the frequency of that behavior.

THE CASE OF ALCOHOL USE

Normally, the GABAergic interneurons inhibit the dopaminergic neurons that project from the VTA to the nucleus accumbens, and modulate the dopamine released after a pleasant sensation. These GABAergic neurons are activated through the action of the excitatory neurotransmitter glutamate.

When alcohol is used in large amounts (for example in binge drinking), dopaminergic neurons are directly overactivated, leading to euphoria, joviality, and disinhibition ; secondly, acute alcohol use induces endorphin release, resulting in activation of mu receptors on the GABAergic neurons (VTA). Moreover, there is an inhibition of glutamate effects on GABAergic neurons due to alcohol leading to decreased GABAergic activity in the VTA, and subsequently increased firing of the dopaminergic neurons, resulting in increased dopamine release in the NAc.

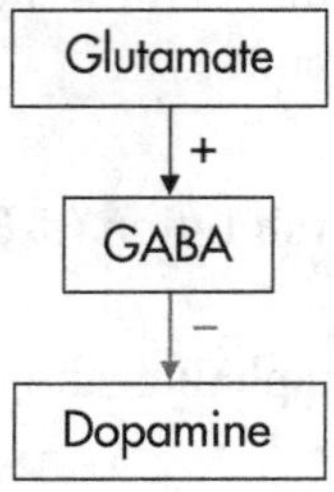

Figure 4
Without alcohol

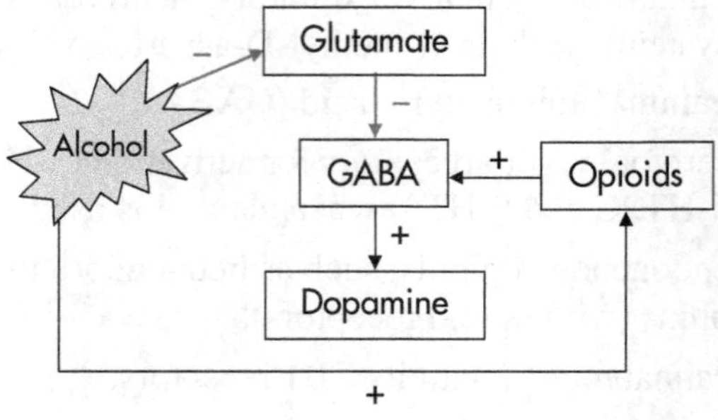

Figure 5
Acute alcohol

During chronic alcohol use, we observe an alteration of NMDA receptor numbers, and also an alteration (desensitization) of dopamine receptors (D2).

During withdrawal from alcohol (after chronic use leading to dependence), glutamate input to GABAergic neurons is increased, leading to decreased dopamine release. Moreover, dopaminergic activity is reduced in the VTA.

Abrupt cessation of alcohol exposure results in brain hyperexcitability, because receptors previously inhibited by alcohol are no longer inhibited. Brain hyperexcitability manifests clinically as anxiety, irritability, agitation, and tremors. Severe manifestations include alcohol withdrawal seizures and delirium tremens. Some medications are proposed to alcoholics during withdrawal to maintain abstinence and reduce craving ; these include naltrexone and acamprosate. Naltrexone (Revia) is an opioid-receptor antagonist and its effects are likely due to the modulation of the dopaminergic mesolimbic pathway. Acamprosate (Aotal) reduces the release of excitatory neurotransmitters like glutamate, which activates NMDA receptors.

Drug addiction is a chronic relapsing disorder, characterized by compulsive drug intake, loss of control over intake, and impairment in social and occupational function. A specific portion of the limbic circuit known as the mesolimbic dopaminergic system is involved in craving, and in the compulsive behaviour described in cases of psychological dependence.

Selective references for further reading

Arvers, P. (2005). Alcohol drinking and alcohol-related problems in France. *Trastornos Adictivos*, *7*, 59-68.

Koob, G. F. & Le Moal, M. (2005). *Neurobiology of Addiction*. New York : Academic Press.

Lejoyeux, M. (2007). *Du plaisir à la dépendance : Nouvelles addictions, nouvelles thérapies*. Paris : Éditions de la Martinière.

Reynaud, M. (2006). *Traité d'addictologie*. Paris : Flammarion Médecine Sciences.

Exercise 33

Questions

1. What are the symptoms of brain hyperexcitability ?
2. Which of the following is *not* generally associated with withdrawal from tobacco ? Anxiety, tearfulness, increased appetite ?
3. How many of the DSM-IV-TR's criteria for substance dependence need to be observed within a 12-month period for a diagnosis ?
4. Someone drinks alcohol in order to avoid unpleasant withdrawal symptoms. What sort of reinforcement is this ?
5. What is the VTA ?

D'autres thèmes de la neuropsychologie à découvrir sur le DVD :

Pour en savoir plus sur les différents types d'Aphasie, reportez-vous au DVD contenant le film intitulé :

Film 20 : Bases of neuropsychology : course 1

Pour en savoir plus sur les différents types d'Apraxie et d'Agnosie, reportez-vous au DVD contenant le film intitulé :

Film 21 : Bases of neuropsychology : course 2

Chapitre 8

RÉPONSES/ANSWERS

EXERCISE 1

1-d, 2-e, 3-b, 4-g, 5-c, 6-f, 7-a

EXERCISE 2

1. Likert scale ; SDS (semantic differential scale) ; IAT (implicit association test).
2. The peripheral route.
3. Metacognition.
4. Affective, cognitive, behavioural.
5. Implicit.

EXERCISE 3

1-g, 2-b, 3-d, 4-f, 5-l, 6-h, 7-e, 8-i, 9-k, 10-m, 11-a, 12-n, 13-c, 14-j

EXERCISE 4

1-b, 2-e, 3-f, 4-c, 5-a, 6-d

EXERCISE 5

1. The cognitive disruption model.
2. MacAndrew and Egerton.
3. The amount thought to have been consumed, according to Bègue *et al.* (2009).
4. Efficient.
5. Decrease (and to increase dispositional attributions).

EXERCISE 6

1. The paradigmatic attitude.
2. 11 years old.
3. Broca's aphasia.
4. False. This is more likely when they are among people with whom they are unpopular.
5. Its interlocutory (communicative) aspects.

EXERCISE 7

1. Territory.
2. A space whose control is shared within a community.
3. Because people do not feel personally responsible for the environment, or capable of resolving its problems.
4. Individual and family.
5. Living in a city is stressful ; green spaces reduce stress and improve health.

EXERCISE 8

1-k, 2-b, 3-h, 4-a, 5-j, 6-f, 7-g, 8-d, 9-i, 10-e, 11-c

EXERCISE 9

1. A Massively-Multiplayer Online Role-Playing Game.
2. Three of : salience, mood modification, tolerance, withdrawal symptoms, craving, relapse.
3. A virtual world which continues after a player stops playing.
4. Jacob.
5. A virtual character representing a player in the game.

EXERCISE 10

1-e, 2-d, 3-f, 4-b, 5-g, 6-h, 7-j, 8-c, 9-i, 10-a

EXERCISE 11

1-e, 2-a, 3-d, 4-c, 5-b

EXERCISE 12

1. Analysis of dreams, slips of the tongue, mistakes and symptoms
2. The Superego
3. The phallic stage
4. Denial, dissociation, projection, idealisation, repression, humour, sublimation
5. Cathexis

EXERCISE 13

1. The need for progressively higher and higher doses to achieve the same effect.

2. Cocaine – stimulant ; cannabis – hallucinogen ; alcohol – depressant.
3. The socio-cultural approach.
4. Reinforcement of behaviour as a result of something unpleasant stopping – for example, taking drugs may relieve a feeling of boredom.
5. Tendency to anxiety or depression ; impulsiveness ; reward-dependence ; sensation-seeking.

EXERCISE 14

1-f ; 2-c ; 3-e ; 4-g ; 5-a ; 6-d ; 7-b ; 8-h

EXERCISE 15

1. Using medication and psychotherapy.
2. OCD (Obsessive-Compulsive Disorder).
3. Repeated panic attacks constitute panic disorder.
4. Conflict between the Id's desires and the Superego's prohibitions.
5. Pathological fear of going out alone.

EXERCISE 16

1-e, 2-j, 3-c, 4-h, 5-b, 6-g, 7-a, 8-d, 9-f, 10-i.

EXERCISE 17

1. Three to four years old.
2. People with autism generally do not demonstrate theory of mind.
3. Dogs have no TOM.
4. Cognitive – concerning beliefs ; affective – concerning emotions.
5. TOM generally disappears with the onset of schizophrenia.

EXERCISE 18

1-f, 2-a, 3-g, 4-b, 5-e, 6-g, 7-b, 8-h, 9-d, 10-c

EXERCISE 19

1. Secure ; insecure-avoidant ; insecure-ambivalent ; disorganised.
2. The mother.
3. Ainsworth.
4. Insecure-ambivalent.
5. A secure base from which to explore and to which to return.

EXERCISE 20

1. Abstraction.
2. Inability to view a situation from any point of view other than one's own.
3. Imitation, drawing, representational activity.
4. Taking other points of view into account.
5. Conservation.

EXERCISE 21

1. Sensory capture and feedback.
2. The Montessori method.
3. Neurodegenerative.
4. Memory loss ; confusion ; agitation ; language/speech problems ; visuo-spatial disturbance.
5. Reality orientation.

EXERCISE 22

1. The unpleasant event.
2. Biology and culture.
3. Snakes in Asia ; pepper in Mexico.
4. False ; a single experience can create an aversion.

EXERCISE 23

1-d, 2-c, 3-b, 4-f, 5-a, 6-e

EXERCISE 24

1-c, 2-e, 3-b, 4-a, 5-d

EXERCISE 25

1-e, 2-b, 3-c, 4-a, 5-f, 6-d

EXERCISE 26

1. Lay people and experts (hepatologists).
2. To see whether knowledge about hepatitis C in the general population improved between 1997 and 2003.
3. Nos. 3, 6, 8, 9, 10, 22, 25.
4. No.
5. Small sample of experts ; lay sample not necessarily representative ; different people questioned in 1997 and 2003.

EXERCISE 27

1. Up to six months.
2. No ; the early symptoms such as fatigue are easy to miss.
3. Cynicism/depersonalization.
4. Distal.
5. Emotional ; informational ; appraisal ; instrumental.

EXERCISE 28

1. Because their job, and people's expectations of them, are broad and ill-defined.
2. Person-role conflict.
3. Inter-sender conflict.
4. Occurs when the cumulative demands of a person's role exceed his/her ability to perform the task.
5. Because role ambiguity causes stress, low commitment to the organisation, and an increased tendency to leave.

EXERCISE 29

1-c, 2-d, 3-e, 4-a, 5-b, 6-f, 7-g, 8-i, 9-h

EXERCISE 30

1-c ; 2-a ; 3-d ; 4-b ; 5-f ; 6-e

EXERCISE 31

1-g, 2-c, 3-f, 4-d, 5-h, 6-e, 7-a, 8-b

EXERCISE 32

1. The brain ; the spinal cord ; the nerves.
2. Freezing.
3. The tongue.
4. It has no pain receptors.
5. By implanting electrodes in the basal ganglia.

EXERCISE 33

1. Anxiety, irritability, agitation, tremors.
2. Tearfulness.
3. At least three.
4. Negative.
5. The Ventral Tegmental Area, a structure of the brain involved in dopamine release.

Chapitre 9

LEXIQUE ANGLAIS-FRANÇAIS/ ENGLISH-FRENCH LEXICON

Abandonment (*n.*)	Abandon (*n.*)
Ability (*n.*)	Aptitude, capacité (*n.*)
Abstract thinking	Pensée abstraite
Acceptance-based therapies	Thérapies basées sur l'acceptation
Accuracy *(n.)*	Justesse, exactitude, précision *(n.)*
Achievement (*n.*) ; achieve *(v.)*	Réussite (*n.*) ; réussir *(v.)*
Acquired *(adj.)*	Acquis *(adj.)*
Act irrevocability	Irrévocabilité de l'acte (voir C. Kiesler)
Acting-out (*n.*)	Passage à l'acte
Action rules (n.)	Règles d'actions (voir J.-R. Anderson)
Activity theories	Théories de l'activité
Actual *(n.)*	Véritable *(n.)*
Acute alcohol consumption	Consommation aiguë d'alcool
Acute episode	Épisode aigu
Acute stress	Stress aigu
Addiction *(n.)*	Addiction *(n.)*
Addictive behaviours	Comportements addictif
Adult Attachment Interview	Entretien *d'*attachement adulte (voir M. Main)
Affect *(n.)*	Affect *(n.)*
Affective *(adj.)*	Affectif *(adj.)*

Affordances *(n.)*	Affordances *(n.)* (capacité d'un objet à suggérer sa propre utilisation, voir J.-J. Gibson)
Agentic state	État agentique (voir S. Milgram)
Agitation *(n.)*	Agitation (*n.*)
Alcohol (*n.*)	Alcool *(n.)*
Alcohol expectancies	Attentes par rapport à l'alcool
Altruistic *(adj.)*	Altruiste, généreux, désintéressé *(adj.)*
Amnesia *(n.)*	Amnésie *(n.)*
Amygdalae *(n.)*	Amygdales *(n.)*
Analytical strategy	Stratégie analytique
Anger *(n.)*	Colère *(n.)*
Anhedonia *(n.)*	Anhédonie *(n.)*. Perte d'intérêt pour les choses agréables.
Anoetic *(adj.)*	Anoétique *(adj.)* : expérience indépendante de la pensée consciente
Anorexia *(n.)*	Anorexie *(n.)*
Anorexic *(adj.)*	Anorexique *(adj.)*
Antidepressants *(n.)*	Antidépresseurs *(n.)*
Anxiety *(n.)*	Anxiété, angoisse *(n.)*
Apparatus *(n.)*	Appareil *(n.)*
Appetite *(n.)*	Appétit *(n.)*
Appraisal *(n.)*	Estimation, évaluation *(n.)*
Arguments *(n.)*	Arguments *(n.)* ou dispute selon le contexte
Arousal *(n.)*	Excitation, éveil *(n.)*
Asperger syndrome	Syndrome d'Asperger
Assertive proposition	Proposition assertive
Assess *(v.)*	Évaluer *(v.)*
Assessment *(n.)*	Évaluation *(n.)*
Assessment tool	Outil d'évaluation

Asymptomatic *(adj.)*	Asymptomatique *(adj.)* : sans symptômes visibles
Attachment *(n.)*	Attachement *(n.)*
Attachment patterns	Patterns (modèle, forme, structure) d'attachement
Attention deficit	Déficit de l'attention
Attentional disorder	Trouble de l'attention
Attitude *(n.)*	Attitude *(n.)*. État mental de préparation à l'action organisé à travers l'expérience, exerçant une influence directe et dynamique sur le comportement (Allport, 1935)
Attribution processes	Processus d'attribution
Attributional model	Modèle attributionnel
Auditory stimulation	Stimulation auditive
Autism *(n.)*	Autisme *(n.)*
Autobiographical memory	Mémoire autobiographique
Automatic activation	Activation automatique
Automation process	Processus d'automatisation (voir J. Leplat)
Autonomous nervous system	Système nerveux autonome (responsable des fonctions automatiques telles que la digestion, la sudation…)
Autonomous state	État d'autonomie, d'indépendance
Autonomy *(n.)*	Autonomie *(n.)*
Availability *(n.)*	Disponibilité *(n.)*
Average *(n.)* (on average)	En moyenne *(n.)*
Aversive conditioning	Conditionnement aversif (voir B.F. Skinner) : L'association d'une conséquence punitive avec un stimulus quelconque peut donner lieu à un conditionnement aversif.
Aversive emotion	Émotion aversive
Avoid *(v.)*	Éviter *(v.)*
Avoidance *(n.)*	Évitement *(n.)*

Avoidance behaviour	Comportement d'évitement
Aware *(adj.)*	Conscient *(adj.)*
Awareness *(n.)*	Conscience *(n.)*
Balanced design	Plan expérimental équilibré
Balanced diet	Régime équilibré
Barbiturates *(n.)*	Barbituriques *(n.)*
Basal ganglia	Ganglions de la base
Basis *(n.)*	Base *(n.)*
Battery *(n.)*	Batterie *(n.)* (de tests)
Bayesian probabilities	Probabilités bayesiennes. (voir T. Bayes et sa théorie des probabilités)
Behave *(v.)*	Se comporter *(v.)*
Behavioral tasks	Tâches comportementales
Behavior-related illnesses	Maladies liées à des comportements (adoptés)
Behaviour or Behavior (American) *(n.)*	Comportement *(n.)*
Behavioural *(adj.)* or Behavioral (American)	Comportemental *(adj.)*
Behavioural constraint	Contraintes comportementales
Belief validation	Validation des croyances
Benevolent sexism	Sexisme bienveillant
Beta-blockers *(n.)*	Béta-bloquants *(n.)*
Bias *(n.)*	Biais *(n.)*
Binding communication	Communication engageante
Binge drinking	Beuverie *(n.)*
Biomedical model	Modèle biomédical
Bipolar adjective scales	Échelle d'adjectifs antithétiques ou opposés (exemples : chaud-froid ; faible-fort)
Bipolar disorders	Troubles bipolaires
Black box	Boîte noire (analogie avec ce qui se passe dans la tête des gens)

Blocking hypothesis	Hypothèse du blocage
Blood *(n.)*	Sang *(n.)*
BMI = Body Mass Index	Indice de masse corporelle
Body image detection device	Dispositif de détection de l'image corporelle
Body image dissatisfaction	Insatisfaction de l'image corporelle
Body image distortion	Distorsion de l'image du corps
Body posture	Posture corporelle
Body Shape Questionnaire	Questionnaire d'insatisfaction corporelle
Body size	Corpulence, gabarit
Borderline *(n.)*	État-limite *(n.)*
Borderline personality disorder	Trouble de la personnalité borderline
Brain *(n.)*	Cerveau *(n.)*
Brain hyperexcitability	Hyperexcitabilité cérébrale
Brain injury	Lésion cérébrale
Brain stroke	Accident vasculaire cérébral (AVC)
Brain tissue	Tissu cérébral
Brain tumor	Tumeur au cerveau
Breaking and entering	Vol par effraction
Caliper *(n.)*	Caliper *(n.)* (instrument de mesure de la masse graisseuse)
Carcinogenesis *(n.)*	Carcinogénèse *(n.)* : naissance d'une tumeur cancéreuse (carcinome).
Carcinoma *(n.)*	Carcinome *(n.)* : tumeur cancéreuse
Cardiovascular disease	Maladie cardio-vasculaire
Caregiver *(n.)*	Personne qui dispense aide et soins
Cartesian mind-body dualism	Dualisme cartésien corps-esprit
Case studies	Études de cas
Castrated *(adj.)*	Castré *(adj.)*
Castration *(n.)*	Castration *(n.)*
Castration anxiety	Angoisse de castration

Categorization *(n.)*	Catégorisation *(n.)*
Category Test	Test de catégories d'après Halstead
Cathexis *(n.)*	Investissement *(n.)*
Causal attributions	Attributions causales (voir B. Weiner)
Cells *(n.)*	Cellules *(n.)*
Censorship *(n.)*	Censure *(n.)*
Central nervous system	Système nerveux central
Central route	Voie centrale
Cerebral activity	Activité cérébrale
Cerebral area	Aire cérébrale
Cerebral function	Fonction cérébrale
Cerebral imaging *(n.)*	Imagerie cérébrale *(n.)*
Chain of neurons	Chaînes de neurones
Childhood *(n.)*	Enfance *(n.)*
Chi-square test	Test du Chi Carré, (voir tests statistiques)
Chronic diseases	Maladies chroniques
Chronic stress	Stress chronique
Chronic use	Usage chronique
Circular madness	Folie circulaire (expression due à J.-P. Falret, psychiatre du XIXe siècle)
Civil behavior	Comportement courtois, poli
Clinical trials	Essais cliniques
Closeness *(n.)*	Proximité, connivence
Clue *(n.)*	Indice *(n.)*
Codability *(n.)*	Fait de pouvoir être codé
Cognitive *(adj.)*	Cognitif *(adj.)*
Cognitive appraisal	Évaluation cognitive
Cognitive aspect	Aspect cognitif
Cognitive disruption model	Théorie de la perturbation cognitive

Cognitive functions	Fonctions cognitives
Cognitive load	Charge cognitive
Cognitive miser	Avarice cognitive (voir S.T. Fiske & S.E. Taylor, 1984)
Cognitive processes	Processus cognitif
Cognitive psychology	Psychologie cognitive
Cognitive resources	Ressources cognitives
Cognitive response model	Modèle de la réponse cognitive (voir A.G. Greenwald, 1968)
Cognitive-behavioural orientation	Orientation cognitivo-comportementale
Collective level	Niveau collectif, du groupe
Commitment *(n.)*	Engagement *(n.)* (voir C. Kiesler)
Communication skills	Compétences communicatives, capacités de communication
Comorbidity *(n.)*	Comorbidité *(n.)* : La comorbidité, ou double diagnostic, est définie par l'Organisation mondiale de la santé (OMS) comme la « cooccurrence chez la même personne d'un trouble dû à la consommation d'une substance psychoactive et d'un autre trouble psychiatrique »
Complaint *(n.)*	Plainte *(n.)*
Complex Figure Test	La figure complexe de Rey
Compliance *(n.)*	Compliance, adhésion, adhérence *(n.)*
Compulsions *(n.)*	Compulsions *(n.)*
Concept *(n.)*	Concept *(n.)* : unité cognitive qui regroupe une classe d'objets, d'événements, de relations, etc, qui possèdent des éléments en commun
Conceptualisation in action	Conceptualisation dans l'action
Conditional reasoning	Raisonnement conditionnel
Conditioned response	Réponse conditionnée

Confederate *(n.)*	Complice, compère, collaborateur *(n.)*
Confidentiality *(n.)*	Confidentialité *(n.)*
Configuration of features	Configuration de traits
Confusion *(n.)*	Confusion *(n.)*
Conscious (adj)	Conscient *(adj)*
Consciousness *(n.)*	Conscience *(n.)*
Conservation *(n.)*	Conservation *(n.)* : concept de Piaget, selon lequel l'aspect quantitatif d'une chose n'est pas affecté par un changement dans l'apparence de la chose.
Constructivist approach or constructivist epistemology approach	Épistémologie ou approche constructiviste : théorie de l'apprentissage fondée sur l'idée que la connaissance est construite par l'apprenant sur la base d'une activité mentale qui lui permet d'éditer ses propres « règles » et « modèles mentaux » pour donner un sens à ses expériences.
Consumption *(n.)*	Consommation *(n.)*
Content *(n.)*	Contenu *(n.)*
Contextual marking	Marquage contextuel
Control condition	Condition contrôle
Control group	Groupe contrôle, groupe témoin : groupe de sujets qui ne subit pas le traitement expérimental et qui sert de point de comparaison. Dans les études médicales, le groupe contrôle reçoit un placébo.
Controllability *(n.)*	Contrôlabilité *(n.)*
Coping strategies	Stratégies de coping (d'adaptation, d'ajustement, de maîtrise = faire face)
Coronary heart disease	Maladies coronariennes
Correlate *(n.)*	Corrélat *(n.)*

Correlational analysis	Analyse corrélationnelle (voir corrélation en statistique)
Cortical area	Aire corticale
Costly request	Demande coûteuse
Counterfactual thinking	Pensée, raisonnement, contrefactuel
Countertransference	Contre-transfert
Craving *(n.)*	Envie *(n.)*, besoin irrésistible
Crossing organizational boundaries	Franchissement des frontières organisationnelles
Cue *(n.)*	Indice *(n.)*
Cure *(v.)*	Guérir *(v.)*
Curve *(n.)*	Courbe *(n.)*
Cut down *(v.)*	Réduire *(v.)*
Cyclothymia *(n.)*	Cyclothymie *(n.)*
Data *(n.)*	Données (d'une étude) *(n.)*
Day center	Hôpital de jour
Daydream *(n.)*	Rêve éveillé
DDT	DDT (un insecticide)
Death drive	Pulsion de mort
Debriefing *(n.)*	Débriefing, désaffabulation *(n.)* : on explique aux sujets expérimentaux le véritable objectif poursuivi dans l'expérience après leur avoir donné une fausse raison au départ.
Decentering *(n.)*	Décentration *(n.)*
Decision-making	Prise de décision
Decision-making under uncertainty	Prise de décision en situation d'incertitude
Defense mechanisms	Mécanismes de défense
Deficiency *(n.)*	Insuffisance, faiblesse, carence, déficience *(n.)*
Delirium *(n.)*	Délire *(n.)*
Delirium tremens	Delirium tremens

Dementia *(n.)*	Démence *(n.)*
Denial *(n.)*	Déni *(n.)*
Dependence *(n.)*	Dépendance *(n.)*
Depersonalization of relationships	Dépersonnalisation des relations
Depressant *(n.)*	Dépresseur ou psycholeptique *(n.)*
Depressed *(adj.)*	Déprimé *(adj.)*
Depression *(n.)*	Dépression *(n.)*
Desensitization *(n.)*	Désensibilisation *(n.)*
Desirable trait	Trait désirable
Developmental psychology	Psychologie du développement
Diabetes *(n.)*	Diabètes *(n.)*
Diagnosis *(n.)*	Diagnostic *(n.)*
Diagnostic disclosure	Révélation du diagnostic
Differentiation *(n.)*	Différenciation *(n.)*
Disability *(n.)*	Incapacité, invalidité, handicap *(n.)*
Disabling *(adj.)*	Invalidant, handicapant *(adj.)*
Disappointment *(n.)*	Déception, désillusion *(n.)*
Disease *(n.)* = Illness *(n.)*	Maladie *(n.)*
Disorder *(n.)*	Trouble *(n.)* : par troubles mentaux et du comportement, on entend des affections cliniquement significatives qui se caractérisent par un changement du mode de pensée, de l'humeur (affects) ou du comportement associé à une détresse psychique et/ou à une altération des fonctions mentales (OMS, 2001).
Disorganisation syndrome	Syndrome de désorganisation (dissociation)
Disorganized patients	Patients désorganisés (voir schizophrénie)
Disorganized attachment	Attachement désorganisé
Disorganized speech	Discours incohérent, désorganisé
Displacement *(n.)*	Déplacement *(n.)*

Disruption *(n.)*	Perturbations, dérèglement *(n.)*
Disruptive behavior	Comportement perturbateur
Dissociation *(n.)*	Dissociation *(n.)*
Distorting mirror	Miroir déformant
Distorting video technique	Technique vidéo de distorsion (corporelle)
Distress *(n.)*	Désarroi, détresse, souffrance *(n.)*
Distressed *(adj.)*	Perturbé, bouleversé, chagriné *(adj.)*
Dominant group	Groupe dominant
Dose-response relationship	Relation dose-effet
Drive *(n.)*	Pulsion *(n.)*
Drug *(n.)*	Drogue *(n.)*
Drug users	Toxicomanes *(n.)*
DSM - IV = Diagnostic and Statistical Manual of Mental Disorders	DSM-IV = *Manuel diagnostique et statistique des troubles mentaux* (4e éd.)
Dyad *(n.)*	Dyade *(n.)* : couple de 2 personnes en interaction
Dysfunction *(n.)*	Dysfonctionnement *(n.)*
Dysfunctional *(adj.)*	Dysfonctionnel *(adj.)*
Dyskinesia *(n.)*	Dyskinésie *(n.)* : perturbation qui se situe au niveau des mouvements et qui se traduit entre autre par de l'incoordination, des spasmes et une diminution de la force musculaire
Dysphoria *(n.)*	Dysphorie *(n.)*
Early mother-infant interaction	Interactions précoces mère-enfant
Eating disorders	Troubles du comportement alimentaire
Ecological pact	Pacte écologique
Economic approach	Approche économique
Effective *(adj.)*	Efficace
Effectiveness *(n.)*	Efficacité *(n.)*

Ego *(n.)*	Moi *(n.)*
Egocentrism *(n.)*	Égocentrisme *(n.)*
Elaboration Likelihood Model	Modèle de probabilité d'élaboration, (voir R.E. Petty et J.T. Cacioppo, 1986)
Elderly *(n.)*	Personnes âgées *(n.)*
Electric shock	Choc électrique
Electrical current	Courant électrique
Electrode *(n.)*	Électrode *(n.)*
Emotion *(n.)*	Émotion *(n.)* : réponses de forte intensité qui comportent des manifestations expressives, physiologiques et subjective.
Emotion regulation	Régulation de l'émotion
Emotional exhaustion	Épuisement émotionnel
Emotional process	Processus émotionnel
Emotion-focused coping *(n.)*	Coping centré sur l'émotion
Empathic *(adj.)*	Empathique *(adj.)*
Empathize *(v.)*	Être empathique *(v.)*
Empathy *(n.)*	Empathie *(n.)*
Encoding context	Contexte d'encodage
Encounters *(n.)*	Rencontres *(n.)*
Enculturation *(n.)*	Enculturation *(n.)*
Environmental field	Champ environnemental
Environmental overload	Surcharge environnementale
Environmental stress	Stress environnemental
Epidemiologist *(n.)*	Epidémiologue *(n.)*
Epidemiology *(n.)*	Épidémiologie *(n.)*
Epilepsy *(n.)*	Épilepsie *(n.)*
Epileptic foci	Foyers épileptogènes
Ergonomics *(n.)*	Ergonomie
Ethiopathogenic *(adj.)*	Éthiopathogénique *(adj.)* : Étude des causes d'une maladie et des processus par lesquels ces causes agissent.

Ethology *(n.)*	Éthologie *(n.)* : Etude scientifique des comportements animaux (voir C. Lorenz)
Ethos *(n.)*	Éthos ou système de valeurs *(n.)*
Etiologic *(adj.)*	Étiologique *(adj.)*
Etiology *(n.)*	Étiologie *(n.)* : relatif aux causes des maladies
Euphoria *(n.)*	Euphorie *(n.)*
Evolutionary psychology	Psychologie évolutionniste
Examination *(n.)*	Examen *(n.)*
Excitatory neurotransmitter	Neurotransmetteur excitateur
Executive functions	Fonctions exécutives (anticipation, sélection d'un but, planification, organisation de la démarche, évaluation des résultats, formulation d'hypothèses différentes, autocritique, auto correction, souplesse mentale, persistance dans la tâche, capacité d'ajustement en cours de route, capacité d'adaptation aux changements)
Exemplar *(n.)*	Exemplaire d'une catégorie, membre d'une catégorie (par exemple, la baleine est un exemplaire de la catégorie des mammifères)
Expectations *(n.)*	Attentes *(n.)*
Experimental psychology *(n.)*	Psychologie expérimentale *(n.)*. Ensemble des connaissances élaborées à l'aide de la méthode expérimentale.
Experimenter *(n.)*	Expérimentateur *(n.)*
Exposure effect	Effet d'exposition
Expressive strategy	Stratégie expressive
External control	Lieu de contrôle externe (voir J. Rotter et son concept du *locus of control*)

Externality *(n.)*	Externalité *(n.)* (voir B. Weiner et sa théorie des attributions)
Extrinsic motivation	Motivation extrinsèque (qui provient de l'environnement de la personne)
Eye task	Tâche d'attribution d'intentions basé sur le regard
Facial expressions	Expressions faciales
Facilitation priming effect	Effet d'amorçage facilitateur
Factual event	Événement factuel, avéré
False belief task	Tâche de fausse croyance
Family support groups	Groupes de soutien familial
Fantasy *(n.)*	Fantasme *(n.)*
Favouritism towards the outgroup	Favoritisme envers l'exogroupe
Fear *(n.)*	Peur *(n.)*
Fear conditioning	Conditionnement par la peur
Fear of failure *(n.)*	Peur de l'échec *(n.)*
Feature *(n.)*	Caractéristique *(n.)*
Feet (foot) *(n.)*	Pieds (pied) *(n.)*
Fever *(n.)*	Fièvre *(n.)*
Field observations	Observations de terrain
Field research	Recherche appliquée, de terrain
Figure rating scale	Échelle de notation de personnages
Flow *(n.)*	« Flux », « expérience-flux », « expérience optimale » ou « négentropie psychique » *(n.)* : par référence à la sensation que l'on ressent lorsqu'on agit avec une implication totale dans ce que l'on fait, au point de perdre, par exemple, la notion de l'heure ou du bruit environnant
Follow-up *(n.)*	Suivi *(n.)*

Food practice *(n.)*	Pratique alimentaire *(n.)*
Foot-in-the-door	Pied-dans-la-porte
Foreclosure *(n.)*	Forclusion *(n.)*
Forgiveness *(n.)*	Pardon *(n.)*
Formal models	Modèles formels
Free association tests	Tâche d'associations libres
Free will compliance	Soumission librement consentie
Freeze *(v.)*	Se figer *(v.)*
Freudian slips	Lapsus *(n.)*
Friendship *(n.)*	Amitié *(n.)*
Frontal lobe	Lobe frontal
Frustration *(n.)*	Frustration *(n.)*
Full-scale	Évaluation complète (totalité de l'échelle)
Functioning *(n.)*	Fonctionnement *(n.)*
Gait disorder *(n.)*	Trouble de la marche, la démarche étant atteinte en raison d'un trouble moteur
Gastroenterology service	Service de gastroentérologie
Gaze direction	Direction du regard
Gender *(n.)*	Genre *(n.)* (rôles des hommes et des femmes)
Generalized anxiety disorder	Trouble anxieux généralisé
Genes *(n.)*	Gènes *(n.)*
Genovese case	Affaire Genovese : l'affaire Ketty Genovese est au départ de la réflexion de Latané & Darley sur l'apathie des témoins.
Give up *(v.)*	Abandonner *(v.)*
Glass ceiling effect	Effet « plafond de verre » ou effet de ségrégation verticale
Glass partition effect	Effet « paroi de verre »
Grief *(n.)*	Chagrin *(n.)*
Groundbreaking *(adj.)*	Révolutionnaire *(adj.)*

Group pressure	Pression du groupe
Guidelines *(n.)*	Lignes directrices
Guilt *(n.)*	Culpabilité *(n.)*
Habits *(n.)*	Habitudes *(n.)*
Hallucination *(n.)*	Hallucination *(n.)*
Hand tremor	Tremblement des mains
Head injury	Blessure à la tête
Heal *(v.)*	Soigner *(v.)*
Health *(n.)*	Santé *(n.)*
Health care system	Système de santé
Health insurance	Assurance maladie
Health policy	Politique de santé
Health-care workers	Personnel de santé
Healthy *(adj.)*	Sain *(adj.)*
Heart rate	Rythme cardiaque
Helping behavior	Comportement d'aide
Helplessness *(n.)*	Résignation, impuissance *(n.)*
Hepatitis C	Hépatite C
Hepatologists	Hépatologue (spécialiste du foie)
Heuristic-Systematic Model	Modèle heuristique-systématique (Chaiken, 1987)
HIV/AIDS	Virus HIV/SIDA
Holistic *(adj.)*	Holistique *(adj.)* : qui prend en compte la globalité d'un phénomène
Homeostatic *(adj.)*	Homéostasique *(adj.)*
Humanistic psychology *(n.)*	Psychologie humaniste (voir C. Rogers comme l'un des pères fondateurs)
Hunger *(n.)*	Faim *(n.)*
Hyperactivity *(n.)*	Hyperactivité *(n.)*
Hypersomnia *(n.)*	Hypersomnie *(n.)* (somnolence excessive)
Hyperthymic *(adj.)*	Hyperthymique *(adj.)*

Hypomania *(n.)*	Hypomanie *(n.)*
Hypomanic *(adj.)*	Hypomaniaque *(adj.)*
Hypothesis *(n.)*	Hypothèse *(n.)*
Hypothesize *(v.)*	Émettre une hypothèse
ICD-10 = International Classification of Diseases	CIM-10 = Classement international des maladies
Id *(n.)*	Ça *(n.)*
Idealization *(n.)*	Idéalisation *(n.)*
Ideation *(n.)*	Idéation ou production des idées *(n.)*
Identification task	Tâche d'identification
Illness *(n.)*	Maladie *(n.)*
Imbalance *(n.)*	Déséquilibre *(n.)*
Imitation *(n.)*	Imitation *(n.)*
Immune functioning	Fonctionnement immunitaire
Impairment *(n.)*	Altération *(n.)*
Implicit Association Test	Test d'association implicite
Implicit attitudes	Attitude implicite, non consciente
Impulse control	Contrôle des impulsions
Incentive *(adj.)*	Motivant, incitatif *(adj.)*
Incentive *(n.)*	Motivation, encouragement *(n.)*
Incidence *(n.)*	Incidence *(n.)*
Incomplete activation hypothesis	Hypothèse d'activation incomplète
Individual variables	Variables individuelles
Industrial-organizational psychologist	Psychologue industriel - organisationnel
Inflammatory bowel disease	Syndrome du colon irritable
Informed consent	Consentement éclairé : permission donnée par un patient pour pouvoir procéder à une étude, une recherche ou une intervention spécifique.
Ingroup *(n.)*	Endo-groupe, ou groupe d'appartenance

Inhibit *(v.)*	Inhiber *(v.)*
Inhibit regret-laden behaviors	Inhiber les comportements menant au regret
Inhibitory priming effect	Effet d'amorçage inhibiteur
Innate *(adj.)*	Inné *(adj.)*
Inpatient medical units	Unités d'hospitalisation
Insecure-ambivalent	Attachement insécure ambivalent
Insecure-avoidant	Attachement insécure évitant
Insomnia *(n.)*	Insomnie *(n.)*
Intake *(n.)*	Consommation *(n.)*
Intended *(adj.)*	Intentionnel, voulu, projeté *(adj.)*
Intentionality bias	Biais d'intentionnalité
Intergroup *(n.)*	Intergroupe (relation d'un groupe à un autre groupe. Exemples : relations entre enseignants et étudiants, conflit entre groupes ethniques, etc.)
Internal control	Lieu de contrôle interne (voir J. Rotter et son concept du *locus of control*)
Internal medicine residents	Internes en médecine
Internalised prohibitions	Internalisation des interdits
Internality *(n.)*	Internalité *(n.)* (voir B. Weiner et sa théorie des attributions)
Internalize *(v.)*	Internaliser *(v.)*
Interneurons *(n.)*	Interneurones *(n.)*
Interpersonal *(n.)*	Interpersonnel *(adj.)* (relation d'un individu à un autre individu)
Interviews *(n.)*	Méthodes d'entretiens
Intimacy *(n.)*	Intimité
Intoxication *(n.)*	Intoxication *(n.)*
Intrapersonal *(n.)*	Intra – individuel, intra – personnel
Intravenous *(adj.)*	Intraveineux

Intrinsic motivation	Motivation intrinsèque (interne, qui provient de la personne)
Intrusive *(adj.)*	Intrusif *(adj.)*
Irritability *(n.)*	Irritabilité *(n.)*
Issue *(n.)*	Problème, question (de recherche) *(n.)*
Items *(n.)*	Items *(n.)* : partie ou questions d'un test, d'un questionnaire
Joint attention	Attention conjointe
Juvenile delinquency	Délinquance juvénile
Language *(n.)*	Langage, langue *(n.)*
Lateralized lesion	Lésion latéralisée
Law of effect	La loi de l'effet établit qu'une réponse est davantage susceptible d'être reproduite si elle entraîne une satisfaction et d'être abandonnée s'il en résulte une insatisfaction
Lay people or lay person	Profane, non-initié *(n.)*
Learned association	Association acquise
Learned helplessness	Impuissance apprise ou acquise (voir M. Seligman)
Learning by doing	Apprentissage par l'action
Learning phase	Phase d'apprentissage
Leg *(n.)*	Jambe *(n.)*
Lethal *(adj.)*	Mortel *(adj.)*
Lethal risk	Risque léthal (qui peut entraîner la mort)
Lexical skills	Compétences lexicales
Lexicometric methods of analysis	Méthodes d'analyses lexicométriques
Libidinal *(adj.)*	Libidinal *(adj.)*
Libido *(n.)*	Libido *(n.)*
Life drive	Pulsion de vie
Light beam	Faisceau lumineux

Likert scale	Échelle de Likert
Limited capacity working memory	Capacité limitée de la mémoire de travail
Linear function	Fonction linéaire : elle implique la proportionnalité (On dit que deux mesures sont proportionnelles quand on peut passer de l'une à l'autre en multipliant par une constante…). Par exemple, on dira que le prix d'un plein d'essence est fonction linéaire (dans les mathématiques élémentaires, les fonctions linéaires sont les fonctions les plus simples que l'on rencontre. Ce…) du nombre de litres mis dans le réservoir car : pour un litre, on paie 1,10 euros, pour 2 litres on paie 2,20 euros, pour 10 litres on paie 11 euros etc.
Locus of Control	Lieu de contrôle
Long term memory	Mémoire à long terme
Longitudinal study	Étude longitudinale : étude qui permet de mesurer un événement chez un groupe de patients à différents moments dans le temps.
Long-range *(adj.)*	À long terme
Loss *(n.)*	Perte, altération, déficit *(n.)*
Loss of interest or pleasure	Perte d'intérêt ou de plaisir
Loss of contact with reality	Perte de contact avec la réalité
Low vs. high in credibility	Forte versus faible crédibilité
Lower part	Partie inférieure
Lung cancer	Cancer du poumon
Lymphocyte rates	Taux de lymphocites
Magic thinking	Pensée magique
Maltreated *(adj.)*	Maltraité, abusé *(adj.)*
Mania *(n.)*	Manie *(n.)*

Manic depressive illness	Maladie maniaco-dépressive (alternance de phases dépressives et maniaques ou d'excitation)
Matching *(n.)*	Appariement *(n.)*
Mean *(n.)*	Moyenne *(n.)*
Mean responses	Réponses moyennes
Mediating role	Rôle médiateur
Medical staff	Personnel médical, soignants
Members of the category	Membres d'une catégorie
Memory *(n.)*	Mémoire *(n.)*
Memory cues	Indices mnésiques
Memory loss	Perte de mémoire
Mental map	Carte mentale
Mental processes	Processus mentaux
Mental states	États mentaux
Mere exposure effect	Effet de simple exposition
Metacognition *(n.)*	Métacognition *(n.)*
Metalinguistic *(adj.)*	Métalinguistique, relatif au métalangage *(adj.)*
Mind *(n.)*	Esprit *(n.)*
Mindfulness approaches	Approches basées sur la pleine conscience
Minority group	Groupe minoritaire
Misconception *(n.)*	Idée fausse, méprise, mauvaise compréhension *(n.)*
Mistakes *(n.)*	Actes manqués (contexte psychanalytique)
Mode of transmission	Mode de transmission
Modelings *(n.)*	Modélisations *(n.)*
Modularity theorists	Théoriciens de la modularité
Montessori method	Méthode développée par M. Montessori
Mood *(n.)*	Humeur *(n.)*

Mood Fluctuation	Changement d'humeur
Moral anxiety	Angoisse morale (d'après S. Freud)
Morbid state	État morbide : état pathologique en lien avec la maladie
Morphosyntactic methods of analysis	Méthodes d'analyses morpho-syntaxiques
Motivated tactician model	Modèle du « tacticien motivé » (voir S.T. Fiske et S.E. Taylor, 1987)
Motor dysfunction	Dysfonctionnement moteur
Motor expression	Expression motrice
Motor fluctuations	Fluctuations motrices (dans la maladie de Parkinson)
Motor function	Fonction motrice
Motor homunculus	Homunculus moteur
Motor representation	Représentation motrice
Motor skill	Capacité motrice
Mourning *(n.)*	Deuil *(n.)*
Multi-faceted plan of attack	Un plan d'attaque multi-facettes
Multiplayer Online Role-Playing Games	Jeu de rôles multi-joueurs en ligne
Multiple Sclerosis	Sclérose en plaques
Muscle *(n.)*	Muscle *(n.)*
Muscle aches	Douleurs musculaires
Musculoskeletal disorders	Troubles squeletto-musculaires
Mutual attunement	Écoute mutuelle
Myth *(n.)*	Mythe *(n.)*
Naive participant	Sujet naïf (dans le sens d'une personne qui ignore les objectifs de l'expérience)
Naive scientist model	Modèle du théoricien naïf (voir Hoffman & Hurst, 1990)
Narcissistic needs	Besoins narcissiques

Natural thinking	Pensée naturelle par opposition à la pensée logique
Nausea *(n.)*	Nausée *(n.)*
Necessary and sufficient properties	Propriétés nécessaires et suffisantes
Neo-reality *(n.)*	Néo-réalité *(n.)* (dans le sens d'une nouvelle réalité, une réalité reconstruite)
Nerve *(n.)*	Nerf *(n.)*
Nervous influx	influx nerveux
Nervous system	système nerveux
Neurobiological basis	Base neurobiologique
Neurodegenerative disease	Maladie neurologique dégénérative
Neuron *(n.)*	Neurone *(n.)*
Neuron firing	Activation neuronale
Neuronal network	Réseau de neurones
Neuropsychological *(adj.)*	Neuropsychologique *(adj.)*
Neuroscience	Neurosciences
Neurosis *(n.)*	Névrose *(n.)*
Neurotic *(adj.)*	Névrotique *(adj.)*
Neurotic anxiety	Angoisse névrotique
Neurotransmitter *(n.)*	Neurotransmetteur *(n.)*
Noetic *(adj.)*	Noétique *(adj.)* : visée d'un objet par la pensée
Nonverbal communication	Communication non verbale (ou mimo-posturo-gestuel)
Norm theory	Théorie normative du raisonnement (voir D. Kahneman & A. Tversky, 1982)
Normative expectations	Attentes normatives
Nucleus accumbens	Noyau accumbens
Nursing home	Maison de retraite
Nurture *(v.)*	Élever, soigner, nourrir *(v.)*
Obedience to authority	Soumission à l'autorité

Obesity *(n.)*	Obésité *(n.)*
Object relationship	Relation d'objet
Observation matrix	Protocole d'observation
Obsessions *(n.)*	Obsession *(n.)*
Obsessive *(adj.)*	Obsessionnel *(adj.)*
Obsessive Compulsive Disorder (OCD)	Trouble obsessionnel compulsif (TOC)
Occupational psychology	Psychologie du travail
Occupational status	Statut professionnel
Oedipal conflict	Conflit œdipien
Oedipus complex	Complexe d'Œdipe
Offence *(n.)*	Délit, offense *(n.)*
Offender *(n.)*	Délinquant, coupable *(n.)*
Office furniture placement	Agencement de l'équipement de bureau
Offspring *(n.)*	Progéniture *(n.)*
Olfactory perception	Perception olfactive
Olfactory processing	Traitement olfactif
Olfactory receptors	Récepteurs olfactifs
One-way mirror *(n.)*	Glace sans tain *(n.)*
Onset *(n.)*	Début, déclenchement *(n.)*
Operant conditioning	Conditionnement opérant
Operationalise *(v.)*	Opérationnaliser *(v.)*
Opioids *(n.)*	Opioïdes *(n.)*
Oral and anal stages	Les stades oral et anal
Organism *(n.)*	Organisme *(n.)*
Organizational psychologist	Psychologue des organisations
Orthogonal factorial design	Plan factoriel orthogonal. Définitions : pour chacun des niveaux d'un facteur, tous les niveaux de l'autre facteur sont associés, et ce le même nombre de fois.
Orthopedic surgeons	Chirurgiens orthopédistes

Outcome *(n.)*	Résultat, issue *(n.)*
Outgroup *(n.)*	Exo-groupe
Overactivate *(v.)*	Suractiver *(v.)*
Overt anxiety	Angoisse devant un danger réel
Overweight *(n.)*	Surpoids *(n.)*
Pain *(n.)*	Douleur *(n.)*
Pain receptors	Récepteurs à la douleur
Painful *(adj.)*	Douloureux *(adj.)*
Panic attacks	Attaque de panique
Panic disorder	Trouble panique
Paradigmatic relation	Relation paradigmatique
Parenthood *(n.)*	Parentalité, condition de parent
Parenting *(n.)*	Éducation des enfants
Parkinson's disease	Parkinson, maladie de Parkinson
Passive smoking	Tabagisme passif
Pavlovian conditioning	Conditionnement pavlovien (voir conditionnement classique ou répondant et le modèle stimulus/ réponse ; père fondateur : I. Pavlov).
Paw *(n.)*	Patte *(n.)*
Peak experience	Expérience paroxystique (plénitude) (voir A. Maslow)
Peer *(n.)*	Pairs *(n.)*
Perceived control	Contrôle perçu
Perinatal period	Période péri-natale (période située entre la vingt-huitième semaine de grossesse et le septième jour de vie après la naissance)
Peripheral route	Voie périphérique
Persecution fears	Peur de persécution
Personal accomplishment	Accomplissement personnel
Personal space	Espace privé
Personalisation *(n.)*	Personnalisation *(n.)*

Person-directed	Dirigé vers la personne
Person-to-group relations	Relations de l'individu au groupe
Persuasive communication	Communication persuasive
Persuasive message	Message persuasif
Phallic stage	Stade phallique
Phenomenological *(adj.)*	Phénoménologique *(adj.)*
Phenotype *(n.)*	Phénotype *(n.)* (l'ensemble des caractéristiques physiques et physiologiques d'un individu, résultant de son génotype et de son environnement)
Phobia *(n.)*	Phobie *(n.)*
Phonological property	Propriété phonologique
Physician *(n.)*	Médecin *(n.)*
Physiological arousal	Excitation physiologique
Placebo *(n.)*	Placébo *(n.)*
Pleasure circuits	Circuits du plaisir
Pleasure principle	Principe de plaisir
Plot *(n.)*	Tracé, graphique
Policy *(n.)*	Politique *(n.)*
Politeness *(n.)*	Politesse *(n.)*
Porteus Mazes	Test des labyrinthes de Porteus
Positive illusions	Illusions positives
Postcentral gyrus	Gyrus postcentral
Post-surgery recovery	En chirurgie, suite opératoire
Post-Traumatic Stress Disorder	Trouble de Stress Post-Traumatique
Practical knowledge or "know-how"	Savoir pratique, savoir-faire
Practitioners *(n.)*	Praticiens *(n.)*
Pragmatic knowledge	Savoir pragmatique, pratique
Praise *(n.)*	Éloges *(n.)*
Precentral gyrus	Gyrus précentral
Preconscious *(n.)*	Préconscient *(n.)*

Prejudice *(n.)*	Préjugé *(n.)*
Preliminary act	Acte préparatoire
Pre-morbid *(adj.)*	Prémorbide *(adj.)* : signes avant-coureurs de l'entrée dans une maladie
Pre-planned selection	Sélection planifiée
Preschool *(n.)*	Maternelle (école) *(n.)*
Prescription analysis	Analyse des prescriptions, des consignes de travail
Pretend play	Jeu symbolique, jeu du "faire semblant"
Prevalence *(n.)*	Prévalence *(n.)* : en épidémiologie, il s'agit du nombre de personnes atteintes d'une certaine maladie à un moment donné dans une population donnée.
Primary attachment	Attachement primaire
Primary care programs	Programmes de soins de santé primaires
Prime *(n.)*	Amorce *(n.)*
Priming *(n.)*	Amorçage *(n.)*
Privacy *(n.)*	Espace privé, intime *(n.)*
Proactive *(adj.)*	Proactif *(adj.)*
Problem-focused coping	Coping centré sur le problème
Problem-solving	Résolution de problème(s)
Process of generalisation	Processus de généralisation
Process-directed praise	Éloge dirigé vers le processus ayant permis de réaliser la tâche
Processing of information	Traitement de l'information
Product-directed praise	Éloge dirigé vers la tâche, la production de quelque chose
Professional didactics	Didactique professionnelle
Professional training processes	Processus de formation professionnelle
Projection *(n.)*	Projection *(n.)*

Projective identification	Identification projective (voir dictionnaire de psychanalyse)
Prophylactic *(adj.)*	Prophylactique *(adj.)* : en rapport avec l'ensemble des mesures permettant de prévenir les maladies.
Prototype *(n.)*	Prototype *(n.)*. En psychologie cognitive, catégorie la plus typique à l'égard de la catégorie qui lui est subordonné (exemple : « la rose » est le prototype de la catégorie des « fleurs »).
Prototypical situation	Situation prototypique
Psyche *(n.)*	Psyché *(n.)*
Psychic *(adj.)*	Psychique *(adj.)*
Psychological distress	Détresse, souffrance, psychologique
Psychomotor retardation *(n.)*	Ralentissement, retard, déficit psychomoteur
Psychophysics *(n.)*	Psychophysique *(n.)* : branche de la psychologie consacrée à l'étude des relations entre les stimuli et les sensations qui en résultent (voir G. Fechner comme père fondateur).
Psychosensorial *(adj.)*	Psychosensoriel *(adj.)*
Psychosis *(n.)*	Psychose *(n.)*
Psychosomatic disorders	Troubles psychosomatiques
Psychotic *(adj.)*	psychotique *(adj.)*
Psychotropic substance	Substance psychotrope : se dit des substances chimiques qui produisent des effets sur le psychisme des individus.
Psychotropic substance	Substance psychoactive
Public health	Santé publique
Pulse rate	Pouls
Punishment *(n.)*	Punition *(n.)*
Purposive activities	Activités intentionnelles

Qualitative methods	Méthodes qualitatives
Quality of life	Qualité de vie
Random *(n.)*	Au hasard
Random strangers	Rencontres dues au hasard
Randomise *(v.)*	Sélectionner ou attribuer de manière aléatoire (au hasard)
Range of olfactory stimuli	Éventail ou étendue des stimuli olfactifs
Rate *(n.)*	Taux *(n.)*
Rates ranging from… to	Taux variant, allant de… à
Rating *(n.)*	Classement, note, évaluation *(n.)*
Raven's Progressive Matrices	Matrices progressives de Raven
Reaction-formation	Formation réactionnelle
Reality Orientation Therapy	Rééducation de l'orientation : technique utilisée dans le cadre de la maladie d'Alzheimer)
Reality principle	Principe de réalité
Rearing, child rearing	Éducation des enfants
Reasoning *(n.)*	Raisonnement *(n.)*
Reasoning in action	Raisonnement dans l'action
Receiver of a message	Récepteur d'un message
Receptor *(n.)*	Récepteur *(n.)*
Recover *(v.)*	Récupérer *(v.)*
Referential strategy	Stratégie référentielle
Referral *(n.)*	Recommandation : le fait d'adresser le patient à un médecin spécialiste
Reflecting abstraction	Abstraction réfléchissante
Regenerate *(v.)*	Régénérer *(v.)*
Rehabilitation program	Programme de rééducation
Reinforcements *(n.)*	Renforcements *(n.)*
Relapse prevention	Prévention des rechutes
Relapsing *(n.)*	Rechute *(n.)*

Release *(v.)*	Libérer *(v.)*
Relevance *(n.)*	Pertinence *(n.)*
Relieve *(v.)*	Soulager *(v.)*
Remedial care	Soins curatifs
Remission rate	Taux de rémission
Removal *(n.)*	Ablation, enlèvement *(n.)*
Reoffending minors	Mineurs récidivistes
Repentance *(n.)*	Repentance, regret de ses fautes *(n.)*
Representation of a thing	Représentation de choses
Representation of a word	Représentation de mots
Repression *(n.)*	Refoulement *(n.)*
Request *(n.)*	Requête, demande *(n.)*
Request *(v.)*	Demander *(v.)*
Research field	Domaine de recherche
Resection *(n.)*	Résection *(n.)*
Resilience *(n.)*	Résistance, résilience *(n.)*
Restless *(adj.)*	Agité, nerveux *(adj.)*
Restorative justice	Justice restauratrice
Retrieval process	Processus de récupération
Reward *(n.)*	Récompense *(n.)*
Rig *(v.)*	Truquer, tricher *(v.)*
Risk factors	Facteurs de risque
Rodent *(n.)*	Rongeur *(n.)*
Role ambiguity	Ambiguïté de rôle (professionnel)
Role conflict	Conflit de rôles (professionnels)
Ruff Figural Fluency Test *(n.)*	Test de fluence graphique de Ruff
Rule of morality	Règle de moralité
Sadistic *(adj.)*	Sadique *(adj.)*
Sample *(n.)*	Échantillon *(n.)*
Scale *(n.)*	Échelle (de mesure) *(n.)*
Schema *(n.)*	Schème *(n.)* (voir J. Piaget)

Scholar *(n.)*	Érudit, savant *(n.)*, les universitaires
Screening *(n.)*	Dépistage *(n.)*
Secure attachment	Attachement sécure
Seizure *(n.)*	Attaque *(n.)*
Selective erasure	Destruction sélective
Self-blame *(n.)*	Auto-accusation
Self-construal *(n.)*	Perception de soi
Self-definition *(n.)*	Quête de soi, définition de soi
Self-efficacy theory	Théorie de l'auto-efficacité (voir A. Bandura)
Self-esteem *(n.)*	Estime de soi *(n.)*
Self-fulfillment *(n.)*	Épanouissement de soi *(n.)*
Self-fulfillment of expectations	Prophéties autoréalisées
Self-healing *(n.)*	Auto-guérison *(n.)*
Selfish *(n.)*	Égoïste *(n.)*
Self-management	Autogestion, prise en charge *(n.)*
Self-monitoring	Monitorage de soi
Self-mutilation *(n.)*	Automutilation *(n.)*
Self-report questionnaire	Questionnaire auto-administré
Self-theory *(n.)*	Théorie du Soi *(n.)* (voir théorie implicite de l'intelligence d'après C.S. Dweck)
Self-validation hypothesis	Hypothèse d'auto-validation
Semantic differential scale	Échelle du différenciateur sémantique
Semantic memory	Mémoire sémantique
Semantic property	Propriété sémantique
Semen *(n.)*	Sperme *(n.)*
Sensation *(n.)*	Sensation *(n.)*
Sensation-seeking	Recherche de sensations
Sensorimotor tasks	Tâches sensorimotrices
Sensory *(adj.)*	Sensoriel *(adj.)*

Sensory capture	Capture sensorielle (voir Technique humaniste)
Sensory homunculus	Homunculus sensoriel
Sensory stimulation	Stimulation sensorielle
Sensory stimuli	Stimuli sensoriels
Separation anxiety	Angoisse de séparation
Shell-shock *(n.)*	État de choc traumatique
Shift *(n.)*	Changement, modification, déplacement *(n.)*
Shock generator *(n.)*	Générateur de chocs électriques *(n.)*
Sign test *(n.)*	Test des signes (voir test en statistique)
Similarity *(n.)*	Similarité *(n.)*
Simulation theory	Théorie de la simulation
Situational variables	Variables situationnelles
Skill *(n.)*	Capacité, compétence, habileté *(n.)*
Skilled *(adj.)*	Compétent, entraîné, expert *(adj.)*
Skinner box *(n.)*	La boîte de Skinner est un dispositif expérimental inventé par Skinner pour mettre en évidence l'apprentissage par essai-erreur chez des animaux (rats/pigeons) en faisant intervenir un stimulus renforçateur du comportement (prise de nourriture pour un renforcement positif, choc électrique pour un renforcement négatif).
Skull *(n.)*	Crâne, Boîte crânienne *(n.)*
Sleep disturbances	Troubles du sommeil
Sleepless night	Nuit blanche, nuit sans sommeil
Slip of the tongue	Lapsus
Social cohesiveness	Cohésion sociale

Social desirability	Désirabilité sociale : tendance à donner une image de soi conforme à celle attendue par *l'endogroupe* (voir ce mot)
Social Identity Theory	Théorie de l'identité sociale (voir H. Tajfel & J.-C. Turner 1986)
Social isolation	Isolement social
Social networks	Réseaux sociaux
Social norms	Normes sociales
Social phobia	Phobie sociale
Social reproduction	Reproduction sociale
Social status	Statut social
Social support	Soutien social
Social workers	Travailleurs sociaux
Socially skilled	Socialement compétent(e)
Somatic *(adj.)*	Somatique *(adj.)* : relatif au corps dans sa dimension physique
Somatic reaction	Manifestation, réaction somatique
Sorting task	Tâche de classification
Source credibility	Crédibilité de la source
Source expertise	Expertise de la source (d'un message)
Speech *(n.)*	Parole *(n.)*
Sphere of close relations	Sphère des relations intimes
Spinal cord	Moelle épinière
Spreading of activation	Diffusion de l'activation
Stability *(n.)*	Stabilité *(n.)*
Stable Cause	Cause stable (voir B. Weiner et sa théorie des attributions)
Stage *(n.)*	Stade *(n.)*
Stage of the relationship	Stade de la relation
Stance *(n.)*	Position *(n.)*
State *(n.)*	État *(n.)*
State anxiety	Anxiété-état (d'après Spielberger)

Stereotypes *(n.)*	Stéréotype *(n.)*
Stomach pain	Douleur abdominale
Storage of information in memory	Stockage de l'information en mémoire
Strange Situation *(n.)*	Situation Étrange : expérience consistant à induire un léger stress par le départ et le retour d'un parent chez des enfants âgés d'un an. La situation se compose de huit épisodes (départ-retour) de trois minutes chacun, dont certains se déroulent en présence d'un inconnu. Les réactions de l'enfant sont examinées et permettent d'inférer le style d'attachement de l'enfant.
Style A or C	Type A ou C
Sublimation *(n.)*	Sublimation *(n.)*
Subliminal priming	Amorçage subliminal
Substance abuse	Abus de substance (voir drogues)
Substance use disorders	Troubles liés à l'utilisation/ consommation d'une substance
Substance-induced disorders	Troubles induits par une substance
Sudden arousal state	État d'excitation (d'agitation) soudaine
Suicide attempts	Tentatives de suicide
Super-ego *(n.)*	Surmoi *(n.)*
Surgeons *(n.)*	Chirurgiens *(n.)*
Survival mechanisms	Mécanismes de survie
Sweat *(v.)*	Transpirer *(v.)*
Swing door effect	Effet « porte pivotante »
Symbolic function	Fonction symbolique
Symbolic value system	Système de valeurs symboliques
Syndrome *(n.)*	Syndrome *(n.)* : regroupement de symptômes caractérisant un état pathologique

Syndromic *(adj.)*	Syndromique *(adj.)*
Syntactical system	Système syntaxique
Syntagmatic relation	Relation syntagmatique
Tactile hallucination	Hallucination tactile
Talking cure (*cf.* S. Freud)	Thérapie par la parole (*cf.* S. Freud)
Target *(v.)*	Cibler, diriger *(v.)*
Target person	Personne cible
Task *(n.)*	Tâche *(n.)* (épreuve, test)
Taxinomic *(adj.)*	Taxinomique *(adj.)* : dont le but est de classifier.
Territoriality *(n.)*	Territorialité, territoire
Theory of commitment	Théorie de l'engagement
Theory of mind (TOM)	Théorie de l'esprit
Theory of personality	Théorie de la personnalité
Theory theory (see TOM)	Théorie de la théorie (voir théorie de l'esprit)
Therapy *(n.)*	Thérapie *(n.)*
Thirst *(n.)*	Soif *(n.)*
Threat of castration	Menace de castration
Threat to self-esteem	Menace à l'estime de soi *(n.)*
Threshold *(n.)*	Seuil *(n.)*
Thyroid disease *(n.)*	Maladie thyroïdienne *(n.)*
Tingling *(n.)*	Picotement *(n.)*
Tinker Toy Test *(n.)*	Test Tinker Toy *(n.)*
Tip-of-the tongue phenomenon	Phénomène du mot sur le bout de la langue
Tip-of-the-nose	Mot au bout du nez
Toddler *(n.)*	Enfant en bas âge, bambin *(n.)*
Token economy	Économie de jeton, technique des jetons : système de récompenses par des jetons, bon points, images…

Tolerance *(n.)*	Tolérance *(n.)* : la tolérance à une drogue oblige à en consommer des quantités croissantes pour avoir les mêmes effets
Tongue *(n.)*	Langue *(n.)*
Tower of London test	Test de la tour de Londres (voir Tour de Hanoï).
Trait-anxiety *(n.)*	Anxiété-trait *(n.)* (d'après Spielberger)
Transference *(n.)*	Transfert *(n.)*
Trauma *(n.)*	Traumatisme *(n.)*
Tremble *(v.)*	Trembler *(v.)*
Trial *(n.)*	Essai *(n.)*
Trigger *(v.)*	Déclencher *(v.)*
Unconditional stimulus	Stimulus inconditionnel : stimulus qui déclenche une réponse de manière réflexe, sans apprentissage nécessaire.
Unconscious *(n.)* or *(adj.)*	Inconscient *(n.)* ou *(adj.)*
Underweight (n.)	Sous-poids *(n.)*
Unintentional	Non intentionnel
Unrealistic optimism	Optimisme irréaliste
Unstable cause	Cause instable (voir B. Weiner et sa théorie des attributions)
Upper part	Partie supérieure
Valenced variables	Variables « valence » : la valence désigne ce qui attire (valence positive) ou repousse (valence négative) un individu
Validation Method	Méthode de validation (d'après N. Feil)
Value *(n.)*	Valeur
Venereal diseases, STD (Sexually Transmitted Diseases), STI (Sexually Transmitted Infections)	Maladies/infections sexuellement transmissibles, maladies vénériennes
Ventral tegmental area	Aire tegmentale ventrale

Visual judgement	Évaluation visuelle
Visual stimulation	Stimulation visuelle
Visuospatial functioning/orientation *(n.)*	Fonctionnement/orientation visuo-spatial *(n.)*
Vocational training	Formation professionnelle
Vomiting *(n.)*	Vomissement *(n.)*
Wavelength *(n.)*	Longueur d'onde
Weight *(n.)*	Poids *(n.)*
Weight given to properties	Poids accordé aux propriétés
Well-being *(n.)*	Bien-être *(n.)*
Wisconsin Card Sorting Test	Test de classement de cartes du Wisconsin
Wish fulfillment	Accomplissement, réalisation de souhait(s)
Withdrawal *(n.)*	État de manque, retrait (*n.*)
Withdrawal syndrome	Syndrome de sevrage, état de manque
Work analysis	Analyse du travail
Working memory	Mémoire de travail
World Health Organisation	Organisation mondiale de la santé (OMS)
Yale Model	Modèle de Yale : modèle élaboré par une équipe de l'université de Yale (Holland, Janis & Kelly)
Yawning *(n.)*	Bâillement *(n.)*

Chapitre 10

LEXIQUE FRANÇAIS-ANGLAIS/ FRENCH-ENGLISH LEXICON

À long terme	Long-range *(adj.)*
Abandon *(n.)*	Abandonment *(n.)*
Abandonner *(v.)*	Give up *(v.)*
Ablation, enlèvement *(n.)*	Removal *(n.)*
Abus de substance (voir drogues)	Substance abuse
Accident vasculaire cérébral (AVC)	Brain stroke
Accomplissement personnel	Personal accomplishment
Accomplissement, réalisation de souhait(s)	Wish fulfillment
Acquis *(adj.)*	Acquired *(adj.)*
Acte préparatoire	Preliminary act
Actes manqués (contexte psychanalytique)	Mistakes *(n.)*
Activation automatique	Automatic activation
Activation neuronale	Neuron firing
Activité cérébrale	Cerebral activity
Activités intentionnelles	Purposive activities
Addiction *(n.)*	Addiction *(n.)*
Affaire Genovese : l'affaire Ketty Genovese est au départ de la réflexion de Latané & Darley sur l'apathie des témoins.	Genovese case
Affect *(n.)*	Affect *(n.)*
Affectif *(adj.)*	Affective *(adj.)*

Affordances *(n.)* (capacité d'un objet à suggérer sa propre utilisation, voir J.-J. Gibson)	Affordances *(n.)*
Agencement de l'équipement de bureau	Office furniture placement
Agitation *(n.)*	Agitation *(n.)*
Agité, nerveux *(adj.)*	Restless *(adj.)*
Aire cérébrale	Cerebral area
Aire corticale	Cortical area
Aire tegmentale ventrale	Ventral tegmental area
Alcool *(n.)*	Alcohol *(n.)*
Altération *(n.)*	Impairment *(n.)*
Altruiste, généreux, désintéressé *(adj.)*	Altruistic *(adj.)*
Ambiguïté de rôle (professionnel)	Role ambiguity
Amitié *(n.)*	Friendship *(n.)*
Amnésie *(n.)*	Amnesia *(n.)*
Amorçage *(n.)*	Priming *(n.)*
Amorçage subliminal	Subliminal priming
Amorce *(n.)*	Prime *(n.)*
Amygdales *(n.)*	Amygdalae *(n.)*
Analyse corrélationnelle (voir corrélation en statistique)	Correlational analysis
Analyse des prescriptions, des consignes de travail	Prescription analysis
Analyse du travail	Work analysis
Angoisse de castration	Castration anxiety
Angoisse de séparation	Separation anxiety
Angoisse devant un danger réel	Overt anxiety
Angoisse morale (d'après S. Freud)	Moral anxiety
Angoisse névrotique	Neurotic anxiety
Anhédonie *(n.)* : perte d'intérêt pour les choses agréables.	Anhedonia *(n.)*

Anoétique *(adj.)* : expérience indépendante de la pensée consciente	Anoetic *(adj.)*
Anorexie *(n.)*	Anorexia *(n.)*
Anorexique *(adj.)*	Anorexic *(adj.)*
Antidépresseurs *(n.)*	Antidepressants *(n.)*
Anxiété, angoisse *(n.)*	Anxiety *(n.)*
Anxiété-état (d'après Spielberger)	State anxiety
Anxiété-trait *(n.)* (d'après Spielberger)	Trait-anxiety *(n.)*
Appareil *(n.)*	Apparatus *(n.)*
Appariement *(n.)*	Matching *(n.)*
Appétit *(n.)*	Appetite *(n.)*
Apprentissage par l'action	Learning by doing
Approche économique	Economic approach
Approches basées sur la pleine conscience	Mindfulness approaches
Aptitude, capacité *(n.)*	Ability *(n.)*
Arguments *(n.)*	Arguments *(n.)* ou dispute selon le contexte
Aspect cognitif	Cognitive aspect
Association acquise	Learned association
Assurance maladie	Health insurance
Asymptomatique *(adj.)* : sans symptômes visibles	Asymptomatic *(adj.)*
Attachement *(n.)*	Attachment *(n.)*
Attachement désorganisé	Disorganized attachment
Attachement insécure ambivalent	Insecure-ambivalent
Attachement insécure évitant	Insecure-avoidant
Attachement primaire	Primary attachment
Attachement sécure	Secure attachment
Attaque *(n.)*	Seizure *(n.)*
Attaque de panique	Panic attacks

Attentes *(n.)*	Expectations *(n.)*
Attentes normatives	Normative expectations
Attentes par rapport à l'alcool	Alcohol expectancies
Attention conjointe	Joint attention
Attitude *(n.)* : état mental de préparation à l'action organisé à travers l'expérience, exerçant une influence directe et dynamique sur le comportement (Allport, 1935)	Attitude *(n.)*
Attitude implicite, non consciente	Implicit attitudes
Attributions causales (voir B. Weiner)	Causal attributions
Au hasard	Random *(n.)*
Autisme *(n.)*	Autism *(n.)*
Auto-accusation *(n.)*	Self-blame *(n.)*
Autogestion, prise en charge *(n.)*	Self-management
Automutilation *(n.)*	Self-mutilation *(n.)*
Autonomie *(n.)*	Autonomy *(n.)*
Auto-guérison *(n.)*	Self-healing *(n.)*
Avarice cognitive (voir S.T. Fiske & S.E. Taylor, 1984)	Cognitive miser
Bâillement *(n.)*	Yawning *(n.)*
Barbituriques *(n.)*	Barbiturates *(n.)*
Base neurobiologique	Neurobiological basis
Basis *(n.)*	Base *(n.)*
Batterie *(n.)* (de tests)	Battery *(n.)*
Besoins narcissiques	Narcissistic needs
Béta-bloquants *(n.)*	Beta-blockers *(n.)*
Beuverie *(n.)*	Binge drinking
Biais *(n.)*	Bias *(n.)*
Biais d'intentionnalité	Intentionality bias
Bien-être *(n.)*	Well-being *(n.)*
Blessure à la tête	Head injury

Boîte de Skinner : dispositif expérimental inventé par Skinner pour mettre en évidence l'apprentissage par essai-erreur chez des animaux (rats/pigeons) en faisant intervenir un stimulus renforçateur du comportement (prise de nourriture pour un renforcement positif, choc électrique pour un renforcement négatif).	Skinner box *(n.)*
Boîte noire (analogie avec ce qui se passe dans la tête des gens)	Black box
Ça *(n.)*	Id *(n.)*
Caliper *(n.)* (instrument de mesure de la masse graisseuse)	Caliper *(n.)*
Cancer du poumon	Lung cancer
Capacité limitée de la mémoire de travail	Limited capacity working memory
Capacité motrice	Motor skill
Capacité, compétence, habileté *(n.)*	Skill *(n.)*
Capture sensorielle (voir Technique humaniste)	Sensory capture
Caractéristique *(n.)*	Feature *(n.)*
Carcinogénèse *(n.)* : naissance d'une tumeur cancéreuse (carcinome).	Carcinogenesis *(n.)*
Carcinome *(n.)* : tumeur cancéreuse	Carcinoma *(n.)*
Carte mentale	Mental map
Castration *(n.)*	Castration *(n.)*
Castré *(adj.)*	Castrated *(adj.)*
Catégorisation *(n.)*	Categorization *(n.)*
Cause instable (voir B. Weiner et sa théorie des attributions)	Unstable cause
Cause stable (voir B. Weiner et sa théorie des attributions)	Stable Cause
Cellules *(n.)*	Cells *(n.)*
Censure *(n.)*	Censorship *(n.)*

Cerveau *(n.)*	Brain *(n.)*
Chagrin *(n.)*	Grief *(n.)*
Chaînes de neurones	Chain of neurons
Champ environnemental	Environmental field
Changement d'humeur	Mood Fluctuation
Changement, modification, déplacement *(n.)*	Shift *(n.)*
Charge cognitive	Cognitive load
Chirurgiens *(n.)*	Surgeons *(n.)*
Chirurgiens orthopédistes	Orthopedic surgeons
Choc électrique	Electric shock
Cibler, diriger *(v.)*	Target *(v.)*
CIM-10 : Classement international des maladies	ICD-10 = International Classification of Diseases
Circuits du plaisir	Pleasure circuits
Classement, note, évaluation *(n.)*	Rating *(n.)*
Cognitif *(adj.)*	Cognitive *(adj.)*
Cohésion sociale	Social cohesiveness
Colère *(n.)*	Anger *(n.)*
Communication engageante	Binding communication
Communication non verbale (ou mimo-posturo-gestuel)	Nonverbal communication
Communication persuasive	Persuasive communication
Comorbidité *(n.)* : la comorbidité, ou double diagnostic, est définie par l'Organisation mondiale de la Santé (OMS) comme la « cooccurrence chez la même personne d'un trouble dû à la consommation d'une substance psychoactive et d'un autre trouble psychiatrique »	Comorbidity *(n.)*
Compétences communicatives, capacités de communication	Communication skills
Compétences lexicales	Lexical skills
Compétent, entraîné, expert *(adj.)*	Skilled *(adj.)*

Complexe d'Œdipe	Oedipus complex
Compliance, adhésion, adhérence *(n.)*	Compliance *(n.)*
Complice, compère, collaborateur *(n.)*	Confederate *(n.)*
Comportement *(n.)*	Behaviour or Behavior (American) *(n.)*
Comportement courtois, poli	Civil behavior
Comportement d'aide	Helping behavior
Comportement d'évitement	Avoidance behaviour
Comportement perturbateur	Disruptive behavior
Comportemental *(adj.)*	Behavioural *(adj.)* or Behavioral (American)
Comportements addictif	Addictive behaviours
Compulsions *(n.)*	Compulsions *(n.)*
Concept. *(n.)* Unité cognitive qui regroupe une classe d'objets, d'événements, de relations, etc, qui possèdent des éléments en commun	Concept *(n.)*
Conceptualisation dans l'action	Conceptualisation in action
Condition contrôle	Control condition
Conditionnement aversif (voir B.F. Skinner) : L'association d'une conséquence punitive avec un stimulus quelconque peut donner lieu à un conditionnement aversif.	Aversive conditioning
Conditionnement opérant	Operant conditioning
Conditionnement par la peur	Fear conditioning
Conditionnement pavlovien (voir conditionnement classique ou répondant et le modèle stimulus/réponse ; père fondateur : I. Pavlov).	Pavlovian conditioning
Confidentialité *(n.)*	Confidentiality *(n.)*
Configuration de traits	Configuration of features
Conflit de rôles (professionnels)	Role conflict

Conflit œdipien	Oedipal conflict
Confusion *(n.)*	Confusion *(n.)*
Conscience *(n.)*	Consciousness *(n.)*
Conscience *(n.)*	Awareness *(n.)*
Conscient (adj)	Conscious (adj)
Conscient *(adj.)*	Aware *(adj.)*
Consentement éclairé : permission donnée par un patient pour pouvoir procéder à une étude, une recherche ou une intervention spécifique.	Informed consent
Conservation *(n.)* : concept de Piaget, selon lequel l'aspect quantitatif d'une chose n'est pas affecté par un changement dans l'apparence de la chose.	Conservation *(n.)*
Consommation *(n.)*	Consumption, Intake *(n.)*
Consommation aiguë d'alcool	Acute alcohol consumption
Contenu *(n.)*	Content *(n.)*
Contexte d'encodage	Encoding context
Contraintes comportementales	Behavioural constraint
Contre-transfert	Countertransference
Contrôlabilité *(n.)*	Controllability *(n.)*
Contrôle des impulsions	Impulse control
Contrôle perçu	Perceived control
Coping centré sur l'émotion	Emotion-focused coping *(n.)*
Coping centré sur le problème	Problem-focused coping
Corpulence, gabarit	Body size
Corrélat *(n.)*	Correlate *(n.)*
Courant électrique	Electrical current
Courbe *(n.)*	Curve *(n.)*
Crâne, Boîte crânienne *(n.)*	Skull *(n.)*
Crédibilité de la source	Source credibility
Culpabilité *(n.)*	Guilt *(n.)*

Cure ou thérapie par la parole	Talking cure
Cyclothymie *(n.)*	Cyclothymia *(n.)*
DDT (un insecticide)	DDT
Débriefing, désaffabulation *(n.)* : on explique aux sujets expérimentaux le véritable objectif poursuivi dans l'expérience après leur avoir donné une fausse raison au départ.	Debriefing *(n.)*
Début, déclenchement *(n.)*	Onset *(n.)*
Décentration *(n.)*	Decentering *(n.)*
Déception, désillusion *(n.)*	Disappointment *(n.)*
Déclencher *(v.)*	Trigger *(v.)*
Déficit de l'attention	Attention deficit
Définition de soi, quête de soi	Self-definition
Délinquance juvénile	Juvenile delinquency
Délinquant, coupable *(n.)*	Offender *(n.)*
Délire *(n.)*	Delirium *(n.)*
Delirium tremens	Delirium tremens
Délit, offense *(n.)*	Offence *(n.)*
Demande coûteuse	Costly request
Demander *(v.)*	Request *(v.)*
Démence *(n.)*	Dementia *(n.)*
Déni *(n.)*	Denial *(n.)*
Dépendance *(n.)*	Dependence *(n.)*
Dépersonnalisation des relations à autrui	Depersonalization of relationships
Dépistage *(n.)*	Screening *(n.)*
Déplacement *(n.)*	Displacement *(n.)*
Dépresseur ou psycholeptique *(n.)*	Depressant *(n.)*
Dépression *(n.)*	Depression *(n.)*
Déprimé *(adj.)*	Depressed *(adj.)*
Désarroi, détresse, souffrance *(n.)*	Distress *(n.)*
Désensibilisation *(n.)*	Desensitization *(n.)*

Déséquilibre *(n.)*	Imbalance *(n.)*
Désirabilité sociale : tendance à donner une image de soi conforme à celle attendue par l'endogroupe (voir ce mot)	Social desirability
Destruction sélective	Selective erasure
Détresse, souffrance, psychologique	Psychological distress
Deuil *(n.)*	Mourning *(n.)*
Diabètes *(n.)*	Diabetes *(n.)*
Diagnostic *(n.)*	Diagnosis *(n.)*
Didactique professionnelle	Professional didactics
Différenciation *(n.)*	Differentiation *(n.)*
Diffusion de l'activation	Spreading of activation
Direction du regard	Gaze direction
Dirigé vers la personne	Person-directed
Discours incohérent, désorganisé	Disorganized speech
Disponibilité *(n.)*	Availability *(n.)*
Dispositif de détection de l'image corporelle	Body image detection device
Dissociation *(n.)*	Dissociation *(n.)*
Distorsion de l'image du corps	Body image distortion
Domaine de recherche	Research field
Données (d'une étude) *(n.)*	Data *(n.)*
Douleur *(n.)*	Pain *(n.)*
Douleur abdominale	Stomach pain
Douleurs musculaires	Muscle aches
Douloureux *(adj.)*	Painful *(adj.)*
Drogue *(n.)*	Drug *(n.)*
DSM-IV : *Manuel diagnostique et statistique des troubles mentaux* (4e éd.)	DSM-IV = *Diagnostic and Statistical Manual of Mental Disorders*
Dualisme cartésien corps-esprit	Cartesian mind-body dualism

Dyade *(n.)* : couple de 2 personnes en interaction	Dyad *(n.)*
Dysfonctionnel *(adj.)*	Dysfunctional *(adj.)*
Dysfonctionnement *(n.)*	Dysfunction *(n.)*
Dysfonctionnement moteur	Motor dysfunction
Dyskinésie *(n.)* : perturbation qui se situe au niveau des mouvements et qui se traduit entre autre par de l'incoordination, des spasmes et une diminution de la force musculaire	Dyskinesia *(n.)*
Dysphorie *(n.)*	Dysphoria *(n.)*
Échantillon *(n.)*	Sample *(n.)*
Échelle (de mesure) *(n.)*	Scale *(n.)*
Échelle d'adjectifs antithétiques ou opposés (exemples : chaud-froid ; faible-fort)	Bipolar adjective scales
Échelle de Likert	Likert scale
Échelle de notation de personnages	Figure rating scale
Échelle du différenciateur sémantique	Semantic differential scale
Économie de jetons, technique des jetons : système de récompenses par des jetons, bons points, images…	Token economy
Écoute mutuelle	Mutual attunement
Éducation des enfants	Rearing, child rearing
Education des enfants	Parenting *(n.)*
Effet « paroi de verre »	Glass partition effect
Effet « plafond de verre » ou effet de ségrégation verticale	Glass ceiling effect
Effet « porte pivotante »	Swing door effect
Effet d'exposition	Exposure effect
Effet d'amorçage facilitateur	Facilitation priming effect
Effet d'amorçage inhibiteur	Inhibitory priming effect

Effet de simple exposition	Mere exposure effect
Efficace	Effective *(adj.)*
Efficacité *(n.)*	Effectiveness *(n.)*
Égocentrisme *(n.)*	Egocentrism *(n.)*
Égoïste *(n.)*	Selfish *(n.)*
Électrode *(n.)*	Electrode *(n.)*
Élever, soigner, nourrir *(v.)*	Nurture *(v.)*
Éloge dirigé vers la tâche, la production de quelque chose	Product-directed praise
Éloge dirigé vers le processus ayant permis de réaliser la tâche	Process-directed praise
Eloges *(n.)*	Praise *(n.)*
Émettre une hypothèse	Hypothesize *(v.)*
Émotion *(n.)* : réponses de forte intensité qui comportent des manifestations expressives, physiologiques et subjective.	Emotion *(n.)*
Émotion aversive	Aversive emotion
Empathie *(n.)*	Empathy *(n.)*
Empathique *(adj.)*	Empathic *(adj.)*
Enculturation *(n.)*	Enculturation *(n.)*
Endo-groupe, ou groupe d'appartenance	Ingroup *(n.)*
Enfance *(n.)*	Childhood *(n.)*
Enfant en bas âge, bambin *(n.)*	Toddler *(n.)*
Engagement *(n.)* (voir C. Kiesler)	Commitment *(n.)*
Entretien d'attachement adulte (voir M. Main)	Adult Attachment Interview
Envie, besoin irrésistible *(n.)*	Craving *(n.)*
Épanouissement de soi *(n.)*	Selfulfillment *(n.)*
Épidémiologie *(n.)*	Epidemiology *(n.)*
Epidémiologiste *(n.)*	Epidemiologist *(n.)*
Épilepsie *(n.)*	Epilepsy *(n.)*
Épisode aigu	Acute episode

Épistémologie ou approche constructiviste : théorie de l'apprentissage fondée sur l'idée que la connaissance est construite par l'apprenant sur la base d'une activité mentale qui lui permet d'éditer ses propres « règles » et « modèles mentaux » pour donner un sens à ses expériences.	Constructivist approach or constructivist epistemology approach
Épuisement émotionnel	Emotional exhaustion
Ergonomie	Ergonomics *(n.)*
Érudit, savant, universitaire *(n.)*	Scholar *(n.)*
Espace privé	Personal space
Espace privé, intime *(n.)*	Privacy *(n.)*
Esprit *(n.)*	Mind *(n.)*
Essai *(n.)*	Trial *(n.)*
Essais cliniques	Clinical trials
Estimation, évaluation *(n.)*	Appraisal *(n.)*
Estime de soi *(n.)*	Self-esteem *(n.)*
État *(n.)*	State *(n.)*
État agentique (voir S. Milgram)	Agentic state
État d'autonomie, d'indépendance	Autonomous state
État de choc traumatique	Shell-shock *(n.)*
Etat de manque	Withdrawal *(n.)*
État d'excitation (d'agitation) soudaine	Sudden arousal state
État morbide : état pathologique en lien avec la maladie	Morbid state
État-limite *(n.)*	Borderline *(n.)*
États mentaux	Mental states
Éthiopathogénique *(adj.)* : étude des causes d'une maladie et des processus par lesquels ces causes agissent.	Ethiopathogenic *(adj.)*

Éthologie *(n.)* : étude scientifique des comportements animaux (voir C. Lorenz)	Ethology *(n.)*
Éthos ou système de valeurs *(n.)*	Ethos *(n.)*
Étiologie *(n.)* : relatif aux causes des maladies	Etiology *(n.)*
Étiologique *(adj.)*	Etiologic *(adj.)*
Être empathique *(v.)*	Empathize *(v.)*
Étude longitudinale : étude qui permet de mesurer un événement chez un groupe de patients à différents moments dans le temps.	Longitudinal study
Études de cas	Case studies
Euphorie *(n.)*	Euphoria *(n.)*
Évaluation *(n.)*	Assessment *(n.)*
Évaluation cognitive	Cognitive appraisal
Évaluation complète (totalité de l'échelle)	Full-scale
Évaluer *(v.)*	Assess *(v.)*
Événement factuel, avéré	Factual event
Éventail ou étendue des stimuli olfactifs	Range of olfactory stimuli
Évitement *(n.)*	Avoidance *(n.)*
Éviter *(v.)*	Avoid *(v.)*
Examen *(n.)*	Examination *(n.)*
Excitation physiologique	Physiological arousal
Excitation, éveil *(n.)*	Arousal *(n.)*
Exemplaire d'une catégorie, membre d'une catégorie (par exemple, la baleine est un exemplaire de la catégorie des mammifères)	Exemplar *(n.)*
Exo-groupe	Outgroup *(n.)*

Expérience paroxystique (plénitude) (voir Abraham Maslow)	Peak experience
Expérimentateur *(n.)*	Experimenter *(n.)*
Expertise de la source (d'un message)	Source expertise
Expression motrice	Motor expression
Expressions faciales	Facial expressions
Externalité *(n.)*. Voir B. Weiner et sa théorie des attributions)	Externality *(n.)*
Facteurs de risque	Risk factors
Faim *(n.)*	Hunger *(n.)*
Faisceau lumineux	Light beam
Fait de pouvoir être codé	Codability *(n.)*
Fantasme *(n.)*	Fantasy *(n.)*
Favoritisme envers l'exogroupe	Favouritism towards the outgroup
Fièvre *(n.)*	Fever *(n.)*
Figure complexe de Rey	Complex Figure Test
Fluctuations motrices (dans la maladie de Parkinson)	Motor fluctuations
Flux « expérience-flux », « expérience optimale » ou « négentropie psychique » *(n.)* : par référence à la sensation que l'on ressent lorsqu'on agit avec une implication totale dans ce que l'on fait, au point de perdre, par exemple, la notion de l'heure ou du bruit environnant	Flow *(n.)*
Folie circulaire (expression due à J.-P. Falret, psychiatre du XIXe siècle)	Circular madness
Fonction cérébrale	Cerebral function

Fonction linéaire : elle implique la proportionnalité. Par exemple, on dira que le prix d'un plein d'essence est fonction linéaire du nombre de litres mis dans le réservoir car : pour un litre, on paie 1,10 euros, pour 2 litres on paie 2,20 euros, pour 10 litres on paie 11 euros etc.	Linear function
Fonction motrice	Motor function
Fonction symbolique	Symbolic function
Fonctionnement *(n.)*	Functioning *(n.)*
Fonctionnement immunitaire	Immune functioning
Fonctionnement/orientation visuo-spatial *(n.)*	Visuospatial functioning/orientation *(n.)*
Fonctions cognitives	Cognitive functions
Fonctions exécutives (anticipation, sélection d'un but, planification, organisation de la démarche, évaluation des résultats, formulation d'hypothèses différentes, autocritique, auto correction, souplesse mentale, persistance dans la tâche, capacité d'ajustement en cours de route, capacité d'adaptation aux changements)	Executive functions
Forclusion *(n.)*	Foreclosure *(n.)*
Formation professionnelle	Vocational training
Formation réactionnelle	Reaction-formation
Forte versus faible crédibilité	Low vs. high in credibility
Foyers épileptogènes	Epileptic foci
Franchissement des frontières organisationnelles	Crossing organizational boundaries
Frustration *(n.)*	Frustration *(n.)*
Ganglions de la base	Basal ganglia
Générateur de chocs électriques *(n.)*	Shock generator *(n.)*

Gènes *(n.)*	Genes *(n.)*
Genre *(n.)* (rôles des hommes et des femmes)	Gender *(n.)*
Glace sans tain *(n.)*	One-way mirror *(n.)*
Groupe contrôle, groupe témoin : groupe de sujets qui ne subit pas le traitement expérimental et qui sert de point de comparaison. Dans les études médicales, le groupe contrôle reçoit un placébo.	Control group
Groupe dominant	Dominant group
Groupe minoritaire	Minority group
Groupes de soutien familial	Family support groups
Guérir *(v.)*	Cure *(v.)*
Gyrus postcentral	Postcentral gyrus
Gyrus précentral	Precentral gyrus
Habitudes *(n.)*	Habits *(n.)*
Hallucination *(n.)*	Hallucination *(n.)*
Hallucination tactile	Tactile hallucination
Hépatite C	Hepatitis C
Hépatologue (spécialiste du foie)	Hepatologists
Holistique *(adj.)* : qui prend en compte la globalité d'un phénomène	Holistic *(adj.)*
Homéostasique *(adj.)*	Homeostatic *(adj.)*
Homunculus moteur	Motor homunculus
Homunculus sensoriel	Sensory homunculus
Hôpital de jour	Day center
Humeur *(n.)*	Mood *(n.)*
Hyperactivité *(n.)*	Hyperactivity *(n.)*
Hyperexcitabilité cérébrale	Brain hyperexcitability
Hypersomnie *(n.)* (somnolence excessive)	Hypersomnia *(n.)*
Hyperthymique *(adj.)*	Hyperthymic *(adj.)*

Hypomaniaque *(adj.)*	Hypomanic *(adj.)*
Hypomanie *(n.)*	Hypomania *(n.)*
Hypothèse *(n.)*	Hypothesis *(n.)*
Hypothèse d'activation incomplète	Incomplete activation hypothesis
Hypothèse d'auto-validation	Self-validation hypothesis
Hypothèse du blocage	Blocking hypothesis
Idéalisation *(n.)*	Idealization *(n.)*
Idéation ou production des idées *(n.)*	Ideation *(n.)*
Idée fausse, méprise, mauvaise compréhension *(n.)*	Misconception *(n.)*
Identification projective (voir dictionnaire de psychanalyse)	Projective identification
Illusions positives	Positive illusions
Imagerie cérébrale *(n.)*	Cerebral imaging *(n.)*
Imitation *(n.)*	Imitation *(n.)*
Impuissance apprise ou acquise (voir Martin Seligman)	Learned helplessness
Incapacité, invalidité, handicap *(n.)*	Disability *(n.)*
Incidence *(n.)*	Incidence *(n.)*
Inconscient *(n.)* ou *(adj.)*	Unconscious *(n.)* or *(adj.)*
Indice *(n.)*	Clue *(n.)*
Indice de masse corporelle	BMI = Body Mass Index
Indices mnésiques	Memory cues
influx nerveux	Nervous influx
Inhiber *(v.)*	Inhibit *(v.)*
Inhiber les comportements menant au regret	Inhibit regret-laden behaviors
Inné *(adj.)*	Innate *(adj.)*
Insatisfaction de l'image corporelle	Body image dissatisfaction
Insomnie *(n.)*	Insomnia *(n.)*
Insuffisance, faiblesse, carence, déficience *(n.)*	Deficiency *(n.)*

Intentionnel, voulu, projeté *(adj.)*	Intended *(adj.)*
Interactions précoces mère-enfant	Early mother-infant interaction
Intergroupe (relation d'un groupe à un autre groupe. Exemples : relations entre enseignants et étudiants, conflit entre groupes ethniques, etc.)	Intergroup *(n.)*
Internalisation des interdits	Internalised prohibitions
Internaliser *(v.)*	Internalize *(v.)*
Internalité *(n.)* (voir Bernard Weiner et sa théorie des attributions)	Internality *(n.)*
Internes en médecine	Internal medicine residents
Interneurones *(n.)*	Interneurons *(n.)*
Interpersonnel *(adj.)* (relation d'un individu à un autre individu)	Interpersonal *(n.)*
Intimité	Intimacy *(n.)*
Intoxication *(n.)*	Intoxication *(n.)*
Intra-individuel, intra-personnel	Intrapersonal *(n.)*
Intraveineux	Intravenous *(adj.)*
Intrusif *(adj.)*	Intrusive *(adj.)*
Invalidant, handicapant *(adj.)*	Disabling *(adj.)*
Investissement *(n.)*	Cathexis *(n.)*
Irrévocabilité de l'acte (voir Charles Kiesler)	Act irrevocability
Irritabilité *(n.)*	Irritability *(n.)*
Isolement social	Social isolation
Items *(n.)* : partie ou questions d'un test, d'un questionnaire	Items *(n.)*
Jambe *(n.)*	Leg *(n.)*
Jeu de rôles multi-joueurs en ligne	Multiplayer Online Role-Playing Games
Jeu symbolique, jeu du "faire semblant"	Pretend play
Jugement/évaluation visuel (le)	Visual judgement

Justesse, exactitude, précision *(n.)*	Accuracy *(n.)*
Justice restauratrice	Restorative justice
Langage, langue *(n.)*	Language *(n.)*
Langue *(n.)*	Tongue *(n.)*
Lapsus	Slip of the tongue
Lapsus *(n.)*	Freudian slips
Lésion cérébrale	Brain injury
Lésion latéralisée	Lateralized lesion
Libérer *(v.)*	Release *(v.)*
Libidinal *(adj.)*	Libidinal *(adj.)*
Libido *(n.)*	Libido *(n.)*
Lieu de contrôle	Locus of Control
Lieu de contrôle externe (voir Julian Rotter et son concept du *locus of control*)	External control
Lieu de contrôle interne (voir Julian Rotter et son concept du *locus of control*)	Internal control
Lignes directrices	Guidelines *(n.)*
Lobe frontal	Frontal lobe
Loi de l'effet établit qu'une réponse est davantage susceptible d'être reproduite si elle entraîne une satisfaction et d'être abandonnée s'il en résulte une insatisfaction	Law of effect
Longueur d'onde	Wavelength *(n.)*
Maison de retraite	Nursing home
Maladie *(n.)*	Illness, disease *(n.)*
Maladie cardio-vasculaire	Cardiovascular disease
Maladies chroniques	Chronic diseases
Maladies coronariennes	Coronary heart disease
Maladies liées à des comportements (adoptés)	Behavior-related illnesses

Maladie maniaco-dépressive (alternance de phases dépressives et maniaques ou d'excitation)	Manic depressive illness
Maladie neurologique dégénérative	Neurodegenerative disease
Maladie thyroïdienne *(n.)*	Thyroid disease *(n.)*
Maladies vénériennes	Venereal diseases, STD (Sexually Transmitted Diseases), STI (Sexually Transmitted Infectious)
Maltraité, abusé *(adj.)*	Maltreated *(adj.)*
Manie *(n.)*	Mania *(n.)*
Manifestation, réaction somatique	Somatic reaction
Marquage contextuel	Contextual marking
Maternelle (école) *(n.)*	Preschool *(n.)*
Matrices progressives de Raven	Raven's Progressive Matrices
Mécanismes de défense	Defense mechanisms
Mécanismes de survie	Survival mechanisms
Médecin *(n.)*	Physician *(n.)*
Membres d'une catégorie	Members of the category
Mémoire *(n.)*	Memory *(n.)*
Mémoire à long terme	Long term memory
Mémoire autobiographique	Autobiographical memory
Mémoire de travail	Working memory
Mémoire sémantique	Semantic memory
Menace à l'estime de soi *(n.)*	Threat to self-esteem
Menace de castration	Threat of castration
Message persuasif	Persuasive message
Métacognition *(n.)*	Metacognition *(n.)*
Métalinguistique, relatif au métalangage *(adj.)*	Metalinguistic *(adj.)*
Méthode de validation (d'après N. Feil)	Validation Method
Méthode développée par M. Montessori	Montessori method

Méthodes d'analyses lexicométriques	Lexicometric methods of analysis
Méthodes d'analyses morpho-syntaxiques	Morphosyntactic methods of analysis
Méthodes d'entretiens	Interviews *(n.)*
Méthodes qualitatives	Qualitative methods
Mineurs récidivistes	Reoffending minors
Miroir déformant	Distorting mirror
Mode de transmission	Mode of transmission
Modèle attributionnel	Attributional model
Modèle biomédical	Biomedical model
Modèle de la réponse cognitive (voir A.G. Greenwald, 1968)	Cognitive response model
Modèle de probabilité d'élaboration, (voir R.E. Petty et J.T. Cacioppo, 1986)	Elaboration Likelihood Model
Modèle de Yale : modèle élaboré par une équipe de l'université de Yale (Holland, Janis & Kelly)	Yale Model
Modèle du « tacticien motivé » (voir S.T. Fiske et S.E. Taylor, 1987)	Motivated tactician model
Modèle du théoricien naïf (voir Hoffman & Hurst, 1990)	Naive scientist model
Modèle heuristique-systématique (Chaiken, 1987)	Heuristic-Systematic Model
Modèles formels	Formal models
Modélisations *(n.)*	Modelings *(n.)*
Moelle épinière	Spinal cord
Moi *(n.)*	Ego *(n.)*
Monitorage de soi	Self-monitoring
Mortel *(adj.)*	Lethal *(adj.)*
Mot au bout du nez	Tip-of-the-nose
Motivant, incitatif *(adj.)*	Incentive *(adj.)*

Motivation extrinsèque (qui provient de l'environnement de la personne)	Extrinsic motivation
Motivation intrinsèque (interne, qui provient de la personne)	Intrinsic motivation
Motivation, encouragement *(n.)*	Incentive *(n.)*
Moyenne *(n.)*	Mean *(n.)*
Moyenne *(n.)* (en moyenne)	Average *(n.)* (on average)
Muscle *(n.)*	Muscle *(n.)*
Mythe *(n.)*	Myth *(n.)*
Nausée *(n.)*	Nausea *(n.)*
Néo-réalité *(n.)* (dans le sens d'une nouvelle réalité, une réalité reconstruite)	Neo-reality *(n.)*
Nerf *(n.)*	Nerve *(n.)*
Neurone *(n.)*	Neuron *(n.)*
Neuropsychologique *(adj.)*	Neuropsychological *(adj.)*
Neurosciences	Neuroscience
Neurotransmetteur *(n.)*	Neurotransmitter *(n.)*
Neurotransmetteur excitateur	Excitatory neurotransmitter
Névrose *(n.)*	Neurosis *(n.)*
Névrotique *(adj.)*	Neurotic *(adj.)*
Niveau collectif, du groupe	Collective level
Noétique *(adj.)* : visée d'un objet par la pensée	Noetic *(adj.)*
Non intentionnel	Unintentional
Normes sociales	Social norms
Noyau accumbens	Nucleus accumbens
Nuit blanche, nuit sans sommeil	Sleepless night
Obésité *(n.)*	Obesity *(n.)*
Observations de terrain	Field observations
Obsession *(n.)*	Obsessions *(n.)*
Obsessionnel *(adj.)*	Obsessive *(adj.)*

Opérationnaliser *(v.)*	Operationalise *(v.)*
Opioïdes *(n.)*	Opioids *(n.)*
Optimisme irréaliste	Unrealistic optimism
Organisation mondiale de la santé (OMS)	World Health Organisation
Organisme *(n.)*	Organism *(n.)*
Orientation cognitivo-comportementale	Cognitive-behavioural orientation
Outil d'évaluation	Assessment tool
Pacte écologique	Ecological pact
Pairs *(n.)*	Peer *(n.)*
Pardon *(n.)*	Forgiveness *(n.)*
Parentalité, condition de parent	Parenthood *(n.)*
Parkinson, maladie de Parkinson	Parkinson's disease
Parole *(n.)*	Speech *(n.)*
Partie inférieure	Lower part
Partie supérieure	Upper part
Passage à l'acte	Acting-out *(n.)*
Patients désorganisés (voir schizophrénie)	Disorganized patients
Patte *(n.)*	Paw *(n.)*
Patterns (modèle, forme, structure) d'attachement	Attachment patterns
Pensée abstraite	Abstract thinking
Pensée magique	Magic thinking
Pensée naturelle par opposition à la pensée logique	Natural thinking
Pensée, raisonnement contrefactuel	Counterfactual thinking
Perception de soi	Self-construal *(n.)*
Perception olfactive	Olfactory perception
Période péri-natale (période située entre la vingt-huitième semaine de grossesse et le septième jour de vie après la naissance)	Perinatal period

Personnalisation *(n.)*	Personalisation *(n.)*
Personne cible	Target person
Personne qui dispense aide et soins	Caregiver *(n.)*
Personnel de santé	Health-care workers
Personnel médical, soignants	Medical staff
Personnes âgées *(n.)*	Elderly *(n.)*
Perte de mémoire	Memory loss
Perte de contact avec la réalité	Loss of contact with reality
Perte d'intérêt ou de plaisir	Loss of interest or pleasure
Perte, altération, déficit *(n.)*	Loss *(n.)*
Pertinence *(n.)*	Relevance *(n.)*
Perturbations, dérèglement *(n.)*	Disruption *(n.)*
Perturbé, bouleversé, chagriné *(adj.)*	Distressed *(adj.)*
Peur *(n.)*	Fear *(n.)*
Peur de l'échec *(n.)*	Fear of failure *(n.)*
Peur de persécution	Persecution fears
Phase d'apprentissage	Learning phase
Phénomène du mot sur le bout de la langue	Tip-of-the tongue phenomenon
Phénoménologique *(adj.)*	Phenomenological *(adj.)*
Phénotype *(n.)* : l'ensemble des caractéristiques physiques et physiologiques d'un individu, résultant de son génotype et de son environnement)	Phenotype *(n.)*
Phobie *(n.)*	Phobia *(n.)*
Phobie sociale	Social phobia
Picotement *(n.)*	Tingling *(n.)*
Pied-dans-la-porte	Foot-in-the-door
Pieds (pied) *(n.)*	Feet (foot) *(n.)*
Placébo *(n.)*	Placebo *(n.)*
Plainte *(n.)*	Complaint *(n.)*

Plan expérimental équilibré	Balanced design
Plan factoriel orthogonal. Définitions : pour chacun des niveaux d'un facteur, tous les niveaux de l'autre facteur sont associés, et ce le même nombre de fois.	Orthogonal factorial design
Poids *(n.)*	Weight *(n.)*
Poids accordé aux propriétés	Weight given to properties
Politesse *(n.)*	Politeness *(n.)*
Politique *(n.)*	Policy *(n.)*
Politique de santé	Health policy
Position *(n.)*	Stance *(n.)*
Posture corporelle	Body posture
Pouls	Pulse rate
Praticiens *(n.)*	Practitioners *(n.)*
Pratique alimentaire *(n.)*	Food practice *(n.)*
Préconscient *(n.)*	Preconscious *(n.)*
Préjugé *(n.)*	Prejudice *(n.)*
Prémorbide *(adj.)* : signes avant-coureurs de l'entrée dans une maladie	Pre-morbid *(adj.)*
Pression du groupe	Group pressure
Prévalence *(n.)* : en épidémiologie, il s'agit du nombre de personnes atteintes d'une certaine maladie à un moment donné dans une population donnée.	Prevalence *(n.)*
Prévention des rechutes	Relapse prevention
Principe de plaisir	Pleasure principle
Principe de réalité	Reality principle
Prise de décision	Decision-making
Prise de décision en situation d'incertitude	Decision-making under uncertainty
Proactif *(adj.)*	Proactive *(adj.)*

Probabilités bayesiennes (voir T. Bayes et sa théorie des probabilités)	Bayesian probabilities
Problème, question (de recherche) *(n.)*	Issue *(n.)*
Processus cognitif	Cognitive processes
Processus d'attribution	Attribution processes
Processus d'automatisation (voir J. Leplat)	Automation process
Processus de formation professionnelle	Professional training processes
Processus de généralisation	Process of generalisation
Processus de récupération	Retrieval process
Processus émotionnel	Emotional process
Processus mentaux	Mental processes
Profane, non-initié *(n.)*	Lay people or lay person
Progéniture *(n.)*	Offspring *(n.)*
Programme de rééducation	Rehabilitation program
Programmes de soins de santé primaires	Primary care programs
Projection *(n.)*	Projection *(n.)*
Prophéties autoréalisées	Self-fulfillment of expectations
Prophylactique *(adj.)* : en rapport avec l'ensemble des mesures permettant de prévenir les maladies.	Prophylactic *(adj.)*
Proposition assertive	Assertive proposition
Propriété phonologique	Phonological property
Propriété sémantique	Semantic property
Propriétés nécessaires et suffisantes	Necessary and sufficient properties
Protocole d'observation	Observation matrix

Prototype *(n.)* : en psychologie cognitive, catégorie la plus typique à l'égard de la catégorie qui lui est subordonné (exemple : « la rose » est le prototype de la catégorie des « fleurs »).	Prototype *(n.)*
Proximité, connivence	Closeness *(n.)*
Psyché *(n.)*	Psyche *(n.)*
Psychique *(adj.)*	Psychic *(adj.)*
Psychologie cognitive	Cognitive psychology
Psychologie du développement	Developmental psychology
Psychologie du travail	Occupational psychology
Psychologie évolutionniste	Evolutionary psychology
Psychologie expérimentale *(n.)* : ensemble des connaissances élaborées à l'aide de la méthode expérimentale.	Experimental psychology *(n.)*
Psychologie humaniste (voir C. Rogers comme l'un des pères fondateurs)	Humanistic psychology *(n.)*
Psychologue des organisations	Organizational psychologist
Psychologue industriel - organisationnel	Industrial-organizational psychologist
Psychophysique *(n.)* : branche de la psychologie consacrée à l'étude des relations entre les stimuli et les sensations qui en résultent (voir G. Fechner comme père fondateur).	Psychophysics *(n.)*
Psychose *(n.)*	Psychosis *(n.)*
Psychosensoriel *(adj.)*	Psychosensorial *(adj.)*
psychotique *(adj.)*	Psychotic *(adj.)*
Pulsion *(n.)*	Drive *(n.)*
Pulsion de mort	Death drive
Pulsion de vie	Life drive
Punition *(n.)*	Punishment *(n.)*
Qualité de vie	Quality of life

Questionnaire auto-administré	Self-report questionnaire
Questionnaire d'insatisfaction corporelle	Body Shape Questionnaire
Raisonnement (n.)	Reasoning *(n.)*
Raisonnement conditionnel	Conditional reasoning
Raisonnement dans l'action	Reasoning in action
Ralentissement, retard, déficit psychomoteur	Psychomotor retardation *(n.)*
Récepteur (n.)	Receptor *(n.)*
Récepteur d'un message	Receiver of a message
Récepteurs à la douleur	Pain receptors
Récepteurs olfactifs	Olfactory receptors
Recherche appliquée, de terrain (*n.*)	Field research *(n.)*
Recherche de sensations	Sensation-seeking
Rechute (n.)	Relapsing *(n.)*
Recommandation : le fait d'adresser le patient à un médecin spécialiste	Referral *(n.)*
Récompense (n.)	Reward *(n.)*
Récupérer (v.)	Recover *(v.)*
Réduire (v.)	Cut down *(v.)*
Rééducation de l'orientation : technique utilisée dans le cadre de la maladie d'Alzheimer)	Reality Orientation Therapy
Refoulement (n.)	Repression *(n.)*
Régénérer (v.)	Regenerate *(v.)*
Régime équilibré	Balanced diet
Règle de moralité	Rule of morality
Règles d'actions (voir J.-R. Anderson)	Action rules
Régulation de l'émotion	Emotion regulation
Relation d'objet	Object relationship
Relation dose-effet	Dose-response relationship

Relation paradigmatique	Paradigmatic relation
Relation syntagmatique	Syntagmatic relation
Relations de l'individu au groupe	Person-to-group relations
Rencontres *(n.)*	Encounters *(n.)*
Rencontres de personnes inconnues, dues au hasard	Random strangers
Renforcements *(n.)*	Reinforcements *(n.)*
Repentance, regret de ses fautes *(n.)*	Repentance *(n.)*
Réponse conditionnée	Conditioned response
Réponses moyennes	Mean responses
Représentation de choses	Representation of a thing
Représentation de mots	Representation of a word
Représentation motrice	Motor representation
Reproduction sociale	Social reproduction
Requête, demande *(n.)*	Request *(n.)*
Réseau de neurones	Neuronal network
Réseaux sociaux	Social networks
Résection *(n.)*	Resection *(n.)*
Résignation, impuissance *(n.)*	Helplessness *(n.)*
Résilience *(n.)*	Resilience *(n.)*
Résolution de problème(s)	Problem-solving
Ressources cognitives	Cognitive resources
Résultat, issue *(n.)*	Outcome *(n.)*
Retrait, état de manque *(n.)*	Withdrawal *(n.)*
Réussite *(n.)* ; réussir *(v.)*	Achievement *(n.)* ; achieve *(v.)*
Rêve éveillé	Daydream *(n.)*
Révélation du diagnostic	Diagnostic disclosure
Révolutionnaire *(adj.)*	Groundbreaking *(adj.)*
Risque léthal (qui peut entraîner la mort)	Lethal risk
Rôle médiateur	Mediating role

Rongeur *(n.)*	Rodent *(n.)*
Rythme cardiaque	Heart rate
Sadique *(adj.)*	Sadistic *(adj.)*
Sain *(adj.)*	Healthy *(adj.)*
Sang *(n.)*	Blood *(n.)*
Santé *(n.)*	Health *(n.)*
Santé publique	Public health
Savoir pragmatique, pratique	Pragmatic knowledge
Savoir pratique, savoir-faire	Practical knowledge or "know-how"
Schème *(n.)* (voir J. Piaget)	Schema *(n.)*
Sclérose en plaques	Multiple Sclerosis
Se comporter *(v.)*	Behave *(v.)*
Se figer *(v.)*	Freeze *(v.)*
Sélection planifiée	Pre-planned selection
Sélectionner ou attribuer de manière aléatoire (au hasard)	Randomise *(v.)*
Sensation *(n.)*	Sensation *(n.)*
Sensoriel *(adj.)*	Sensory *(adj.)*
Service de gastroentérologie	Gastroenterology service
Seuil *(n.)*	Threshold *(n.)*
Sexisme bienveillant	Benevolent sexism
Similarité *(n.)*	Similarity *(n.)*
Situation Étrange : expérience consistant à induire un léger stress par le départ et le retour d'un parent chez des enfants âgés d'un an. La situation se compose de huit épisodes (départ-retour) de trois minutes chacun, dont certains se déroulent en présence d'un inconnu. Les réactions de l'enfant sont examinées et permettent d'inférer le style d'attachement de l'enfant.	Strange situation *(n.)*

Situation prototypique	Prototypical situation
Socialement compétent(e)	Socially skilled
Soif *(n.)*	Thirst *(n.)*
Soigner *(v.)*	Heal *(v.)*
Soins curatifs	Remedial care
Somatique *(adj.)* : relatif au corps dans sa dimension physique	Somatic *(adj.)*
Soulager *(v.)*	Relieve *(v.)*
Soumission à l'autorité	Obedience to authority
Soumission librement consentie	Free will compliance
Sous-poids *(n.)*	Underweight *(n.)*
Soutien social	Social support
Sperme *(n.)*	Semen *(n.)*
Sphère des relations intimes	Sphere of close relations
Stabilité *(n.)*	Stability *(n.)*
Stade *(n.)*	Stage *(n.)*
Stade de la relation	Stage of the relationship
Stade phallique	Phallic stage
Stades oral et anal	Oral and anal stages
Statut professionnel	Occupational status
Statut social	Social status
Stéréotype *(n.)*	Stereotypes *(n.)*
Stimulation auditive	Auditory stimulation
Stimulation sensorielle	Sensory stimulation
Stimulation visuelle	Visual stimulation
Stimuli sensoriels	Sensory stimuli
Stimulus inconditionnel : stimulus qui déclenche une réponse de manière réflexe, sans apprentissage nécessaire.	Unconditional stimulus
Stockage de l'information en mémoire	Storage of information in memory
Stratégie analytique	Analytical strategy

Stratégie expressive	Expressive strategy
Stratégie référentielle	Referential strategy
Stratégies de coping : d'adaptation, d'ajustement, de maîtrise = faire face)	Coping strategies
Stress aigu	Acute stress
Stress chronique	Chronic stress
Stress environnemental	Environmental stress
Sublimation *(n.)*	Sublimation *(n.)*
Substance psychoactive	Psychotropic substance
Substance psychotrope : se dit des substances chimiques qui produisent des effets sur le psychisme des individus.	Psychotropic substance
Suite opératoire en chirurgie	Post-surgery recovery
Suivi *(n.)*	Follow-up *(n.)*
Sujet naïf (dans le sens d'une personne qui ignore les objectifs de l'expérience)	Naive participant
Suractiver *(v.)*	Overactivate *(v.)*
Surcharge environnementale	Environmental overload
Surmoi *(n.)*	Super-ego *(n.)*
Surpoids *(n.)*	Overweight *(n.)*
Syndrome *(n.)* : regroupement de symptômes caractérisant un état pathologique	Syndrome *(n.)*
Syndrome d'Asperger	Asperger syndrome
Syndrome de désorganisation (dissociation)	Disorganisation syndrome
Syndrome de sevrage, état de manque	Withdrawal syndrome
Syndrome du colon irritable	Inflammatory bowel disease
Syndromique *(adj.)*	Syndromic *(adj.)*
Système de santé	Health care system
Système de valeurs symboliques	Symbolic value system

Système nerveux	Nervous system
Système nerveux autonome (responsable des fonctions automatiques telles que la digestion, la sudation…)	Autonomous nervous system
Système nerveux central	Central nervous system
Système syntaxique	Syntactical system
Tabagisme passif	Passive smoking
Tâche *(n.)* (épreuve, test)	Task *(n.)*
Tâche d'associations libres	Free association tests
Tâche d'attribution d'intentions basé sur le regard	Eye task
Tâche de classification	Sorting task
Tâche de fausse croyance	False belief task
Tâche d'identification	Identification task
Tâches comportementales	Behavioral tasks
Tâches sensorimotrices	Sensorimotor tasks
Taux *(n.)*	Rate *(n.)*
Taux de lymphocites	Lymphocyte rates
Taux de rémission	Remission rate
Taux variant, allant de… à	Rates ranging from… to
Taxinomique *(adj.)* : dont le but est de classifier.	Taxinomic *(adj.)*
Technique vidéo de distorsion (corporelle)	Distorting video technique
Tentatives de suicide	Suicide attempts
Territorialité, territoire	Territoriality *(n.)*
Test d'association implicite	Implicit Association Test
Test de catégories d'après Halstead	Category Test
Test de classement de cartes du Wisconsin	Wisconsin Card Sorting Test
Test de fluence graphique de Ruff	Ruff Figural Fluency Test *(n.)*
Test de la tour de Londres (voir tour de Hanoï).	Tower of London test

Test des labyrinthes de Porteus	Porteus Mazes
Test des signes (voir test en statistique)	Sign test *(n.)*
Test du Chi Carré, (voir tests statistiques)	Chi-square test
Test Tinker toy *(n.)*	Tinker Toy Test *(n.)*
Théoriciens de la modularité	Modularity theorists
Théorie de la personnalité	Theory of personality
Théorie de la perturbation cognitive	Cognitive disruption model
Théorie de la simulation	Simulation theory
Théorie de la théorie (voir théorie de l'esprit)	Theory theory (see TOM)
Théorie de l'auto-efficacité (voir A. Bandura)	Self-efficacy theory
Théorie de l'engagement	Theory of commitment
Théorie de l'esprit	Theory of mind (TOM)
Théorie de l'identité sociale (voir H. Tajfel & J.-C. Turner 1986)	Social Identity Theory
Théorie du Soi *(n.)* (voir théorie implicite de l'intelligence d'après C.S. Dweck)	Self-theory *(n.)*
Théorie normative du raisonnement (voir D. Kahneman & A. Tversky, 1982)	Norm theory
Théories de l'activité	Activity theories
Thérapie *(n.)*	Therapy *(n.)*
Thérapie par la parole (*cf.* S. Freud)	Talking cure (*cf.* S. Freud)
Thérapies basées sur l'acceptation	Acceptance-based therapies
Tissu cérébral	Brain tissue
Tolérance *(n.)*. La tolérance à une drogue oblige à en consommer des quantités croissantes pour avoir les mêmes effets	Tolerance *(n.)*
Toxicomanes *(n.)*	Drug users

Tracé, graphique	Plot *(n.)*
Trait désirable	Desirable trait
Traitement de l'information	Processing of information
Traitement olfactif	Olfactory processing
Transfert *(n.)*	Transference *(n.)*
Transpirer *(v.)*	Sweat *(v.)*
Traumatisme *(n.)*	Trauma *(n.)*
Travailleurs sociaux	Social workers
Tremblement des mains	Hand tremor
Trembler *(v.)*	Tremble *(v.)*
Trouble anxieux généralisé	Generalized anxiety disorder
Trouble de la marche, la démarche étant atteinte en raison d'un trouble moteur	Gait disorder *(n.)*
Trouble de la personnalité Borderline	Borderline personality disorder
Trouble de l'attention	Attentional disorder
Trouble de Stress Post-Traumatique	Post-Traumatic Stress Disorder
Trouble obsessionnel compulsif (TOC)	Obsessive Compulsive Disorder (OCD)
Trouble panique	Panic disorder
Trouble *(n.)* : par troubles mentaux et du comportement, on entend des affections cliniquement significatives qui se caractérisent par un changement du mode de pensée, de l'humeur (affects) ou du comportement associé à une détresse psychique et/ou à une altération des fonctions mentales (OMS, 2001).	Disorder *(n.)*
Troubles bipolaires	Bipolar disorders
Troubles de l'alimentation	Eating disorders
Troubles du sommeil	Sleep disturbances
Troubles induits par une substance	Substance-induced disorders

Troubles liés à l'utilisation/ consommation d'une substance	Substance use disorders
Troubles psychosomatiques	Psychosomatic disorders
Troubles squeletto-musculaires	Musculoskeletal disorders
Truquer, tricher *(v.)*	Rig *(v.)*
Tumeur au cerveau	Brain tumor
Type A ou C	Style A or C
Un plan d'attaque multi-facettes	Multi-faceted plan of attack
Unités d'hospitalisation	Inpatient medical units
Usage chronique	Chronic use
Valeur	Value *(n.)*
Validation des croyances	Belief validation
Variables « valence ». La valence désigne ce qui attire (valence positive) ou repousse (valence négative) un individu	Valenced variables
Variables individuelles	Individual variables
Variables situationnelles	Situational variables
Véritable *(n.)*	Actual *(n.)*
Virus HIV/SIDA	HIV/AIDS
Voie centrale	Central route
Voie périphérique	Peripheral route
Vol par effraction	Breaking and entering
Vomissement *(n.)*	Vomiting *(n.)*

55143 – (II) – (1) – OSB 80° – TYP – MLN

Dépôt légal : janvier 2011, suite du tirage : février 2013
Achevé d'imprimer par Dupli-Print
N° d'impression : 223456
www.dupli-print.fr

Imprimé en France